WHEN LIFE THROWS YOU FOR THE LOOP

When Life Throws You for the Loop

H_2O + 6,000 miles + 1 year @ 8 knots = America's Great Circle Loop Waterway

A voyage that will change your life!

Captain Chuck Hewitson

Portland • Oregon
inkwaterpress.com

Copyright © 2011 by Charles E. Hewitson

All rights reserved. No part of this book may be reproduced or transmitted in any form or by any means whatsoever, including photocopying, recording or by any information storage and retrieval system, without written permission from the publisher and/or author. Contact Inkwater Press at 6750 SW Franklin Street, Suite A, Portland, OR 97223-2542. 503.968.6777

ISBN-13 978-1-59299-578-3
ISBN-10 1-59299-578-0

Publisher: Inkwater Press | www.inkwaterpress.com

Printed in the U.S.A.
All paper is acid free and meets all ANSI standards for archival quality paper.

1 3 5 7 9 10 8 6 4 2

Contents

Foreword 9

Acknowledgments 11

Prologue 13

Loopet 1: Putting Her Back Together 29

Loopet 2: The Mighty Mississippi Davenport, Iowa to Cairo Illinois
and the Ohio River.. 33

Loopet 3: Kaskaskia River Confluence with the Mississippi to
Kentucky Lake 47

Loopet 4: Kentucky and Tennessee 53

Loopet 5: The Tenn-Tombigbee and Tombigbee-Black Warrior
Waterway 69

Loopet 6: Last Leg to Mobile Bay and Inter-Coastal along the
Northern Gulf 81

Loopet 7: Florida's Big Bend on the Gulf to Madeira Beach Florida 95

Loopet 8: Madeira Beach Florida to Stuart Florida (via Lake
Okeechobee) 107

Loopet 9: Stuart Florida to the Florida Keys 123

Loopet 10: Stuart Florida to Fernandina Beach Florida (Solo) 131

Loopet 11: Georgia and the Carolinas 149

Loopet 12: Georgetown, South Carolina to the Dismal Swamp in
    North Carolina.. 163

Loopet 13: Virginia and the Chesapeake to Chesapeake City,
    Maryland 175

Loopet 14: Chesapeake City to New York City 185

Loopet 15: New York City through the Erie and Oswego Canals 195

Loopet 16: Lake Ontario to Georgian Bay and Lake Huron via the
    Trent-Severn.. 203

Loopet 17: Georgian Bay, Lake Huron to Byng Inlet Ontario 219

Loopet 18: Byng Inlet on Georgian Bay to Little Current, Ontario 227

Loopet 19: My Mom and Life without Her or the Loop 239

Loopet 20: Closing the Loop – The Final Chapter 245

Photos... 254

About the Author.. 272

*This book is dedicated to my fabulous wife
and first mate Chris,
who took her fair share of time at the wheel
and flawlessly piloted Essi-Anna through the locks
of the Erie Canal and the Trent Severn.*

*We also dedicate this journey to our moms
who passed on a love for the water
through their Norwegian heritage.
We reflect on their lives and cherish the memories
we had with them aboard Essi-Anna.*

Foreword

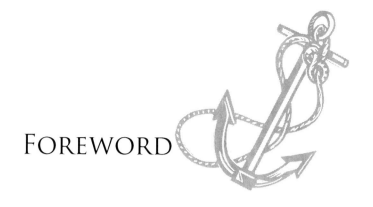

(Paul wrote this while he was docked at Coon Island on the Multnomah Channel connecting the Willamette and Columbia rivers — dreaming of cruises yet to come!)

We all relish those quiet times when in a moment's peace we allow our minds to listen to our heart's dreams. For some it might be soaring with eagles in a silent glider. For others it's hearing the roar of the crowd as they kick the game winning field goal or drop the impossible putt. Those of us as Chuck puts it, who have that "common gene" which calls us to adventure on the water, gravitate toward visions of handsome vessels, offshore passages, beautiful islands, quiet anchorages, quaint waterfront hamlets, and seamanship well practiced.

When Life Throws You for the Loop is the account of just such an adventure.

Chuck and Chris Hewitson, accomplished Northwest cruisers with many years experience in the incomparable islands and channels of the Inland Passage, had earlier, casual thoughts of cruising along the "other coast," but became fully enamored with the possibility after meeting the diehards of America's Great Circle Loop Association. Blessed with the time, drive and resources to make such a dream reality, they, and fellow friends and Northwest cruisers Bill and Gail Stuenkel committed to the adventure and never looked back!

There are other narratives of the Great Circle Loop journey, as well as excellent cruising guides detailing every navigational hazard and hideaway along the route. Chuck treats us to the former with a unique twist, weaving lessons learned along the voyage as metaphors of the pleasures and storms encountered as we steer the course of life. With an engaging style and a format of letters (well emails actually) back home to friends and family, the reader opens each new update "as it happens"— sometimes just a quick note to be detailed later, others fully developed with all the sights and sensations of the moment.

Whether you might be contemplating your own cruise of the Loop or just love a good yarn, you're sure to enjoy "When Life Throws You for the Loop." As Chuck's granddad would put it, "It'll put a smile on your haircut!"

—Paul Pfeifer,
Commodore Tollycrafters Northwest Boating Club

Acknowledgments

Thanks to our dads who cared for our moms during the year we were gone. Thanks to our great boating friends of twelve years, Bill and Gail Stuenkel, who planned the trip and traveled the Loop with us on JUWIKA. Thanks to Paul and Stacy Brannon who joined us on the Chesapeake as the third member of our flotilla and became dear and close friends. Finally thanks to Erica Schwenneker who did a masterful job of editing my manuscript and to our good friend and mariner Paul Pfeifer who took the time to craft the foreword.

Prologue

THERE is a journey that makes no economic sense at all. It is a loop in life that most people have never heard of, nor would ever consider traveling. It is a journey that morphs you so slowly that when the transformation is complete and you say quits – entering mainstream life again with all that it can throw at you – you look for your soul and realize that little pieces of it have been left along the many miles of America's "Great Circle Loop Adventure." Some never do return to life as they knew it before they were thrown for the "Loop". They continue to make the merry-go-round following summer and sharing last year's memories and experience with novice "loopers" getting their feet wet for the first time.

You realize that who you were when you started out has been replaced with the soul of a waterway; demanding, diverse and beautiful. Rivers lead through America's expansive heartland where echoes of our history call out for you to stop and explore: azure, clear and sparkling shallow waters on the Gulf of Mexico, forays on the mighty Atlantic, and lazy meanderings through protected channels just inside the coastal barriers that allow small boats to make their way in safety. Lakes and canals, swamps and channels, bridges and locks and lifts, small towns and large metropolitan areas pepper the route with their own special seasoning as the miles drift by.

The fickle weather throws its fury and its force like the knockout punch of a boxer as easily as it can caress you in the warmth of the ocean breezes and sunshine that beckon you to close your eyes and bask in their peace.

As you read this narrative about what is one of America's best kept secrets to us on the west coast, sit back in your private, imaginative helm chair and be the captain of your own life. Leave behind all the responsibilities that come with living on land. Let the focus of your mind concentrate on each new bend in the river or each page on the chart that must be turned to make safe passage. Better yet, load that vessel of yours aboard a trailer – 25 feet will do – and forget about all the excuses why such an adventure shouldn't be undertaken. With wide open eyes and a heart for an experience that will change you forever let your imagination become reality and let your soul be thrown for "The Loop".

The Dream

EVERY great adventure or accomplishment begins with a dream. We had dreamed of time on the water and decided that being there was more important than having all the creature comforts of the perfect cruising boat which may seem necessary to create the illusion of contentment we are accustom to on land.

For years we had plied the waters of the Cascade lakes, west coast rivers, the Puget Sound, San Juan Islands, Canadian Gulf Islands and Coastlines of British Columbia and had ventured as far north as Petersburg, Alaska. Budgets had always constrained our aquatic wanderings. So many hours on the water had been spent on someone else's boat, rented boats, the Alaska Ferry system, rafts, canoes and eventually our first runabout; a 16'Glasply with an old 50 horse Mercury that took us as far as Victoria, B.C. We graduated in time to larger boats that could be hauled by trailer and eventually to those that needed a full time home in the water.

Today we are the proud owners of a 39' 1990 Tollycraft Euro-sport which has been part of our family for the past 11 years. Her name is Essi-Anna and her beckoning has brightened our winters with memories of summers spent between her home in Poulsbo, Washington and the waters of S.E. Alaska and now the "Great Circle Loop".

Owning and spending time on Essi-Anna is one of the most exciting parts of our lives. With ownership comes the responsibility of caring for her and staying up on all the most modern nautical technologies and opportunities. This means attending boat shows in January to ward off the rainy blues that make the Northwest green and gorgeous in the summer but almost intolerable during the darker and dreary months between November and April.

If you check around the country there are all kinds of opportunities to expand your knowledge about boating and explore boating in other regions of our great country. Seattle always has a wonderful show and we religiously attended services there each year. Living in Vancouver, Washington, we attended the Portland show as well; giving in to the beckoning bill-boards, smelling of summer breezes and time on the water. In 2005 we found ourselves talking about warmer climates and attending a boat show where the sun was actually shining. So we booked our flights and headed for the February show in Miami – "the mother of all boat shows".

Like our great boating friend, Bill says, "Just because you own a piece of art, doesn't mean you stop going to the art galleries." It is the same with boats – to quench your appetite for something bigger or newer or fancier all you have to do is go to the shows and kick a few gunnels and inspect a few price tags to appreciate what you have and come away with more dreams for what may lay ahead.

These shows are full of booths advertising everything from "doggie lifts" for the old pooch that can't get aboard anymore, to the latest buzz lure that hums a tune to the fish and calls out their name by specie, to the Coast Guard's version of "Little Toot" the safety tug. There are the latest in navigational tools, boat rental companies, organizations selling magazines, memberships and even timeshare boats for the person who wants to arrive, cruise and walk away without doing any healthy manual labor at all. Small runabouts to huge mega yachts line the aisles and docks with scantily glad models luring empty-walleted lookers and honest to goodness high rolling buyers alike.

Within such a palace of pleasure our eyes caught the booth of, "America's Great Circle Loop Adventure." A book by the name of, "Honey, Let's Buy a Boat," had been on our previous reading list. Here in broad view were the people who had made their dream come true and had put the "Loop" on the map, writing their humorous stories of inexperience, adventure and lifelong memories of their journey on the loop.

We approached the booth with caution. We had been bitten by the boating bug, the bigger boat bug and the cruising lifestyle bug. Now several thousand miles from the waters we call home, saliva was flowing as we considered the possibilities of making our own loop dream come true.

Our introductions were casual as we explained where we were from and what we had done in our cruising lives. We had lived their trip vicariously through the book but to meet the faces behind the words was refreshing and real.

They shared with us the opportunity to join the Great Circle Loop Association and receive the newsletter packed with information and testimonials of those who had completed the loop or were on the loop. It included details about how government funding or actually the lack thereof could jeopardize the waterway, due to silting, low water levels and the lack of funds for dredging in certain areas of the loop by the Army Corp of Engineering. This would either require boaters to venture into dangerous waters on the ocean, limit deeper draft boats, or close off certain portions of the loop or all of the above.

Many of those who do the loop are located somewhere along the waterway or very close, making the entry points very convenient. For us in the Northwest there are a number of unique obstacles – like how do we get over the "Rocky Mountains"?

They explained that due to the cost of shipping larger boats across country by barge through the Panama Canal or by low boy semis with pilot cars, most loopers were from the east coast or had access to the waterways along the Midwest, Southern and East Coast waterways. The other option was for west coasters, like us, to buy a boat somewhere along the route and sell it when they received their "loop laureate"; a graduation certificate you receive when you cross your own wake wherever you started the loop, completing the journey.

Many people say the best two days of owning a boat are the day you buy it and the day you sell it. We have never found this to be true but we did believe in the theory that being a "two boat owner" was worse than having five in diapers at the same time. We would have to think about our options and our dream of such a voyage.

Toting plastic nautical, advertising bags filled with boating brochures and freebee key chains that float when dropped accidentally overboard, we ended a long but fruitful day of dreaming and discussing what the following year might bring.

We have boated many years with good friends who own a 32 Island Gypsy Trawler, the same vintage as our Tollycraft. When we got home from our exploratory trip we immediately called them to discuss the loop. They said they would like to think about making the journey in their boat, with us. The only hitch was, they both were working and hadn't considered quitting quite yet. They asked us what our plans were and we told them that the summer of 2005 we would venture north again into the wilds of British Columbia where we would think long and hard about the possibility of doing the loop, starting the fall of 2006. We invited them to think about their options and arrive at a plan that might fit into this time frame.

We also invited them to meet us for a week in the Broughtons and explore Knight Inlet on the mainland side of British Columbia, parallel to the northern tip of Vancouver Island. It is a wild place of mountain rimmed fjords covered with green blankets of evergreen and hardwood forests, crowned with snow and shrouded in puffy white clouds; with waterfalls that plummet to the salty, long reaches carved by glaciers many years ago. Wildlife includes: grizzly bears, wolves, dolphins, killer whales and humpbacks. It is also a place where a dip of the nets can produce prawns and crab in abundance and the dropping of a hook can put a variety of fish on the barbeque, at the whim of a hungry crew. It is an unbelievable place to relax and be challenged by nature. It is also a prime spot to sit back and imagine a trip like the one we were planning.

So when we picked Bill and Gail up at Port McNeil, a place we both had passed thorough on our routes to and from Alaska several years prior, they were armed with a plan that solidified the dream of the loop for both of us. They had also read, "Honey, Let's Buy A Boat" and, in fact, had been the ones who had bought us a copy of it years before. Both couples never really thought such a trip would be reality for either of us. The east coast and the Mississippi were a long ways away.

"We have decided to retire and ship JUWIKA." (This is an Indian name for - Let's have another beer.) Just kidding! It is a name which includes the letters of their three kids. "If it is OK with you guys we want to make the journey with you. We have decided that we will both retire in June of 2006. We will sell our house and when we return home after a year we will remodel and move into our rental in Gig Harbor."

This was a huge step of faith after living in one place for over 29 years. They, like us, were both young to be retired, but not getting any younger for a trip like the "Loop".

Chris and I had retired several years earlier and had spent the summer months aboard "Essi-Anna". This is also a name that includes the names our two daughters. Both couples had lots of experience aboard boats and had cruised together aboard our two vessels for the last ten years. Unlike the book we had read, where the authors' maiden voyage was the loop, we felt that the trip would be very manageable yet very different from our usual cruising experiences. After a week of dreaming and talking and vowing to keep this to ourselves until the formal announcements of their retirements had been carried out, we parted ways with a year of preparation ahead of us. We had awakened from the dream and now the clock was ticking down the months, days, hours and minutes to August 20, 2006.

The Plan

WHEN summer was over and Essi-Anna was put away for the winter in her covered slip at the Poulsbo Yacht Club, we ventured home with less than a year to get the wheels in motion and make all the arrangements for the trip. Bill would formally announce his retirement in January and Gail would leave her teaching post at the end of the year. Having subscribed to the newsletter on the "Loop", we were able to start gleaning information about the trip. Bill had also subscribed, so we spent many late fall hours discussing our options.

This trip, agreeing from the start not to be an economic decision, would have to be filled with compromises that had to be considered in spite of the fact they all meant spending money to an extent that some would think foolish and excessive. Some of the first considerations were: whether to ship our boats, where to ship them to, whom we could trust to handle the shipping for us, what were the insurance considerations and the all important yet bite-the-bullet question of "How Much?" A twist in this shipping scenario was; "Do we ship our boat or buy another boat on the west coast and have it shipped – selling it out east when we finish? Or do we leave our boat under cover for a year in Poulsbo, buy another boat back east in Chicago, or on the Illinois River or Mississippi and sell it when we are done with the journey?"

Buying boats is a tricky and expensive business. Even when you have done your due diligence and had a good marine survey you never really know what you have until you find yourself out on the water and usually in difficult weather conditions. We had just replaced our engines in Essi-Anna a couple of years prior and had the transmissions gone through. We had shaken her down in rough weather and cruised north without any problems. We knew her inside and out and she was a trusted member of the family who could be counted on in tough situations. Her bones were good and her reputation as a brand preceded her. Those were the positives. JUWIKA was the same.

After much consideration we arrived at the conclusion that she was going despite some of the negatives which were primarily financial in nature. One of the down sides was that with a stripped height of 13'10" and beam of 14'6" she was going to be a spendy one to take along. Estimates had come in between $12,000.00 to $23,000.00 one way and fuel prices were estimated to rise prior to departure. Should our final decision be to ship her, we had chosen our pick up point to be Olympia, WA, at SwanTown Marina, where we would take off all the additional accessories that would make her too high to ship and prep her for trucking. Our home port of Poulsbo was a night's journey to this most southern most point in the Puget Sound where we would haul her and load her aboard a flat bed, low boy designed for transporting yachts of her pedigree.

We had also chosen the starting point on the loop to be Rock Island, Illinois for JUWIKA and Davenport, Iowa, just across the Mississippi from Rock Island and one lock further up river, just a matter of a long bike ride apart, for Essi-Anna. We would need to do some fairly extensive refitting on Essi-Anna so we had chosen Wakeen's Family Boating Center, in Davenport; a highly respected, family owned, marine service organization who could set us up on blocks next to the Mississippi while we worked on her. They have an ancient looking lift that reminded me of some sort of outdated carnival ride which would pick us off the truck and when splash time came, hoist us over the wall and into the Big Muddy. This lift was more than adequate and had been a relic left over from building Lock 15 which would be our first lock just upstream from JUWIKA, on our float down the Mighty Mississippi.

Even though we had all this information we didn't make our final decision until we had to firm up shipping dates in the spring of 2006. Evaluating the cost analysis and the comfort and safety factors of buying something else versus shipping our boat we finally decided that things were close to a wash. The unexpected repairs of owning another unknown boat to make this passage and the fact that any other boat in the 32 foot plus range was going to be costly, with possible major repairs and a discount and brokerage fee at sale time, as well as facing a year on a smaller boat, without a generator and our own stuff made us realize that the additional cost for taking Essi-Anna along would far outweigh the negatives. Besides, to leave a member of the family home when JUWIKA was going for sure was just out of the question.

Preparation

UNDERSTANDING your yacht or boat insurance and close coordination with your insurance carrier is critical as you ship your boat across country and enter into tornado and hurricane infested areas of the U.S. The shipping company had things covered from their standpoint but we asked our agent to add an additional rider should the insurance not cover a mishap in strange waters or on the road leading to and from Davenport. In addition, there would be a substantial increase in insurance premiums – double – due to traveling in waters which were unfamiliar to us. Plus, there would be limitations on how early and how late we would be able to be south and north of the 32 degree parallel in order to stay out of hurricane season. It all made sense to us. The annual almanac had estimated a lower incidence of tropical storms for the year, a projection which was welcomed by us. There were a few times when the rain, lightning, thunder, wind and waves dealt us a healthy blow, which delayed our travel but never took its hefty toll. We sat for a couple of days, storm tied to a hefty Kentucky dock as a few tornadoes passed within miles of us. We sought shelter in a small but adequate safe harbor during a major storm, the worst in 20 years in North Carolina; and swung on anchor during a major rain, lightning and wind storm that dumped bathtub loads of rain and wind on the Mississippi. With a twelve to one rode ratio we appreciated having oversized and tested ground tackle.

Our insurance agent was on our blog list so we kept her informed as the trip progressed. We never had to call her and make a claim for any issue. All yacht insurances have some sort of towing limit. Since it can be very expensive and/or the limit inadequate for longer tows or un-groundings and due to the skinny water we would transit, we decided to take out towing insurance from Boat U.S.A. This is a no questions asked, no hassle way for what I considered to be a very reasonable price to insure us of what many boaters say is an inevitable part of being on the water. As one of our good friends who owns a gorgeous, wooden 50 foot Grand Banks called the "Wooden Shoe" puts it, "When your draft exceeds the depth of the water, you are surely run aground." We never used the insurance but saw many a captain that had not done the math quite right and found themselves in too little water for their draft. Needless to say you must keep your agent informed through the whole process in and out of the water since a large investment like this needs all the consideration it can get.

When preparing your boat for transport you have to take into consideration what the journey will be like and what might rattle loose. It is a different type of ride than being on the water in rough seas. The cushioned ride and constant jiggle of the road, along with a wind howling at the speed of the truck and trailer adds different dimensions to the preparation to be done. After all, boats aren't meant to travel on land but on the water.

The trucking company we had chosen was very helpful in setting the stage for the transport. We probably over killed the process, boxing up all the dishes, taking down everything off the walls, packing away all the books and stowing everything that could move, rattle or rub; so that when we were ready for transport any professional moving company would have hired us gladly. To get our boat to the lowest possible height we took down the radar arch and removed and packaged all the equipment on the arch. This meant disconnecting wiring on the dual radars and antennas for the GPS. The venturi, bimini, canvas, carpets, stainless framework for the venturi, steering wheel and everything that travels on the deck while cruising had to be put inside. This included: the helm seats, cushions, fenders, lines, inflatable, bikes, motor for the inflatable and any other canvas work or add on panels that were part of the sun bridge.

We made sure the fuel, water and waste water tanks were as empty as possible. The anchor was removed wrapped up and stowed inside and the boat was stripped to its lowest possible height.

After taping cupboards closed with blue painter's tape and all doors and windows on the exterior were locked and taped with a white 2" non-residue tape used for shrink wrapping boats, Essi-Anna was ready for loading. The fridge was empty, dry and taped shut as to not end up with spoiled food or mold when the five day journey across country came to an end in Davenport.

It was also important to turn off the battery switches to the engines, turn off all the panel switches and shut off the fuel lines. We also made sure our bilge areas were dry and that the bilge pumps were active just in case there happened to be a freak storm which dumped heavy rains on our now vulnerable yacht. We also used the white tape to mask over any holes left from removing hardware to keep as much rain and dust out of the holes and interior as possible. The use of duct tape is not recommended as it will leave extensive residue and create a lot of unnecessary cleanup.

Choosing a reputable hauling company is a decision that will make all the difference when you meet your boat at both ends of the land journey. There are other options like shipping your boat on a water transport vessel from Florida through the Panama Canal to Vancouver B.C. or the reverse of that route but it is substantially more expensive to do so. We met a couple who had done just that with their 42 foot Grand Banks and spent upwards of $40,000.00 each way. That math didn't compute to me so we went with trucking her overland.

We chose a local broker who arranged transport for a number of individual haulers; each person owning their own tractor and lowboy trailer, of which there are huge differences. It is essential you know the exact dimensions of your boat and communicate them clearly to the trucker so they can add in their own trailer specs to come up with a doable height, width, and price. Different states have different regulations for travel days, durations, heights, widths and permits which are all variables in the overall cost. In addition there are state regulations requiring the use of a pilot car or multiple pilot cars. These also add to the transport bill. If you are as fortunate as we were to get a professional team who oversaw the loading of Essi-Anna like a mother goose protecting her clutch of incubating eggs, the little extra you may pay for the care taken will be well worth it. Our hauler had a perfect record over 20 years, had a sharp looking, spotless, color coordinated rig with matching pilot car and an assistant pilot car driver who made all the arrangements across the country as easily as buying a ticket to go to the movies. The route is computer generated based on the load's dimensions, starting point and ending point to make it the most efficient, safe and passable route through all the states that must be transited.

As Essi-Anna was pulled out of the water in Olympia for an early morning load we were confronted with a shaft that had slipped forward making it impossible to remove one of the props. This could have increased our overall height. Fortunately the keel and lay of the boat were such that Essi-Anna sat bow down and gave clearance for leaving the prop on. We figured we would deal with the shaft issue at the other end. The lowboy we were loaded on was as low as you could go. Clearance to the road was a matter of a few inches with a steel plate which ran the entire length of the trailer to protect the keel. The trailer also had large fenders which are important so as to not throw dirt, pebbles and debris into the overlapping hull while the boat is moving down the road. Kenny, our professional hauler, had the ability to increase, through the use of air shocks, the clearance off the road to a whopping six inches when height allowed. It was truly amazing how little room for error there would be as our boat sped toward her destination, six to seven times faster per mile than her usual cruising speed.

Our driver took great care to balance and straighten the load and after he was satisfied with the way she sat, he padded all the tie downs with soft carpet pieces where they intersected with the hull, inspected the interior and exterior for proper taping and for any pre-existing scratches, chips and then, with a smile, handshake and a last, "Don't worry about a thing," our girl slid slowly through the gate at SwanTown Marina on a 2300 mile journey, like a giant fiberglass Conestoga Wagon heading for our jumping off place in Iowa. It was a strange feeling to know that five days later we would be reunited in a strange but exciting place – ready to put her and our lives back together in preparation for the journey of a lifetime.

With no need for a car and with everything except a couple of small suitcases in hand and everything we needed for life on the water for a year heading east in the cupboards and closets and holds of Essi-Anna, we caught a ride from a friend to Seattle, where we would attend a board meeting of our church for three days, prior to our departure by plane to Iowa. The timing for our arrival would coincide with that of our friends who were on a family retreat in Montana and would be traveling by car to Rock Island, Illinois just across the Mississippi from Davenport. It is amazing how, when your life interacts with geography and history these places take on new meaning. These obscure names, which had only been passing words in our vocabulary, were now as familiar as an old friend and would become temporary homes for us as we made final preparations for the final leg on land.

Chris and I had made arrangements for Wakeen's in Davenport to lift us off the truck and block us up literally feet from the Mississippi when Essi-Anna arrived. We wanted to be there for the reunion and greet her after her arduous trip over mountains and prairies. Our friends' boat would be loaded in Portland under the supervision of our church friends and make her way to Rock Island a few days after we had landed.

On arrival day we waited patiently for our behemoth, fiberglass girl to show. When she came in sight she dwarfed the semi tractor and trailer. To enter the boatyard, which was now deserted for the summer but which, when the cold winter winds blow and snow and ice block travel on the river, would be wall to wall with shrink-wrapped, winterized boats of all descriptions; Essi-Anna would have to clear one last hurdle. Her last right-of-passage was a mound upon which sat the tracks of the local railroad. Like the pro he was, Kenny made the turn, shifted down, picked up just enough speed and made the jump, sliding over the rails like a high jumper arching his back, brushing the bar without knocking it off and clearing the record breaking height while the crowd gasps with awe and rises to their feet in jubilation. There she sat, a little dirty, but without a blemish or a broken bone or even a hair out of place.

After slinging her off the trailer with the ancient crane used in the building of a nearby lock many years prior, we said our goodbyes and gladly paid the delivery, like a first time father cheerfully pays the hospital account in full after the birth of his first child. With a little extra for a job well done we waved adios to the guardians who had brought our girl to her new life on the Great Circle Loop.

A big part of the preparation is the learning and studying that takes place as you become familiar with new waters and new rules governing safe passage on any waterway. Whether it be Alaska, British Columbia, the Washington Coast or the Puget Sound and now the GCL it is important to have the right charts, cruising guides, tide table (if applicable) and current information, rules of navigation, electronics and electronic charts and equipment, and know how to use them.

We had been members of the Great Circle Loop Association, had read the newsletters and journals of other loopers and actually had been in personal contact with a few couples who had finished the loop. While searching for boats we had run into a couple who had made the trip in a 27 foot Carver. They wanted us to buy their boat and make the journey as they had, but to save our marriage and our sanity we decided to decline their offer. We did, however, glean lots of good information which they were happy to share, and we did purchase from them for less than half price, all the paper charts and cruising guides to accomplish the journey. Most people do this trip once in a lifetime so these books, if not sold afterwards, become very expensive fire starters. This particular couple's record over the route was impressive with nine groundings – two of which required towing and a few propeller replacements.

Our goal was to improve on those statistics, which we did. Not only each day on the cruise did it require refreshing on the immediate leg of the journey and the associated challenges; but prior to the trip many hours were spent reviewing the waterway, becoming familiar with the way the charts worked, reading about points of interest and examining alternate routes should one or more become necessary to use due to closures, weather or low water. That's what dreams are made of, and that's what I saw each night as I closed my eyes for peaceful rest, months before the trip, in anticipation of the adventure that lay ahead. You live it in your mind long before you experience it with your body.

In addition to the cruising charts and books we run Nobeltec Navigational Software and a special blend of charts specific to the Great Circle Route. These electronic charts included the narrow route of the rivers, lakes, inland waterways and coastal waters we would be traveling on. Traveling on the rivers and canal system is like climbing aboard a Disney Ride on rails that takes you either up or down stream. There are not many possibilities to get off track but there are many other hazards to keep an eye on. Even though you would have to try hard to get lost, the wing dams, turn outs behind island and cities and marinas marked on these charts made it possible to plan our mileage and our anchorages much more accurately. They also came in handy when traveling off the well beaten channels where the river flooded over shallow plains adjacent to the channel making the ditch invisible except for pin point GPS accuracy. Nobeltec is software we have been running for the last ten years. It has assisted us with safe passage as far north as Petersburg, Alaska and has been a lifesaver cruising the waters of British Columbia and Washington. It was essential for travel on the shallow Gulf, along the Atlantic, through the many large sounds and bays with the breakers of the Atlantic in clear view, where buoys are not visible from each other, in the fog and at confusing intersections where a wrong turn could place you in harm's way at the many shallow bars entering and exiting the ocean. We do not have all our electronic systems integrated but did have redundant radars, depth sounders and a handheld GPS that we kept on track mode to follow safe passage in or out of a tricky entrance to anchorages well off the beaten path.

That covers the dream, the preparation and a few notes about expectations for a trip like this. The following chapters are a compilation of letters describing the journey itself. The places, names, facts and adventures on the "Great Circle Loop" echo memories that will only be erased when life on this fabulous planet is over for us. This book will serve as a chalkboard for others dreaming of an adventure that is beyond imagination. It is not meant to be a literal cruising guide with all the detail necessary to make your way through the route. It does however, knit together the route in specific sections that will serve as a wonderful planning tool, outlining in narrative form what should be experienced and what should be avoided. The chapters are meant to start you thinking and dreaming about doing something extra ordinary, something beyond comprehension, to take a step toward an adventure that will change your life forever. It is an opportunity to live the trip in your mind and maybe, just maybe, you will decide to make living it vicariously through our journey a reality of your own.

If you undertake this voyage it will open up the geography, history, biology, sociology, meteorology and economics of a vast part of the United States and Canada. I promise, you will be challenged and stretched beyond your wildest imagination. For the rest of your life you will have to pinch yourself and wonder if it all took place in a dream – only to realize that dreams could never leave your heart so touched and so satisfied.

So get comfortable, sit back and slowly let your soul fall in love with the placid yet intense rhythm of one of America's greatest boating treasures and I guarantee your life will be, "Thrown for the Loop".

LOOPET 1

PUTTING HER BACK TOGETHER

GREETINGS Family and Friends,

We are ecstatic and it is hard to believe we have the boat in Davenport, Iowa just feet from the Mississippi and just north of Lock 15 – Mississippi Mile 482.9. The propeller issue and spun shaft issue is still a major obstacle to contend with before being able to be on the water when JUWIKA arrives in five days.

The boat doctor has told us there is no way to break the shaft loose from the collar and pull it out in a conventional manner. The spun shaft had actually welded itself to the collar by the spinning action of the shaft slipping in the sleeve which is attached to the transmission. This means one of the boat surgeons has to perform a tricky operation, while standing on his head in the engine room. He will have to cut the 1 ¾ inch stainless steel shaft with a reciprocating saw and tungsten blades in the tight quarters around the V- drives. This will be a long and expensive process. In addition, using the specification manual that was part of the original documentation on Essi-Anna, we ordered another shaft and collar. It had to be manufactured several hundred miles away and flown in to expedite the reassembly. Unfortunately, the transmissions used on this particular yacht were different from the ones called out in the book; thus, the shaft we ordered was 2.5 inches too short – not long – so it will have to be discarded and another ordered.

Fortunately, Tom, the owner of Wakeen's Family Boat Center, in Davenport negotiated a great expedite price for the second shaft and it arrived quickly and the correct length. One shaft for the price of two – expensive, but we said when we started this dream that we weren't going to keep track of cost – ouch!

The team at Wakeen's worked hard and long hours to get everything back together in the engine room as Chris and I worked hard to reassemble the bridge, electronics and inside of the boat. We had packed her up as though she was a moving van. It literally felt like we were moving back in.

There we sat on our blocked up perch, connected to electricity by a long extension cord to the maintenance shop; the only way to get aboard, a step ladder to the swim platform some six feet in the air. The door to the shop was left open all the time so we could make our way to the privy much the same way pioneers made their way to an outhouse.

In addition to putting Essi-Anna back together we waxed the hull and rub rails, remarked the anchor chain every ten feet and knocked off residual barnacles from the props, shafts and rudders. It would be a while before sea life, as she had known it in the Northwest, would attack her bottom. Not for several months would Essi-Anna bask in the salty brine of the Gulf, connecting in some way with the waters she had known in the Northwest. The zincs were changed, the inflatable was blown up and the bikes, which were our only means of transportation other than our God-given legs, would be loaded at the last minute; the needed groceries bought and we would be ready for splashdown.

Fortunately our companions on this journey had their car there. They had chosen to traverse the country ahead of JUWIKA, where they would leave their car in safe keeping with family in Rock Island. They were staying with relatives there so with the hospitality of our friends and their family we were able to have access to a car and some great meals and nights away from the boat.

The humidity and the bugs in Davenport during August and early September are both things to be contended with. They say the humidity is caused from all the respiration of the corn? The bugs, which must be left over from one of the plagues when God punished Egypt, are at times so thick they take up more room in the air than oxygen. Every morning we vacuumed up a myriad of them who had gone to their maker on our deck – the large boatyard light above us at night attracted them in hoards. The juice some of them secreted was a lime green color that stained the deck, making us look like a float being readied for a St. Patty's Day Parade. The other clouds of tiny white bugs that invaded at night covered the decks and black canvass like talcum powder on a geisha girl. We would be glad to be on the water.

Tollycrafts are unique to the Northwest even though there are a few in the Midwest, East Coast and Great Lakes. A 1990, 39 Tollycraft Eurosport, one of 15 actually manufactured and one of 10 still in existence, is even more of an attraction; and the same craft with Portland, Oregon, tattooed on the transom, at rest on stilts at Wakeen's, is as rare as a unicorn.

Members from the Lindsey Yacht Club, a mile up river, came in their boats and by car to gawk as we reassembled Essi-Anna at the edge of the Mississippi. They paid their visit and offered assistance and local knowledge on a daily basis. They were a wealth of information and hospitality, offering cars, rides and invites to the club for showers and meals.

We were ready to go on September 5, 2006. It had been thirteen days since Essi-Anna had been loaded aboard her chariot in Olympia and now she was ready to make the short hop over the wall and into the inviting waters of the Mississippi.

JUWIKA had been baptized in the Mississippi on September 1. She had experienced a little tussle with a tree and overpass on her journey east and had some damage to the bridge rails and steps leading to the bridge. Bill put things back together in a safe and workable fashion and negotiated $1000.00 for the damage which would have to be repaired to his total satisfaction another day. We decided to wait before leaving from our reassembly marinas on the first leg of our journey until Labor Day was over, to avoid traffic on the river; besides, we still had some finishing touches to put on Bill and Gail's boat prior to departure.

The entrance to the Rock Island Marina is a tricky one with a very shallow and narrow channel. The water level was dropping daily and their window of opportunity to make it onto the Mississippi was closing. At this point the hull of JUWIKA might have to plow some mud to make it out. We had one last dinner with the Stuenkel family in Rock Island, final checks and rechecks and we were ready to make our moves.

LOOPET 2

THE MIGHTY MISSISSIPPI DAVENPORT, IOWA TO CAIRO ILLINOIS AND THE OHIO RIVER

DEAR Family and Friends,
September 7 the day broke as clear and warm as usual with plenty of bug protein on the deck and the ancient crane exercised its bare wire, worn cable control box, ready to make another pick-up and delivery. Bill and Gail had made their last trip to the grocery store and would pull out a little ahead of us with our destination being an anchorage or dockage at Fairport 20 miles downriver. They would enter the river just below lock 15 so we would always hold the record of doing one more lock on the loop than they did or so we thought.

We would do our first test run of the shaft installation and proceed up river to fill with fuel a half mile upstream, before heading south on the Mississippi. All went off as planned but the day was two thirds spent when we finally radioed JUWIKA and entered the upriver gate of Lock 15. They had made it out of the marina with inches to spare and were moseying down the river, on a warm September evening with a light breeze in their faces and the sounds of the river to enhance their euphoric spirits. We would be spit out on the other end of the lock heading south within the hour and catch them about the time the sun went down at an anchorage across from a little restaurant in Fairport, Illinois that specialized in pulled pork sandwiches and beer. These homey riverside pubs are wonderful places of gathering with large screened in porches to keep the flocks of insects at bay.

Rounding the bend we spotted JUWIKA resting peacefully along the side of the river well outside the reach of any barge traffic that runs day and night. We hailed them on the radio and amidst the setting sun, humming of the insects and croaking of the frogs in the shoreline vegetation, we angled our way to the Iowa side of the river and set our hook, for the first time, in the soft mud of the "Mighty Mississippi". There we rested comfortably at the end of our anchor chain in 14 feet of water being caressed by the gentle flow of the river. The flicker of a third anchor light affixed to a very small cruising boat was visible just upstream from our two boat flotilla. Tomorrow we will go visiting to introduce ourselves to the neighbors.

Returning to the boats by inflatables in darkness along the Mississippi after a screened in porch feasting on the house specialty of pulled pork sandwiches; we tethered them to their cleats on 6 foot painters. We sat out on our bridges, the stars filling the heavens – reveling in the splendor of the peace; filled with satisfaction and thankfulness for all that we had been afforded. Sleep came with the counting of the first sheep and then it was morning.

We opened our eyes with excitement as the sun filtered through our curtains. As I emerged from our aft cabin through the back door into the bright sunshine I could hear faintly the sound of, "Amazing Grace" echoing across the water. Maybe we really had died and gone to heaven.

Since cruising would be our life for the next year, we had business cards made with all the particulars about who was aboard our boats, what kind of boat we were on and where they could find us by email on the water and by phone and home while on land. They made introductions more pleasant and allowed us to connect and reconnect with new friends and acquaintances on the trip who readily exchanged their cards for ours. I still have several under my plastic protector on my desk at home and often make a call to someone on the other side of the country just to check in; even a year after completing the trip. Emails drift in and out of my folder from those we became very close to and there are many homes around the country that would welcome a visit as we would welcome "loopers" into our home.

Our introduction to the early morning musician set the mood for the launching of our trip. They had been gone for a year and were just returning home to Davenport after completing the loop. Their boat was spartan and compact - not more than 25 feet long but with all the necessities for safety – not necessarily comfort to the level that we would enjoy. They told us of their experiences and gave us some local knowledge on the Mississippi which we absorbed like sponges. We said our farewells and returned to our boats, ready to venture forth on a pristine, sunny day – the first of 365 that would follow in the footsteps of each other, hearkening to the call of the loop.

With anchors pulled and charts reviewed we tuned our radios to 13 to keep tabs on any tugs and tows in the area as we motored lazily downstream to Locks 16, 17, and 18. We would also encounter our first bridge today at MM 403.1. The largest swing bridge in the United States would allow us to make passage to our second night's stop along the waterfront of Burlington, Illinois. Their city sported a fancier lit suspension bridge which crossed the river; a main arterial just a short distance and overhead from where we landed along the shoreline at a very small and rickety dock next to the boat launch. Before boldly motoring up to the wooden fishing pier, with small circular cleats meant more for smaller, recreational fishing boats I dropped the dinghy in the water while the bigger boats stayed in the channel. With the "Hummingbird" sounder measuring the depth, I scouted the ledge next to the dock and signaled the other boats on my portable VHF that the coast was clear and that we had at least a foot to spare under our keels. This would be the first of many nights docked or anchored in shallow water. In the Northwest we are accustomed to setting the hook in water 15 to 80 feet deep. It would take some time getting used to this skinny water.

This was our first look at small town America along the Mississippi. The people were friendly and inquisitive as we tied off to anything solid we could find on the dock, running some of the lines down under the dock planks themselves. Once secure we were excited to explore. As would become the norm for our trip, we were blessed with a riverfront concert less than a block away.

The day had been spent lazily drifting south toward the confluence of the Ohio River many miles downstream where we would turn our bows against the current and buck our way into Kentucky and Tennessee along the Tennessee River. While heading south on the Mississippi we would be flanked first by Iowa on the west and Illinois to the east. Just south of Lock 19 we would pick up Missouri to our west. It was one giant compass rose geography lesson custom made for us.

After dinner at Big Muddy's, a great night of sleep tied to a dock and well out of the way of any barge traffic, a taxi ride to a far off laundromat and a trip up Burlington's version of San Francisco's Lombard Street, our stay at Burlington was over.

The next stop would be Fort Madison, a half a day's journey south. This is the location of a famed fort and one of the top ten casinos on the water – the "Catfish Bend Casino" – a floating paddlewheel river boat tied to the shore of this quaint little town. In order to land at this little berg we had to pass under one of the many bridges along the Mississippi which had limited clearance. The concrete abutments or metal girders or both on these bridges display the current level of the river and the clearance from the surface. It was crucial our math was perfect and that a radio call on Channel 9 to the bridge tender was made a couple of miles in advance of our arrival, if we felt a need to have it opened for our arrival. Based on traffic – both auto and train – crossing the bridge or approaching it, the bridge tender would tell us how long we would have to wait or if it would swing or be lifted when we arrived. Trains take priority. Cars can be detained if necessary and if you could clear without an opening then no call was necessary. There is no room for error as thousands of pounds of boat being pushed by the Mighty Mississippi would be crushed like a matchstick and decapitated should your height exceed the clearance. It is needless to say, what damage could be done to traffic that crossed the river on a regular basis. It is also the boat's duty to lower anything including antennas that could be lowered to avoid an opening. This became a regular fire drill as we proceeded downstream. We had heard that the Florida Inter-coastal would be even worse.

In the case of the double-decker train/auto bridge we were approaching; it would have to be opened. The infamous bridge master, who in this case was a woman, and known to be a bit cantankerous, did not live up to her reputation. We were pleasant and she was very much so to us. She had the bridge ready and wished us a safe journey.

Directly after passing under the bridge we inquired by radio about a little marina to our starboard (that is the green side or right side facing forward for all you landlubbers).

The harbor master said he was the only thing going for a short stop to visit the town and casino. He said there was at least five feet at the entrance to his little harbor and that he had a couple spots he could land us and let us tie up for a while. Essi-Anna was in the lead so after making a hard right we slid through with the depth sounder reading "1" and a muddy soup churning behind us.

We pulled halfway into the slip he had assigned us and bottomed out with the bow unable to proceed. A quick reverse set us free as we radioed Bill to tell him our situation. Fortunately our props were still in deeper water and clear of the sticky mud bottom. Bill and Gail were already coming into the harbor plowing a trench with JUWIKA's keel which extends lower than her protected prop. Unlike the Northwest, there were no rocks, just a thick layer of mud to push through. Minutes later with less than a half a foot under our keels we tied up to the deepest dock in the marina and went ashore for a short visit.

This was only our second day but we were beginning to have an appreciation for reliable depth sounders. We would also be more cautious in the future with the calculations given to us by harbor masters along the river and do our own investigations via dinghy next time since our drafts were deeper than most of the boats that called this moorage and ones like it home. A short visit was all we needed and off we went with thanks, trying to find the trough we had plowed coming in and then we were back into the well marked channel of the river.

The evening of September 10 we scouted a wide bend in the river well outside of the markers and anchored in ten feet of water just as the sun snuck behind the horizon. In the distance to the east we could see what looked like the castle at Disneyland lighting up the early evening sky. There was no place to land the dinghies to cure our curiosity. The shorelines were filled with lily pads and bulrushes. Besides, this fairytale scene was some distance away. We speculated that it must be some huge church steeple of sorts. Only after a peaceful night of rest gently rocked in the arms of the river to a lullaby of insects and frogs and following our arrival at Quincy, Missouri, Yacht Club the next day, would we discover that it was Nauvoo, Illinois, the site where Joseph Smith had been killed and Mormons pilgrimage today to commemorate his legacy. It is the Mormon version of Williamsburg.

We had traversed locks 19, 20 and 21 on the way south and were now approaching Quincy, Illinois. They have their own yacht club so we pulled in and asked some of the members if we could stay the night and what the charge would be. They were happy to have us and their curiosity as to where we had come from and how we got there was so thick you could part it with a comb. Hospitality was their middle name except for one rather persistent man who had been refreshing himself at a funeral reception in the clubhouse who insisted we pay $20.00 for each boat for our short stay. Rather than create hard feelings and in opposition by the other members, we forked out our dues and thanked him for his generosity. We hope the yacht club benefited from our contribution and not the local tavern. Quincy is at MM 324.9 some 250 miles downriver from our starting point.

The Mississippi is a river with rules that must be followed if you plan on being more than a statistic of disaster which happens to many boaters each and every year. Besides the huge amount of commercial traffic and the many dams and locks, there are the wing dams to contend with. These are piling or rock jetties that jut out into the river from both sides to channel the current to the middle which keeps the dredged channel deep and silt free as long as possible. These can be tremendous hazards to navigation if the water is so high that their tops don't indicate their whereabouts. The river charts show most of them. But should you stray from the channel or during the exploration of an anchorage (which may be found between two of these dams) forget to pay them heed, you will find yourself pinned against one of these protrusions with gaping holes in your hull, props and shafts badly damaged and listing heavily in the swift current of the river. This would be our worst nightmare and most likely the end of the trip.

Aboard our little river boats, making our way down the Mississippi, one can conjure up what it must have been like to travel this historic waterway a hundred years or more ago aboard a massive, churning, steam –powered paddle wheeler. We haven't run into any yet but as we make our way toward Hannibal, Missouri, mile marker 309.07 we can't help but visualize Tom Sawyer and Huck Finn lazily floating downstream on a makeshift log raft – corn cob pipes in their mouths – spinning tales of pirate's treasure and stolen booty.

A small dock made of plastic planks at the river's edge below a modest Hannibal Yacht Club clubhouse was our next landing point, the cleats of which were intended for much smaller boats. The sign on the dock said "For Yacht Club Members Only;" but as we landed, having no other options, we were greeted by a member who welcomed us as though we were part of the "Thatcher Family" and told us to tie off as best we could and explore the town.

The arch at the entrance to this most enchanting, literarily famous town is that of a huge ship's wheel reminiscent of those on the great sternwheelers of the Mississippi. A statue of Mark Twain also adorns the waterfront. His thick mustache and grinning face retell the stories of a life full of adventure along these ever-changing banks of America's infamous river highway.

During my college days I played the part of Huckleberry Finn, so this visit plucked at my heart strings and drew me back into not only days long gone by on the Mississippi but also days long past in my own life. My Becky Thatcher is named Chris, and the fears recounted when throwing cats after ghosts in eerie graveyards have been replaced by real losses of those who have gone on before me.

A plaque in the Tom Sawyer museum put it best. Tom and Huck were talking and Tom said to Huck, "Perhaps if we are good enough then maybe God will allow us to be pirates." In spite of not being good enough, He had allowed us to be pirates and travel this mystical river on our own boats and for this we are ever grateful. My soul was renewed as we said good-bye to Hannibal aboard our plastic pirate ships – having relived the tale - our eyes seeing the river in a new light.

That evening we pulled off river into a wide and shallow lake-like back water behind a large island called Cridder at mile marker 202.9. There was lots of swinging room and the night was calling for heavy winds and lightening so we anchored up separately, well out of the channel – putting out lots of chain rode in case the weather threw its fury our way. We could watch the barge traffic in the main channel a couple of hundred yards away and hear the train as it whistled its way along the shoreline. River boats and trains tend to follow the same parallel routes.

As night fell, dinner was done and a movie plugged in to the DVD player, we were just settling down for a relaxing evening. Bill and Gail's dinghy was tied to the back of Essi-Anna when our boat was shaken by an unexpected gust of wind, flash of lighting and a clap of thunder so powerful it lit and shook the sky like an atomic explosion.

This was the first dynamite stick blast of what became an unbelievable storm which spun our boats on their anchors like the spinning blades of a helicopter. The rains that accompanied were torrential and the heavy wind and light and sound show created such a clatter themselves that the thunder was drowned out. The water came in buckets, without relenting and soon the companion ways on the sides of Essi-Anna flooded with water. Fortunately the drains kept up with the torrent, but barely, and no water entered through the door into the cabin. Bill and Gail were unable to return to their boat. Bilge pumps went off to rid the engine room of water seeping in there; and Bill and Gail's dinghy, viewed through our aft window, looked like a kid's wading pool.

In the midst of the storm and between lightning strikes I lowered the antennas and dropped our dinghy into the water; before the bottom was torn out due to the weight of the water building up. I was drenched in a matter of seconds as I dashed around trying to prevent any damage and lower our profile on the water.

At one point Gail asked what that light was making circles back and forth in the distance. "JUWIKA," was Bill's answer, as he watched her revolve wildly in the flashes, looking as though she was illuminated by the huge lights in a big league baseball stadium. We believe in our Claw anchors and have sworn by them for all our years boating in the Northwest. We gave thanks for them and for divine intervention as we and they had been tested to the extreme on the Big Muddy which tomorrow would live up to that name.

Two full hours later the storm passed and we surveyed the results as Bill and Gail made their way back home. All was well except for flooded dinghies. Everyone was safe, no damage done. On our radios we thanked God that we were well out of the main channel tucked behind this island; which would shield us from the barrage of debris that would race downstream during our peaceful rest and into our continued course toward the confluence of the Illinois River a day's journey away.

Along the banks of the Mississippi the homes are testaments to the vengeance this river deals out on a regular basis. Many of the homes, in fact, most of the homes, to include mobile homes, sit on stilts or airy foundations a good ten feet off the ground to allow the rising flood waters to pass under them without destroying them. Someone asked me what the Mississippi is like. I said, "It is: wide and narrow, winding and straight, deep and shallow, populated and desolate, full of scenery and wildlife and always muddy. Today was no different but just as magnificent.

There is a little hint of chill in the air September 12, 2006 as we make our way 75 miles downstream toward Alton, Illinois. The storm the night before gave us the kick we needed to make great time on this long leg. We traveled by huge flocks of white pelicans which were a strange sight for us. We were not expecting to see them this far north. Duck and goose blinds dotted the shallow flats and the sound of guns popping in the distance made us anticipate that at any moment we could have a gift of fresh waterfowl drop, with a thud from the heavens onto our decks.

We had only been on the river five days but it seemed as though this beginning to the loop was preparing us for the loop of a lifetime. We had only paid for dock space one night and as we passed by the confluence with the Illinois River, headed for the Alton Marina – a world class five star complex with floating swimming pool and hot tub, great ship's store and private suite bath and shower facilities, we looked forward to rejoining civilization again for a change of venue. Time would dictate that we could only linger here for a day and then proceed on our journey downstream.

The hillsides on our approach were peppered with large caves and the highway followed the route of the river – cars, trucks and other vehicles firing by at hyper-speed velocity compared to our meager eight knots. Three huge locks had been transited in rapid succession, one of which we floated through without tying off, with the permission of the Lock Master, like two rubber ducks in a bathtub. Then we were tied to a real dock with real cleats in a larger town on the outskirts of St. Louis. This is an historic spot for the Lewis and Clark expedition, which we felt we had just come off of. Except for the drone of traffic on the bridge directly overhead our slips, we rested well, after having a great Italian dinner out with relatives of Bill and Gail's. They drove down to get a glimpse of these crazy mariners from the west.

We began the last stretch of 150 miles of the Mississippi and then onto the Ohio River before entering Kentucky Lake and eventually the Tenn-Tombigbee and the Tombigbee - Black Warrior canal system that would take us to the Gulf of Mexico at Mobile, Alabama. This final leg is a long stretch of the river with few marinas and supply stations, so we would fuel up and re-provision, fill with water and pump out our holding tanks before leaving Alton.

St. Louis, just a short ways south past lock 11, another day to the south, would have been a great place to plan a stop but we had been told the dock for transient boats was an old barge in an uncomfortable part of the city so we would give it a wide berth and check it out before landing. We preferred the solitude of the backwaters but always enjoyed a change of pace in the cities.

The Mississippi is well marked. The channel has a guaranteed depth of nine feet in the channel which is essential for the commercial tugs and barges to make their way up and down this super highway. Out of the channel there are no guarantees so before we left the ditch to tuck in someplace safe for the evening Chris took the helm of Essi-Anna and I lowered the dinghy. With the depth sounder on the dinghy I scouted out the area for depth, snags, wing dams and any other things that could go "bump in the night". When I believed all was safe I radioed Chris on our walkie-talkies or portable VHF radio and she relayed the message via radio to Bill and Gail. I then went back to the channel and led the boats into our private evening anchorage.

We were the talk of the river, river captains and those we encountered on shore who were astounded and enthralled when they heard of our adventure and where we were from. It made for great conversation and some crazy questions about the fabled Northwest Passage and Panama Canal.

Enough for now; banana pancakes for breakfast an early morning dip in the hot tub and then off to St. Louis. The section of water between Alton and St. Louis is heavy with working river traffic and riddled with no wake zones and canals that lead to the heart of the city. There are a few locks and one diversion canal that must be negotiated in order to miss a dead end that would lead us over a dam and overfall and not through the lock system. The signage is excellent and no problem unless you are asleep at the wheel.

After passing through lock 11 the St. Louis Arch frames the entrance of the city like a colorless rainbow and the bridges that span the river and the ancient rust-colored and dilapidated metal factory buildings along the river to the east stand like monsters out of some eerie "Waterworld" set I had seen at Universal Studios. Trains transit the bridges to and from the west side where the modern city skyscrapers starkly contrast this wreckage with towering smokeless smokestacks and what seem to be millions of windows framed in metal, long since washed or repaired, each an eye into an era gone by. It was not a safe or welcoming looking place.

A call on the radio to the infamous tie up barge, where we could spend the night, and which we had not yet seen as we dodged paddle-wheelers loaded with tourists, raised a voice which seemed to echo the ambiance of the strange eastside landscape. It invited us to come and stay in a tone that equaled a sardonic monster, assuring us we would be well taken care of. In the background we could hear other chatter and talk – something about ordering us a pizza. We responded with silence as we slipped stealthily down river and out of sight of their watchful eye as they requested one last time that we come and linger! We moved on without a word. Good-bye St. Louis.

Downstream just out of the city limits between two wing dams, and within grand view of what appeared to be an academy of sorts high on a cliff on the opposite shore, we dropped anchor for the night. The current runs strong and so care was taken to set the anchors well and put out an appropriate amount of rode. The flow keeps you straight in the river with no fear of swinging so it is possible to set anchor close to the shoreline without worry of being on the sandy beach in the morning. We could hear the chiming of the bells at the academy as we leisurely relaxed on our bridge enjoying a glass of wine and a beautiful sunset, joking about what the night might have been like in downtown St. Louis. Whenever we anchored in swift water or in windy conditions we always anchor separately. Only in settled weather and safe surroundings and conditions that allowed us time to respond in good order to an emergency or where there was only room for us to raft did we do so.

Bill and Gail usually rafted next to us. The current keeps you straight and with 70 feet of chain and an oversized anchor out in twelve feet of water we sleep as soundly as if someone had put us in a cryogenic chamber and turned on the machine for eight hours.

We woke to the first real fog of the trip, so we decided to wait a while, relax and read as the descending current continued to drum its sleepy rhythm against the hull. An hour later JUWIKA cast off her lines and lazily drifted downstream in the glorious rays of sunlight that had evaporated the fog and let us loose of her grip. We followed in lazy pursuit toward our midday destination of Kimswick, Illinois, and the heritage homes and culinary delight of a restaurant named the "Blue Owl" where we would enjoy a lunch out.

This is also the home of Hoppie's, which is a riverside dock consisting of ancient rust laden barges tied together to make a safe river side tie a few hours by boat south of St. Louis. It was not our goal to stay there over night, but "The Hoppies" are the foremost experts on the Mississippi south of their marina, so we looked forward to gleaning any information about water conditions and weather that we could expect to encounter on the stretch of this sparsely populated and wild river as we made our way toward the Ohio. They had been serving boaters along this route since 1934, seven days a week, 24 hours a day.

Kimswick is a short walk from Hoppies. The Mrs. welcomed us in her bathrobe and pointed the way to town. I asked her what her favorite pastry from the "Blue Owl" was and she smiled as I told her I would bring her a few delights for her hospitality and knowledge of the river.

The town itself is a historical masterpiece ¾ of a mile from the dock with log and lap sided homes dating to the 1780's. Old bridges span a creek on the road to town. The "Budweiser People" have an exquisite equestrian center on its outskirts used for therapy for individuals with certain disabilities.

When the lunch bell rang, like the hoard of others from the surrounding area we flocked to the Blue Owl. We ate generous helpings of mouth watering white bean chili – a house specialty, and took with us dessert for the evening – a mile high apple pie topped with caramel and crumbled cinnamon crust made of sugar and pecans – no bigger than a pot pie but piled and bulging over ten inches high with slices from six perfectly cooked apples. This is a nationally renowned treat and not to be missed.

Delivering the promised treats to Mrs. Hoppie, who was still in her robe, we asked our critical, exploratory questions and then bid our farewells and drifted south, bathed in the warmth of another grand day compliments of our friend, "The Mississippi".

With Missouri on our starboard and Illinois to port we rounded a bend to the sound of water churning through what sounded like a large washing machine on a slow wash cycle. This was our first meeting with the royalty of the river – "The Mississippi Queen". She was making her way north – paddles flailing as she churned her way upstream, sporting her name in large, bold and colorful red letters and adorned with all the golden gingerbread and lacework of a real lady. We passed her on the two whistle, which meant that we kept her to our starboard, and cranking our necks, stood at attention as we gawked at her splendor until her Majesty rounded the bend and was out of sight. This brief encounter with history and a time when river pilots and steamboats were what astronauts and space shuttles are today we reestablished our rhythm on the river and sharpened our senses to the Mississippi's majestic past.

The Kaskaskia River is a small tributary at mile 117.3. All along the river system there are markers attached to trees or poles that correspond with the charts and tick off the miles of the river so that those traveling can keep track of their progress. We had heard that the lock master who tended the lock on the step up or down from this feeder river to the Mississippi would allow us to tie off on the waiting wall for the evening, out of the way of the sparse traffic traversing his chambers. He also gave us his blessings to use the concrete dam for a dining platform.

A radio call confirmed our stay as we snaked our way through visible deadheads breaking the surface of the water, which were stuck fast in the muddy bottom. We savored a simple dinner in expectation of devouring our apple pie which stood like a mountain of delight upon our small but adequate picnic table. It had been eight days since we had left our friends in Davenport, Iowa. There were only two nights where we had paid for space at the Quincy and Alton Marinas. We have been captured by the cadence of the river which penetrates your body and flows steadily through your veins like the life blood which flows with every beat of the heart.

Fuel had been very reasonable on the river ranging from $2.39 to $2.89 a gallon with diesel being surprisingly a little more. Over the last eight years we have conserved on our fuel consumption and hours on our engines, which also decreases oil changes, by running on one engine and alternating each hour. This allows us to travel at trawler speeds burning less than ¾ of a gallon per mile. With a kick in the pants from the flow of the Mississippi we have gotten as good as ½ a gallon per mile which is phenomenal for big block 8.1 liter high output, fuel injected Merc-Cruisers. We recommend this method only after checking with your transmission company to see if free-wheeling your inactive, neutral transmission will damage it. In our case it does not and with the exception of running in heavier seas or needing the power through tricky current filled channels up north, or out running a storm at 22 knots, this is the normal mode of operation for us. Eight to nine knots at 1900 to 2100 rpms on one engine is very economical and very comfortable. The auto pilot also steers her just fine on one engine.

Good night from Kaskaskia Lock. Visions of apple pie, dancing in our heads.

LOOPET 3

KASKASKIA RIVER CONFLUENCE WITH THE MISSISSIPPI TO KENTUCKY LAKE

DEAR Family and Friends,
After having let the Mississippi rock us in her arms for almost 500 miles we arrived at the mouth of the Ohio two days ago.

Our last night on the Little Diversion Canal off river on the Mississippi reminded us of being in the swamps of the everglades minus the alligators and mangroves. Turtles lined up on the logs like tin soldiers in a military parade, and hundreds of fish surrounding the boats gulped air from the surface of the still water which made up this little backwash of the Mississippi. The current just outside the canal opening flows steadily and swiftly, so to make our entrance we had to pass her by and approach from downstream to keep from getting slammed into the downstream bank. A wonderful walk along a huge sandbar on the far side of the river, only accessible by our inflatables, as the sun painted her collage of autumn colors in the sky, was the ending to another magical day.

The deafening sounds of the night insects filled the starlit evening air. There were no biters so we sat outside and enjoyed the millions of stars that filled the heavens. This was close to Cape Girardeau 49 miles N of the mouth of the Ohio.

Tugs and tows, going by in the evening, passed by our safe little anchorage which was tucked 100 yards up this narrow channel. They could see our anchor lights and flashed their high powered spotlights that can illuminate buoys a mile or more away, on us. It was almost as though we were playing a marine version of hide and seek; as they passed noisily by, their powerful engines huffing and puffing and their huge propellers churning the waters to combat the flow of this mighty river. Then they were gone and it was pitch black again leaving only the sounds of night along the river.

The last part of the Mississippi winds like a snake and the scenery is magnificent. There was a little barge traffic until we hit the Ohio at Cairo, Illinois. So far we have not left Illinois since we started even though we had left Missouri behind and now entertained Kentucky to our starboard. The barge traffic is amazing with huge trains of barges, as many as 35, being pushed by powerful tugs and skillful captains and crews, mounded high with coal or covered with lids protecting the grain or other precious cargo inside. To be dwarfed in a huge lock and have a monster tug and tows grind its way in behind you scrapping both sides, metal against concrete, and then to come to a snail's pace halt feet from your stern is an experience that will be embossed in my mind for a lifetime.

The water remains warm - around 72 degrees - and the Ohio is as muddy as the Mississippi. Only now we are pushing a '2' knot current and the traffic is thick. Much of our trip had been through rural America so this was like a huge traffic jam of tugs and radio communication as we negotiated our way through the maze. Chris has filled three pages with tug names like: Miss Chris, Wally Roller, Super America and Bill Elmer. These tugs, which took the place of the steam sternwheelers carrying cargo to and from America's heartland, have enormous engines with horsepower in the thousands. Many have telescoping pilot houses allowing them to raise and lower their heights so they can pass under bridges without having to wait for bridge tenders to grant passage. Men scramble about these humungous rafts of barges checking and double checking high tension lines and cables that bind them together like handcuffs on a criminal; the current of the river trying to wrench them into separate pieces of these floating commercial puzzles.

Sadness filled our eyes as we turned the corner and bucked the current north on the Ohio. The lower end of the Mississippi from the Ohio to the Gulf of Mexico at New Orleans is a trough with no navigational value for pleasure boaters and few stops along the way so a turn up the Ohio was the route which would lead us to more adventures and beauty on our way to the Gulf.

The Ohio would take us 50 miles to Paducah where we will choose between the Cumberland or Tennessee River, each of which will take us to the fresh clear water of Kentucky Lake and the resort area of the "Land Between the Lakes".

We anchored well off the channel at mile 27 on the Ohio and had a grand evening just upstream from a new dam they are building that will take fifteen years to complete. We dropped the hook in shallow water a quarter of a mile away from the main channel on a wide stretch of the river, tucked behind a sandbar so no floating debris would awaken us in the evening. We had spent a couple of long days on the rivers. Yesterday had been eleven hours. We passed over what is called a wicket dam. It is basically a huge fence that is lowered when the water level will accommodate traffic over top of it when the river is high enough to bypass the locks. If the wickets are up you have to use the locks. The wickets came down only a day ago. Prior to that there was so much backed up river traffic a three day wait was required as boats waited their turn to get upstream or downstream beyond this point on the Ohio.

The currents over the wickets, when down, are a little extreme- kind of like Deception Pass at a ¼ flood or ebb speed, where water rushes from the Straits of Juan de Fuca into the Puget Sound; but not a problem.

Arriving at the meeting of the Cumberland and Tennessee Rivers at Paducah in the early afternoon, we decided to take the shorter route up the Tennessee to Kentucky Lake. We would return to this quaint little town by car once we settled in above Kentucky Lake Dam. We called the Lock Master, even though we were three hours away, and asked him to tell us what kind of wait to expect. He said to get there as fast as possible and perhaps we could time our lockage close to perfect so we did.

The Tennessee is beautiful. Turtles - big and small - lined the shores, basking in the sunshine on logs at the river's edge. It was so hot my Keens started to melt so we wet down our tee shirts and hung up towels from the bimini to block out the sun. The river is much narrower than the Ohio and Mississippi which allowed us to be up close and personal to the shorelines where industry and coal fired factories lined part of its banks close to Paducah.

We arrived at the locks as a barge was going in and the lock master told us he would take him up the 59 feet to the lake, come back down and get us, taking us up by ourselves in this huge old style lock, before the next tug arrived from the south. This was very fortunate

This lock is very old and when the lock master lets water into the chamber there is extreme turbulence for small boats. You rise to the level of the lake or lower to the level of the river tied only to the middle cleat on the boat and floating bollards that moves up or down as you do. It is necessary to put out fenders at several levels along your rub rail on the side tied to the wall and then try and hold your boat off the wall as you ascend or descend. It is very difficult and the boat gets smashed against the wall smashing our 12 inch diameter fenders as slim as a piece of paper. Without them and constant vigilance the boats would be totally scrapped up. While we were wrestling with Kentucky Lock we heard a sound like a freeway rush hour traffic coming toward us. A huge cloud was racing across the river towards us as we wrestled against this concrete monster. On the assent to the lake mother-nature had turned on her fire hose drenching us to the bone. We gave thanks for health and strength to finish the task. At the top we were dripping, hot and dirty from the slimy walls of the lock, which weep their ooze of scum onto you like the drool of a Saint Bernard.

We told the lock master that this was wilder than a Disneyland ride and thanked him. He said he was new and was just getting use to the old girl. That explained a lot as this was the toughest lock we had experienced on the trip thus far. At the top, the highest point of our trip since leaving the Mississippi and before our fall toward Mobile, an expansive and placid Kentucky Lake greeted us. But a storm was brewing so we needed to find a place to tuck in and drop the anchor. It was getting late with about an hour to total darkness. The sun had already set behind the trees. We navigated the cut between the lake and the Cumberland River and discovered a wonderful little bay and anchored, shared dinner and listened to our church tape from New Heights, thanks to Esther and Steve, our daughter and son-in-law and then hit the sack in a downpour that lasted almost all night. Super hot and wet were the words for the day as we closed our eyes in exhaustion.

We had put 600 miles under our keels and had a ton of memories, with three great American rivers behind us.

We would relax at Green Turtle Bay on the Cumberland River side of the Land Between the Lakes tomorrow and call, our other son-in-law's, Jeff's grandparents who would meet up with us and show us their beautiful area.

Goodnight - Sleep well and let us know what is happening in your lives,

Blessings,

Chuck and Chris

LOOPET 4

KENTUCKY AND TENNESSEE

GREETINGS to Friends and Family,

We have spent the last three days taking it easy at docks. After our long day getting to Kentucky Lake we anchored that evening and woke to a mixed day of sun and rain.

We paddled over to Green Turtle Bay - one mile - and stayed with them for a couple of days. For the first time the "Loopers" - as we are called - showed up in mass with stories of their journeys. Most had been on the loop longer than us and some were taking a breather from the journey, leaving their boats at the dock for a month or so or abandoning them altogether. We are probably the youngest in the bunch. All kinds of boats and all kinds of people! Many are in their late 60's and early 70's and are doing it for the first time - first boat. They have sold everything and are living the dream they had years ago. Green Turtle is full of turtles of all sizes and of course green.

Fall is settling in with coolness in the evening air but the days are still warm so we haven't had to hang up our shorts for confining long pants. The swarms of insects we came to intimately know have started to put on their winter coats. It is September 22.

This general area is called "Land between the Lakes". It is the area between the Tennessee River and The Cumberland River. There are lots of wilderness areas, resorts, summer homes and lovely permanent places along its shorelines which extend some 200 miles.

While at the dock, Channel Six Television station was filming a story on water levels on the lake and river systems and "there I was", less than 24 hours in the area, commenting on the need for the Army Corp of Engineers to keep the water levels higher. For some strange reason I was the only American on the dock at the time so they chose me to comment as their expert witness. That night I was on the news - "Chuck Hewitson - Boater". We laughed so hard.

The highlight of our stay at Green Turtle was meeting up with our son-in-law's grandparents from "Possum Trot" Kentucky. Jeff's grandparents were so gracious and hospitable. They came to the boat for breakfast at Green Turtle. It was a glorious sunny day. Then they toured us around the countryside in their Suburban, took us grocery shopping and to an open air veggie market. We visited the town of "Metropolis", Home of Superman. Let your imaginations run wild and you will see the infamous newspaper, gigantic statue on the town square and cut outs on the street where you can insert your head and snap your own private photo session, which allows you for the moment to be, "It's a bird! It's a plane! No!! It's Superman!!!"

We also visited Fort Massac, a remnant from the French and Indian Wars. Then we took in a wonderful barbecue lunch with St. Louis Style ribs. We relived our experience at St. Louis with them.

A visit to Paducah, (William Clark settled here after the westward expedition) - named after "Chief Paduke", with all its wonderful water front murals and river boats was exceptional. A tour of "Possum Trot" and Fran and Neil's was a highlight. Neil shared with us that their city limit boundary signs are in high demand and need to be replaced often, as people collect them for their garages or to hang in their bedrooms which has to bring a smile to their faces on a regular basis.

Since they only had a two seat GMC, Bill and I took turns sitting in the back like we use to do when we were kids. Bill looked funnier than I did back there since his knees stuck up higher and with the groceries packed in around him he looked like the Schwann delivery man. We had a memorable day with Fran and Neil and are so happy we could connect with our family in Kentucky.

One of the things that Neil showed us in his backyard was where the crayfish live under the mud; making conical dirt chimneys which act as vents, or so we were told. The holes and mounds were all over the yards and gardens at their home. "This was Very Strange"! We have moles in the northwest – they have crayfish.

Fishing in this area is huge! - crappies, bass, blue gill and of course catfish are all on the menu. There are thousands of high powered, sleek and expensive race horse bass boats. House boats in the 50 to 80 foot range are also a dime a dozen.

While at Green Turtle we walked to a small town about a mile away to have the world famous "Pattie's Pork Chop". It is 2 inches thick and the best that $$$$ can buy. Each couple split an order which came complete with all the trimmings and a mini loaf of freshly baked bread served in its oven hot terra cotta flower pot. We topped it off with lemon meringue pie that had that white, luscious, sugar oozing, golden crusted topping reaching well into the next county north - but not for long. No dinner that night. We found out later that Pattie's family owns most of the town including the "Harley Davidson Dealership" in a town of 400; but sporting a huge summer vacation population.

Last night was another "White Squall" evening with high winds and lots of "Cats and Dog rain". We anchored at a state park on the Kentucky side of the lake. Tonight we are at a dock in Paris Landing, which is a state park in Tennessee. These parks are amazing, to include: lodges, conference centers, trailer parks and camp grounds, lakefront cabins, 18 hole golf courses, marinas and wonderful trails to hike and bike. We were glad to be tied up and cozy in our little motor homes on the water as another round of rain and high winds was expected.

Today we rented a car and visited "Home Place", a living museum from mid 1800 rural Kentucky life. We also visited a place where the "deer and the antelope" - actually where the "elk and the bison range".

Well enough for now!

Bill and Gail send their greetings.

Keep in touch. We love the new church web site and staying in touch with church family and others that way. Nice job Cyndy!

For those of you who know them - we have heard from Sherwoods who are traveling the country in their motor home and LeCounts who are helping to rebuild New Orleans with a group called Laborers for Christ. We will try and rendezvous with them in the near future.

God's Blessing to all and healing where it is needed, guidance and wisdom when sought and health, peace and joy to you and your families.

You are in our thoughts and prayers.

Stay in touch!

Fondly,

Chuck and Chris

Greetings to all our family and friends,

Wow, have we had the rain and wind, lightning and thunder; and if you have been watching the weather channel or the national weather news, even tornados. We thank God we have been spared the experience of being directly hit by one of these destructive natural and customary phenomena's even though they have been close enough to brush us with their breath. We have storm tied our boats with double lines and battened down the hatches today in preparation, as huge black storm clouds bellow above the tree lines just miles away. One night we got 4 inches of rain and the sky was lit up like the blast of atomic explosions. In spite of it all it passed without harm to us and the humidity wasn't too bad except for a few nights.

We stayed put at the dock in a place called Paris Landing State Park on Kentucky Lake in the beautiful state of Tennessee. This wonderful little marina is home to a coast guard station and a little marina store. It is also close to the little town of Paris so we were able to rent a car and go exploring. On this swath of land between the Tennessee River and the Cumberland River there were many tobacco farms in the 1800's and in the 1900's. During the prohibition this was also the home of some of the finest high quality "moonshine" made. The area, at that time, was called "Golden Pond".

Today there is a museum and an interpretive center located there, which tells the story of that bootlegging era gone by. We saw no sign of customized Fords hauling mason jars filled with this potent elixir.

The area is peppered with over 200 cemeteries. The tombstones tell the story of church and family life in this unique part of the United States.

These sacred grounds and the roads leading to them are considered off limits to outsiders.

We also visited a working farm from the 1850's called the "Home Place".

This living museum depicts, in a very real way the life of a middle class farmer during that era.

Farms during that time were very self-sufficient. The exhibits included the raising and growing of food, tobacco for sale, daily life, the construction of log homes which were sometimes made from rafts used to float down the rivers, and all the crafts and provisioning needed to make a life for them and their families.

We sat in a small log home on handmade wooden chairs from the 19th century, huddled around the rustic, crackling fireplace as the man of the house, dressed in soiled overalls, told us about his farm and life in the 1850's. His wife was peeling potatoes in preparation for the evening meal. We then were invited to join him as he slopped the pigs and tended to the drying and curing of his tobacco crop in a crude barn made of sassafras logs. Smoke from smoldering fire pits in the drying shed seeping aromatic plumes of smoke from the cracks in the roof.

Later in the day we passed modern barns, smoke seeping from cracks in their roofs, as they cured their cash crop of tobacco. We were told that a farmer could make a good living on six acres of good ground with a healthy tobacco crop.

The scenery here is magnificent. Huge rolling, green lawns freshly mown are the norm and long white or brown rail fences grace the fashionable homes. The trees are predominately hard wood and mostly oak with an interspersing of pine. In a week or so the colors of autumn will start to sew their mosaic into the landscape and the forests will be ablaze with crimson, yellow, orange and all shades of green.

The people here exude southern hospitality. We are offered rides as we walk along country roads and many strangers have offered to let us use their cars to get into nearby towns from the lakeshore.

This is also an area very much steeped in the history of the Civil War. Cemeteries, battlefields, confederate flags, wall plagues and historical markers tell the story of the struggle and pain and its impact on the families of this area and our nation.

We went for a walk yesterday and came upon a "cricket farm" in a gentleman's garage so I stopped and asked him if he would give us a tour. He was very hospitable and the farm was very interesting - raising crickets for bait and feed for all kinds of snakes, lizards and frogs.

He had lots of confederate memorabilia hanging in his shop and his mailbox was decorated like a confederate flag. His license plate also told the story of his allegiance. On a crude table under the gallery of Confederate Generals was a jar of pickled eggs which we imagined would be consumed in a late evening meeting where discussions of how the fish were biting and what it would have been like if the south had won would be carried on. The owner, with a hospitable yet skeptical eye, peering over his glasses, asked us where we were from since we didn't sound much like we were from those parts. In spite of our heavy northern accent, he was very kind and shared his story and the story of his little enterprise.

Traveling by water we move very slowly. It is a tremendous way to let the scenery, people, history and geography sink into our bodies, minds and souls. At seven to eight miles per hour there is much opportunity to reflect and think about who we are and where we have been. It also gives us time to appreciate the variety and uniqueness that makes up these wonderful United States.

Today we left Paris Landing and meandered lazily south on Kentucky Lake. There were memories of holding an owl at the Paris lodge. We met a lady who was doing Tennessee golf course reviews, who was more interested in our story and may include us in her magazine. With a seafood buffet, including hush puppies, catfish and frog legs still under our belts, we couldn't help but think of how blessed and fortunate we are to be a part of this huge experience.

Good night - at anchor in a little bay called Pebble Isle under a clear sky and a blanket of a million stars.

Blessings,
Stay in touch and let us know what is happening in your lives.
Chuck and Chris

Greetings to family and friends,

It has been a lazy last 10 days. We have only done about 100 miles and have enjoyed exploring Kentucky Lake and The Land Between the Lakes. The area is very beautiful and is a wonderful recreational area for off-road vehicles, hiking, camping, hunting and boating.

We have arrived at a place called, "Pebble Isle" Marina. It is owned by two brothers and by one of the brother's wives. It is a peaceful place on a gorgeous little bay. The osprey screech above the lake, white egrets grace its shore and the water is full of turtles, blue gill and catfish that we feed stale biscuits from the little restaurant to. It is very reasonable to stay here and since Bill and Gail need to go home for Julie and Joel's birth of a new son or daughter? - We will hang out here and wait for their return. We booked dock space for a month even though we will only be here for three weeks since the weekly or daily rate would have been more expensive. At $175.00 per month it is almost free in comparison to dock space we expect to rent in Florida and along the east coast.

The marina borders a park where General William Bedford Forrest (confederate cavalry) defeated the Union Navy. It is near a little town called New Johnsonville. This general eventually became the founder of the KKK, which, as far as I am concerned, takes away from his heroic status.

There are beautiful roads for bike riding and trails for hiking. We see a copper colored mother fox and her kits sitting on the side of the road almost every evening. She watches us intensely, making sure that the coast is clear before giving the signal for her kits to scamper in and out of sight, chasing each other's flaming red and white paint brush tails in a game of tag.

This part of the lake is also an area where they culture fresh water pearls because the lake has so many fresh water mussels. You see dive boats all around the lake. There are also catfish long lines, which are used to commercially fish these huge delectable suckers.

One young diver I met had rigged a crude hose like apparatus to a small air compressor and with hose clamps and duct tape had created his own little aqua-lung. He weighted himself down with a lead belt and heavy boots with forked prongs on the front to gain traction. He literally would go overboard with a rope tied around his waist and to the front of his boat; and with compressor humming in his rickety skiff, went walking on the bottom like some strange sea monster in search of these fresh water pearls – his life just seconds away from hanging on the edge of disaster. He was relatively poor but made his living this way.

A strange sport here is bare hand wrestling of the huge catfish, which live in the lake or in holes along the banks of the streams and rivers. "Noodlers", as they are called, wade through shallow water and stick their arms or legs in the large caverns along the muddy riverbanks. The fish suck onto their body and they wrestle them until one or the other gives up. Some are very large and require the "Noodler" to become totally submerged - holding their breath until they can tire out the strange whiskered prehistoric looking creatures and surface for a gulp of well needed air with arm or hand or leg or foot bloodied from the match; a toothless smiling wrestler holding one of these giant aquatic foes.

The marinas and the people we have met along the way are always offering us the use of their cars. Many of the marinas have courtesy cars to run to town or go exploring or shopping in. Wal-Mart Super Stores are the store of choice and dot the landscape in every little town or burg.

One of the couples we met the other evening was from Tennessee. They were completing part of the loop. They were neat Christian people. Chris, Betty and Gail took the courtesy van and visited Loretta Lynn's home and grounds, to include a tour of a coal mine associated with this coal miner's daughter. Bill and I worked on the boats. We had dinner together and told stories of our adventures. They thought we were OK Yankees. Very nice people!

Yesterday we locked up the boats and headed for Nashville in an Enterprise car, to drop Bill and Gail off at the airport. Believe it or not Enterprise drove an hour to the marina to pick us up, drove back to the Enterprise office, rented us the car and when we dropped the car off in Nashville drove us back to our hotel; all for $39.95 - Wow! We are Enterprise believers!

We got a hotel room and then met up with friends - Sherwoods - who were traveling through in their motor home. It is crazy to think of where we all are.

We will meet my brother and sister-in-law here tonight and are scheduled to go to the Grand Ole Opry tomorrow night. We will also explore Tennessee with them and then return to the boat.

The weather is off and on. The tornado weather we waited out in Paris

Landing Marina was severe for Paducah - 7 people were killed - only an hour away. We were blessed that we were not in its path.

More adventure - more memories- more blessings!

Thanks for staying in touch with us. Trust all is well with you and your families.

God's richest blessings to all.
Chuck and Chris

Greetings to all,
(Paragraphs for you sis!)

We have been on land for the last week since we dropped Bill and Gail off in Nashville. They headed home for the birth of their granddaughter and we met up with my brother and his wife; Matt and Marsha, who came down from Minneapolis for a road trip through the back roads of Tennessee.

Nashville was wonderful with lots to do and of course, there was music wherever you turn. There were night concerts on the river, the Grand Ole Opry and the Wild Horse Saloon; not to mention the many would-be stars strumming and twanging up and down the side streets.

Nashville is the sister city to Athens and so there are Greek festivals and architecture - to include a full scale version of the Parthenon which graces a park in Nashville.

Chris and Marsha swooned over Trace Atkins until he took off his hat but still want to buy his CD. A couple of groups were religious and some of the costumes were right from the time of Tex Ridder or the Lone Ranger. We toured the homes of the rich and the filthy rich and saw the country estates of Minnie Pearl and Dolly Parton.

We also visited the plantation home of our 7th president - Andrew Jackson, 'Old Hickory', who was a slave owner and quite the guy. The home is outside of Nashville and is 99% authentic.

From Nashville we traveled the byways through the mountains (much like our coast range) toward the Smokeys. But we got sidetracked and ended up in Chattanooga. "Pardon me, boys, is that the ... Choo Choo?" rang through our heads as we explored this fabulous little city. The train station there is now a hotel and the train proudly rests in its tracks outside the back door of the station.

There are walking bridges and quaint restaurants, theaters, saltwater and fresh water aquariums, historic homes and a wonderful riverfront with gorgeous facilities for boats of all sizes – complete with gas lamp torches and a spectacular fountain. We spent two days here and hated to leave.

Real estate is booming and the old section of craftsman style homes is being snapped up and renovated. Prices are inexpensive on the homes even though the townhouses and condo's downtown have been discovered and demand a healthy price.

From there we traveled the small roads through the woodlands toward the little town of Jasper. There were not many evergreens, lots of waterfalls, streams and hidden back woods residences concealed in the dense forests. Many of these towns and their people are still in an era gone by and are quite guarded toward, "usuns", if we were to find ourselves on the wrong road or up a driveway that is marked private property. The family hound dog would announce our arrival probably followed by a greeting from a shot gun carrying resident. In spite of what we had been told, we still found the people friendly and helpful even though the opposite can be the norm.

Marsha's cousin owns a motel in Jasper. The name is Acuff's. Roy Acuff was the father of country music and one of the few to be inducted into the Music Hall of Fame while alive. Marsha's cousin is related - thus the name.

After lunch with them we rapidly made our way to "Lynchburg" - Home of the Jack Daniels Distillery. It is located in a dry county - of which there are quite a few and thus only souvenir bottles of the finest whiskey could be purchased because of the redeeming quality of the collectable container. Lemonade samples were given in the gift shop which promoted even more of a hankering to find a store in the neighboring county, where "Old # 7" could be purchased. It is a fascinating process learned by Jack - 5' 2" with shoe size 4 who starting learning it from, yes, "a Lutheran Pastor" whom he lived with at the age of six. The pastor had to decide between making whiskey and his wife and pastoral call so he gave the right to make the whiskey to Jack at the age of thirteen and thus the story goes. Federal taxes on the product are huge for Jack Daniels, bottling over 90 bottles a minute. The closest we got to a taste was through the vapors coming off the charcoal vats when our "southern lady" guide flapped the top for us. You breathe through your mouth because if you take it in through your nose it will knock your socks off! The vaporized taste was zesty and invigorating.

Dinner was had at Davey Crockett's restaurant, (complete with memorabilia and a stuffed backwoods "baar" who's fur and nose had seen extensive rubbing). Ribs cooked in Jack Daniel's and a healthy heaping of sweet potatoes was the fare. Then off for a night's stay at Murfreesboro. This is the site of one of the bloodiest civil war battles of the entire war. Over 80 thousand men assembled and when the three days of fighting were over 23,000 men and boys were dead. This is where the phrase, "Hell's Half Acre" comes from. The union army prevailed after suffering huge losses. The confederate army sustained tremendous losses as well. A haunting cemetery echoes its past as part of this historic battlefield. This was the second most deadly battle next to Gettysburg.

That war and all wars are terrible. I don't have any answers but pray that peace could come to our world and that our men and women who sacrifice so much could come home to their families. The night before the big battle at Murfreesboro took place both armies played "Home Sweet Home" and many of the men and boys from both sides prayed to the same God for protection and victory.

As always we have a hoot traveling with M&M and always find ourselves on wild and crazy adventures which take us off the beaten path and into the lives of many wonderful people.

We got back to the boat last night and watched a movie on the boat in sweltering heat and humidity after downing a fabulous catfish dinner at our marina. The boats are good - all is well - we tried deep fried dill pickles and are looking forward to Bill and Gail's return and the continued journey toward the Gulf.

God is good,
We miss you all,
Stay in touch! We love to hear from you.
Blessings,
C&C

Greetings to all of our family and friends,

Since returning from Nashville and a trip around Tennessee last week we have been blessed with wonderful but chilly weather interspersed with the last strikes of summer heat. The hoards of insects have given way to a few small squads of invaders. We have been through gorgeous evenings with a full moon and the coyotes heralding in the onset of autumn.

Visitors to the marina, from up north, who are meeting friends along the route, share stories of an early winter; with snow storms in October, which is quite unusual! Boats from the marina and those of us who are called, "transients", are fleeing south with the butterflies, geese and white pelicans to avoid the necessity of long pants, coats and stocking hats. Chris has donned her earmuffs and wishes she had brought her long johns. But she wears earmuffs in Hawaii so she is not a good barometer of the weather. We are told that the Monarchs we see zigzagging their way across the lake are headed for a little city called Carrabelle on the "big bend" of Florida where they will also winter. It is the place we will decide either to head directly south to Tarpon Springs or make the bend and "Gunkhole" in the little rivers, towns, islands and estuaries in the undeveloped part of NW Florida along the northwestern Gulf. Water depths and local advice and weather will help us make that decision in a month or so. Really the days have been pleasant and the nights cold, with little rain and lots of sun.

The lake has been at low winter levels. I have been acting as pilot boat in our inflatable for some of the larger vessels as they negotiate the shallow channel on their way to the dock at Pebble Isle. With the depth sounder on the dinghy, this has been helpful in keeping them from running aground. Depths are 6 feet and some of the boats churn the muddy bottom as they arrive and leave. JUWIKA and Essi-Anna need only four feet so we still have a couple feet to spare.

Along with the low water depths come the stranding of large carp and other fish in the pools left isolated near the shoreline. There is a type of carp here that travels in "packs" and are herded by fishermen into nets. When they are not being herded they swim near boats and often leap high into the air - landing on people's laps, in their cabins and onto their decks as they demonstrate their acrobatics, only to slime up and bleed all over their landing strips.

We have also been swimming in the lake until we read that this area is heavily populated with many poisonous snakes - some of which live in the water. There have been two sightings of water moccasins near the dock with one on the swim platform of a boat. I am more anxious about the no-seeums since they are voracious and with multiple bites in the tens and twenties around one ankle you wish you had died - with little relief but to wait out the itch for a week or so. We understand some of the islands in Florida are infested with rattlesnakes and other vipers - so we will be on our guard as we travel south. We are getting in lots of walking and hikes. We've had wonderful bike rides and gazed at and assisted the myriad of looper boats as they land and depart.

We have met many nice people from all walks of life and areas of the U.S. Some are seasoned world travelers and others are first timers. We have shared dinner with both and always enjoy hearing their stories of adventure. Like fish stories many of the wave heights encountered in their harrowing tales seem to be exaggerated or they wouldn't be here to tell about it.

Some of the people took off many years ago and never returned home - selling it all and living the life of a vagabond. Others - like us - have other irons in the fire and are out for a new adventure, wanting to return home to friends and family at sometime in the future!

Tonight we had a pig roast at the restaurant, which has some of the best food around. Catfish and hush puppies are their specialty. We have completed most of the projects on the boat and await Bill and Gail's return on Thursday. We will paddle south, arriving below the 32nd parallel north no earlier than November 1; well after hurricane season is over. We are getting antsy and at the same time have enjoyed Pebble Isle and the new friends we have met.

We are so blessed to have our health, our church family, our friends and family and the opportunity to have this adventure together. My first mate is the best and is a wonderful balance to my spontaneous, adventure-some spirit.

God's Richest Blessings,

We pray often for each of you and for our church family.
Fondly,
Chuck and Chris

Greetings from none other than Tennessee,

Either Tennessee is awfully big or we are really slow! We actually are moving and have made significant progress toward the south since getting back on the Kentucky Lake and the Tennessee River.

The nights have been very cold - in the 30's. So anchoring out the last three nights have necessitated three blankets and the flannel sheets. Chris is obviously wearing her earmuffs and she has checked at our favorite shopping center - WalMart Super Stores - for long johns; but to no avail.

It was sad to leave Pebble Isle but it was either that or winterize the boat and stay.

We rented a car and picked up Bill and Gail in Nashville on the evening of the 19th of October and spent a couple of days giving them the tour of the city.

We don't pay Tennessee taxes here but feel that we have invested a goodly amount of time and money exploring that state and love it. The people here are most hospitable and the scenery is easy on the eyes - not to mention the unique music scene in Nashville. Having taken the "Tommie's Tour" of the town with Matt and Marsha, we retraced our steps and showed them the sights.

We spent Friday afternoon on the music strip downtown going from club to club listening to the up and comers, strumming and twanging away in hopes of being discovered. We introduced B&G to deep-fried pickles, hush puppies and catfish and had a wonderful evening at the Grand Ole Opry on its 81st birthday – sponsored by Martha Whites Biscuits.

Returning to the boats, which we had cleaned up and gotten ready to go, we took one last day to re-provision and say good bye to friends at the marina and on the dock. Then off we went, leaving behind a month of emotions, experiences and lots of fond memories.

The autumn leaves have truly turned to crimson and gold and the crisp days and evenings have brought out a panorama of color which can only be seen and not described! The days on the lower Tennessee before it turns east have been some of the most beautiful we have experienced. The river twists and turns and is very different from the lake-like area called Kentucky Lake which is actually the dammed up Tennessee River closest to Kentucky Dam.

We have passed by beautiful plantation homes on the bluffs of the river and have stopped in little towns along the way which could only be described as the "Home of Andy of Mayberry ". While walking their streets the echo of "hound dogs" reverberates across the countryside and the signs outside each little cafe attest to someone's "southern style home-cooking".

One little marina we stopped in at had a no smoking sign on the door but everyone in the place had a cigarette in one hand and a beer in the other. We moved on to an anchorage up river.

Until we reach the Tenn-TomBigbee Waterway we are heading upstream with a 1 knot current against us. Once we pass through Pickwick Locks we will be on Pickwick Lake and 9 miles past that start our descent toward the Gulf of Mexico some 450 miles to the south. We are looking forward to warmer and drier weather since Tennessee has been unseasonably cold and wet.

As I write this chapter of our journey we are anchored in a small cove just south of Pickwick Dam. We passed through the lock last night and rose 55 feet to a beautiful area of high bluffs and picturesque scenery. Yesterday as we made our way up river we passed the site where the Battle of Shiloh took place.

We considered anchoring off the river but decided to make our way through Pickwick and try to find a way back to the battlefield and museum by road. Since there was just a rustic stairway going up the river bank we would have had to make our own beach landing with the dinghies on the jagged rocky shoreline.

After a restful night on anchor we went ashore and walked to the lodge which is part of the unbelievable state park system of Tennessee - as mentioned in earlier reports these parks are amazing. We checked on a taxi for the trip back to Shiloh. But it had to come from 15 miles away just to pick us up and then wait to return us only to drive another 15 miles back to the home station. It would be $50.00 for all four - too much! Just as we had resolved we would miss this amazing and sad part of American history, where in a two day battle during the first year of the Civil War, over 23,000 men were killed, a man walked by and headed for the exit door of the lodge.

I followed him and asked if he was from the area. He said, "No". But when I told him we were trying to get to Shiloh he said he and his wife were going that way too. After a brief conference with his wife and after unloading their car (new Lincoln Navigator) of all the laundry and camp supplies they had stowed in the back, the four of us loaded in. We spent a day with our new friends, Jackie and Glen, from Houston, Texas. They were our guardian tour guides for the day and even stopped for groceries that we needed to top off our supplies. They also swung in for a fresh supply of gallon size Vodka bottles, of the least expensive type, to top off the milkshake size cups they had been coyly sipping at during our tour.

Tonight we are just relaxing and relearning bridge from Bill and Gail. Tomorrow we will travel a short day to the beginning of the great engineering route of the Tenn-TomBigbee waterway which will eventually deliver us downstream and 12 locks later into the salty water of the Gulf and sunnier days.

>   Blessings to all,
>   Trust all is well with you.
>   Keep those emails coming - we love to hear from you!
>   New pictures coming tomorrow.
>   Chuck and Chris

LOOPET 5

THE TENN-TOMBIGBEE AND TOMBIGBEE-BLACKWARRIOR WATERWAY

GREETINGS from the Tenn-Tombigbee Waterway!
It is Halloween night, or All Saints Eve if you prefer, and we are at mile marker 360 along the fabulous feat of engineering of the Tenn-Tom. The mile marker means that we are that many miles from Mobile Bay and the beginning of pure salt water and the Gulf influence. We will start to feel the tides and some brackish water at approximately mile marker 100.

The Tenn-Tom, (Tenn stands for Tennessee and Tom stands for Tombigbee - two rivers which make up a majority of this canal), as it is affectionately called; is a canal system which was built to offer an alternate route for shipping besides the Mississippi. It was first envisioned by the French during the initial exploration of this area. The amount of dirt removed to connect this waterway with the other rivers and lakes was greater than that removed in the building of the Panama Canal. The elevation drop is around 400 feet to the Gulf which necessitates travelers going both ways to negotiate 12 locks. One section of the Tenn-Tom has 6 locks within a 40 mile stretch which makes for a long day and some extra duty at fenders and lines. Most have drops of around 30 feet and are a challenge in timing and coordination with other boats locking through.

Upstream from each lock and dam there is a backwater lake which provides large estuaries and recreational areas loaded with wonderful scenery and anchorages. Because many of these areas have been flooded due to the backwaters of the dams there are trees and stumps that create an eerie swamp-like atmosphere. Trees line the water and in many cases the depths are very shallow with stump farms clogging what appear to be large open bays.

Below each dam is usually a long stretch of trough which reminds one of punting on the canals of Europe. The water flows gently and the autumn leaves lining these navigable ditches make for a relaxing pace with only the occasional challenge of passing a tug and its tow at close quarters. Depths range between 10 - 15 feet.

All this sounds very technical but it is a magnificent pathway through this region of our great country, not only for us water travelers but also for migratory birds heading south. This water path is a road through small town America. The cities and towns we encounter along the way are quaint and the people are the epitome of southern hospitality and congeniality. With the use of our bikes, legs and courtesy cars at the marinas we have been able to get a glimpse at some amazing, historical places close by: the Shiloh Battlefield, Corinth, Mississippi, Aberdeen, Mississippi, with its huge and beautiful Antebellum homes (pre Civil War) and Second Empire homes; which were built after the war and were a combination of Italian and French architecture.

Before the first of six locks in close succession we held up in a pristine off the beaten path place, tucked behind several little islands, called Bay Spring Lake. It was magical with shorelines covered in autumn and a light fog over the water when we awoke. There wasn't even a breath of air that night and we slept soundly - the silhouettes of our boats reflecting picture perfect images of themselves in the mirror like water.

The next day we traversed four locks and anchored in a pool above a lock near a little place called Smithville. The calm pond was just above the first of two locks we would negotiate first thing the next morning. A dinghy ride to shore at a small boat ramp led us on a walk through freshly picked cotton fields and along some sunny country roads. When you are that close to a lock you can call the lock master and ask when it is convenient and how long the wait would be to lock through. They usually like to have a small flotilla go through together so they wait until a few boats bunch up and then let everyone in. All of these locks have floating bollards so you just hook your center cleat with a line and float up or down in the lock until you reach the level you are going to, then the gates are opened to release the gaggle of fiberglass ducklings. It is important to watch the assent or descent though because often times the bollard hangs up and if you don't let the lock master know and make adjustments you could rip the cleats out of your boat or end up hanging from the side of the lock.

As we approached Aberdeen Lock we decided to spend the night in a tranquil anchorage off the main channel. We found a wonderful little area called Blue Bluff. We went ashore on a rickety dock close by, which attached us to a stairway ascending to a local park which was vacant and closed for the season. On the walk over the hill Bill and Gail spotted an armadillo and Chris and I found the same imitating a road pizza on the shoulder of the rural county road as we hoofed it into town. We visited a little store on the outskirts and met Lois and Judy - two very fun older ladies, who were baking potatoes for a party in the back of this old meat market/beer market/deli/grocery/candy store. The store shelves were sparsely stocked with one or two cans of staples. Trophy mounts of animals lined the walls. In the center were a couple of picnic tables where the locals could enjoy biscuits and gravy for breakfast or "poboy sandwiches" for a quick lunch. They said we were really nice Yankees and very friendly! OK!

In the morning we wound our way to the other side of the channel and through a Halloween, eerie swamp to Aberdeen Marina. The channel leading in is lined with trees growing in the water and boasts depths of six to eight feet which leaves us with about two to three feet under our keel. Some of the markers are attached to trees and the stumps and brush along with the various water plants truly gives the impression of a deep woods bayou. We have now officially arrived in alligator country but have not seen one yet. At the visitor center down river we got a chance to see some of the fauna of the area which displayed some very large water snakes and the rattlers that live in the area, along with beaver, muskrat, otter, fox, coyote and all kinds of birds.

We refueled at Aberdeen Marina, which is a marina on one side and a highway gas station on the other with a convenience/deli in between. Gas on the waterside of the station was an amazing $2.17 for gas and $2.15

for diesel. We have found fuel on this trip to be less than it is at home on the roadway - so we filled up before docking for the evening.

Some acquaintances arrived shortly after on a boat called Trinity. Their daughter; Jaycee, who is home schooled and about eight years old was dressed for the day - Halloween. We had left them in Pebble Isle and didn't expect to see them again before Halloween so had left Jaycee a goodie bag upon our departure but here they were again. It was fun to see her in her costume and she came over to thank us for the treats.

Our hope for the next day was to tour some Antebellum - Pre-Civil War homes; and what we later came to know as Second Empire homes - Post Civil War; which are a combination of Italian and French architecture. The marina owner was also one of the principles in the tourism industry of the area so he called his friends and set up free tours of two exquisitely restored mansions which are actually residences of the people and families who welcomed us into their homes. What an experience!

The antebellum home was 6000 square feet, with twelve foot ceilings and a gigantic pillared, white porch and ornately furnished rooms restored to the original 1850 standards. It was furnished with antiques and original furnishings bought with the home that we estimated to be worth a million dollars. When Tom and his wife bought it they actually found old silver and stock certificates in the walls. The grounds consisted of five acres in the city, full of plants including pomegranate and huge yellow and white trumpet flowers and palm trees. Never had we seen such a place! It was a living museum much like the pictures of the plantation homes you can conjure in your minds.

The other home was built in 1879 and is very colorful and different. The windows on the front opened from floor to ceiling so when the owner entertained or had a dance the guests could dance out one window and into another room after gliding across the porch with a few fancy steps. All the window tops were curved; there were 14 Italian columns holding up a huge front porch and a widow's walk and cupola sat like a crown of jewels at the highest point on the roof. The stair cases in both were awesome with newel posts at the bottom of each stairway. Atop each main newel post was a button which signified that the home was paid for in full. During this era the bank would hold the deed and the button until the last payment was made and then the deed was put in the post and the button filled the hole telling all who entered the home that there was no debt owed.

Mike, the owner of the second home, was unbelievably hospitable and a true gentleman. He shared his 1870's mansion with us and told us about his family and his goal to be a great pianist, which would come later in life since he had only taken three lessons. I told him about my brothers who were also learning to play. He showed us his exquisite, antique, rosewood grand piano and with a smile said it was an overkill but loved the looks of the furniture and the price was right - $300.00. He was in the process of mastering "Jingle Bells" from memory which he wanted to perform by Christmas. Mike also shared a beautiful and touching rendition of "Amazing Grace", sung by a young lady in his community who sang it for her grandfather's funeral. The acoustics, setting and sound system in this special place blended to make it very touching and memorable.

As we said goodbye to Mike on his front porch, we made our way down a sidewalk steeped in history, under the umbrella of a 130 year old Magnolia tree and out the heavy iron-gate next to a drive lined with lighted, gas street lamps. What gracious hosts - southern hospitality and congeniality at its best. You can't buy a day like the experience we had!

Returning to the marina, as the youngsters were starting their rounds for bag loads of candy, we put the well worn, loaner Lincoln Town Car back in her stall, ate supper and turned in for the night.

The following morning we awoke to torrential rain. It was as though God had turned on the fire hose and we were the fire. Papa - the marina owner's father-in-law mans the small kitchen and makes exceptional biscuits. So before shoving off we all decided to take advantage of a great thing and eat breakfast out in one of the tiny booths which shared room with the gas station counter and small convenience store. As we were getting ready to cast off for the day's journey I looked toward the swamp and a large cat caught my eye. After closer examination I recognized it as a bobcat. It sat and watched me for some time atop a golden roll of hay that was being harvested in a field at water's edge. A moment later this seldom seen member of the feline family jumped into the water and swam to the other side of the little bay and disappeared into the brush.

Our next destination would be Columbus, Mississippi, where we would take a side river and anchor below the bluff and within walking distance of the town. Several times that day and once during a locking exercise we had been drenched to the bone by more fire hose rain. As we ventured up the river toward our destination several hours later our water highway was lined with the brilliant orange and reddish autumn colors of the Bald Cypress trees. A low, transparent, fog hung on the water and the wind started to whistle down the channel. Our plan was to each set an anchor in the river with the boats facing opposite directions and raft together, which we have done several times to keep us from swinging in close quarters. Due to the heavy downpour which ran like a torrent down our boats and drenched us again, we decided to wait for a break in the weather before attempting this. We had not seen it rain that hard and that long since that unforgettable night on the Mississippi.

I set our anchor closer to the shoreline in hopes that Bill would bring JUWIKA alongside soon. The current would keep me straight while I waited. A sudden, very strong gust of wind came out of nowhere and started to set me onto the shoreline so I drug Essi-Anna away from the shore with the anchor to get the props and rudders off the soft mud - avoiding any damage or a more solid grounding.

After pulling anchor and resetting closer to the middle we tied stern to bow. It was now dark and the wind started to howl again after what we thought had been its last blow. Bill's generator starting giving him trouble so he was working on it and I was working on our boat when I noticed that JUWIKA's anchor was slipping. We were going to be sideways in the river soon so I signaled to Bill to start his engine and we started ours. With the divine intervention of our guardian angels and Chris's expert handling of Essi-Anna, Bill, Gail and I got the two boats untangled and back in the river and anchored separately, one in front of the other in the coal black night. The wind continued at a fairly strong pace, making the boats shudder on their anchor chains. Both our anchors held well but as a precaution we did anchor watches till midnight and then set our clocks for two hour intervals to check our position. We had to make sure the wind wasn't getting stronger, that our anchors weren't dragging in this narrow channel and that the torrential rains were not causing a major flooding situation. After many, many hundreds of nights at anchor through our boating careers you learn to trust that little piece of metal attached like a tether lifeline to the front of the boat. The skies eventually cleared and the temperature dropped into the 30's.

Morning came slowly but when it did the sun was shining brightly even though the wind was still gusting strongly. Our anchors had held. It was a new day and we were grateful for the safety we had been afforded. After heating up our cabins and taking a brisk dinghy ride to a small park dock nearby for a walk through town, we continued our journey south in search of more adventures and a lifetime of memories.

Trust all is well with you and your families.
Let us know how you are doing.
Blessings to all,
Many of you are in our prayers daily as you work through your own challenges.
Chuck and Chris

Greetings family and friends,

It is now day 82 since leaving the comfort of our home in Vancouver and venturing into the "Great Adventure of the Loop". We have been on the rivers of mid-west, mid-south and south since we left from Davenport, Iowa on September 7th. We have completed 26 locks on the Mississippi, Ohio, Tennessee, Tenn-Tom and Black Warrior-Tombigbee canal system. We have traveled some 1150 miles at a pace that allows one to become fully immersed in the culture, climate and people of the small towns of America along this great waterway. We have been through torrential rains and horrendous lightning and thunder storms and have swatted, smashed and squished more bugs and spiders than one hopes to encounter in a lifetime.

Our little islands of security we call home have been at anchor in: tight little streams where a shoe horn was needed to squeeze in; the water runs brown with tannin from the swamps upstream; the noise of the insects is like the hum of machines in a factory; the stars and moon light up the sky like God's street lamps; and the depths leave no margin for error, with only a foot or two of water under our keels at times. Yet we continue to sleep well and rise in the morning refreshed and ready for a new set of challenges and relationships as custom made by the river. We have filled four pages in our log with tugboat names we have danced with as we and they maneuver the serpent like curves on our ways up and down this waterway.

As I share this part of the journey we are anchored in a remote little swamp in Alabama 100 miles north or upstream of Mobile Bay. We have meandered our way through parts of: Iowa, Illinois, Missouri, Kentucky, Tennessee, Arkansas, Mississippi and now Alabama. The Black Warrior-Tombigbee is the lower section of this assault toward the Gulf and very remote; with virtually no towns, one fuel stop and many miles between anchorages. Our cell phone and internet coverage is nonexistent. We have collected boating cards from many people from all walks of life and many locations throughout the U.S. who are also living this dream of a lifetime, most of whom are pushing south for the winter - destination unknown. We are racing against the November 14th week long closure date at the Coffeyville Dam and Lock, the last drop to the Gulf before climbing our way up to Lake Okeechobee in the southern part of Florida several months from now.

The cold mornings and chilly evenings, where frost glistens on the decks of Essi-Anna and JUWIKA is now turning into milder, warmer evenings and sunny mornings. The coffee is still tasty but no longer necessary to take the chill off the cabin and one's hands, as they grasp the wheel for the first time that day.

Evenings sitting on the deck as the sun goes down, after or before dinner, prepared by one boat's galley slaves or the other (we alternate evenings), give opportunity to reflect on the events still fresh in our minds, which passed at eight miles per hour and are now embedded for a lifetime. Mental images of the real thing run back through your eyelids like a film loop in an infomercial. Those caught with the camera and those that happened too quickly are embedded there for future use when sitting at a street light or waiting in line to check out at a grocery store. Perhaps later in life when eyes and ears are clouded with age and the body can no longer make such trips (or make it to the bathroom alone): our mind will recall a huge alligator basking in the sun along a brown and slippery clay bank just above the splash line on the river; the sound of hooting owls and coyotes crying and barking in the dark in the eerie swamp just yards away from where you are anchored; deer swimming frantically across the river, eluding hunters in the woods, dressed in camouflage gear hoping to get a shot at filling the freezer; trees laden heavy with ferns and long bearded moss, like tinsel on a Christmas tree; armadillos scurrying through the woods like tiny tanks, bulldozing everything in their paths; and fitness walks along remote roads leading through forests ripe with the falling leaves of autumn.

Several nights ago we anchored in a small twist in the river called, "Rattle Snake Bend". Before dinner we took an exploratory excursion upstream in the dinghies to look for wildlife and enjoy the peace and solitude of a beautiful sunset. The wind was calm and the opposing current was weak so the boats doe-see-doed around the anchors – rodes hanging limply. In the evening the animals come alive and make their way to the river for water, in search of food. We came upon a small inlet which led into an estuary filled with stumps and snags - the shoreline thick with fan palms and emblazoned colored cypress trees with roots exposed and reaching toward the water like the knees of a lanky basketball player. The water was like a mirror and the picture was the same looking into the water or onto the shore. At one of the visitors' centers along the river we had seen a display of the animals that lived on the river. The muskrat was missing and Chris wanted to see one of these furry critters. After eyeing several raccoons and egrets one was provided for our entertainment as he or she (Muskrat – Muskrat; you remember the song), swam by our boat and slid onto the shoreline just feet away.

With warmer weather and water come the insects - again. It appears we have caught up with the butterflies we saw in Kentucky Lake and the Lady Bugs have joined us on their trip south. There are tiny boating communities tucked into the side waters of this great river. Tonight we have anchored in a small nook called Bates Lake 54 miles from Mobile Bay. Several other boats have joined us and everyone is sitting on their floating decks enjoying the sunset and looking forward to the millions of stars that will light the sky. Each boat is on its own journey and at the same time we have a common bond and camaraderie that can only be understood after many miles of navigation and page turning to make sure you are out of harm's way and heading in the right direction. There must be a common gene that we all have that calls us to such an adventure.

We differ when it comes to the speeds at which we all travel. While one boat's maximum speed is seven knots another may be capable and wanting to travel this narrow highway at much greater speeds. Sport Fish Yachts heading for the fishing grounds on the Gulf churn the water in a frenzy to get to where the big ones are biting. Most people are very considerate and do what is called a "slow pass" as they go by.

There is a rule of the road on the water that says each captain is responsible for his or her own wake and the damage it does. Fishermen and locals along the river are very conscious of the fact that many of us are visitors and some take advantage of that situation. There are stories of boats either seeing and ignoring or not seeing small fishing boats near the shoreline being rocked or damaged. This sets off either a feud, which can result in shots fired or a call to Uncle Bob, who is the local river police officer downstream. He will meet the perpetrator down river at the next lock, only to fine and or impound the boat until the damage can be assessed and the wake crime settled. Even if there is no crime committed there are some who contrive one in order to collect a few extra dollars paid over the barrel and not claimed on any income tax statement.

Last night we met an older gentleman in a very small flat bottomed John Boat who pulled alongside us as we anchored and introduced himself as Alton Moat. His teeth were stained and encrusted with tobacco from years of use and neglect. He was wearing a matted and soiled life jacket which appeared to be more for warmth than flotation. His hands were permanently varnished with the color of the bait slurry of cheesy looking curds in the bucket beside him. He was a catfish trapper. In the front of his little boat were two chicken mess traps that resembled large prawn traps which he told me had caught several hundred pan sized catfish. He gave a half toothed grin with pride as we shook hands; he asked us in a very solemn tone to watch for him on the river and go very slow if we saw him so that he wouldn't be swamped and capsized. He was very serious and gave us the thumbs up and a huge southern smile when we told him we were settling in for the night and wouldn't have to worry about us. Off he went, as quickly as Saint Nicholas up a chimney to set his traps.

Sorry for the problems with the pictures. I will send them when I send off this email. Some friends have told me of web sites to use where you can view them all at your convenience. Until then you will have to put up with my incompetence.

Blessings to each of you from us.
We think of you often and miss our family and church family.
Many of you are in our prayers and thoughts daily - knowing you are struggling with things in your lives.
We look forward to a rendezvous with some of you in Florida. It will be great to see familiar faces. We are blessed to be traveling with good friends and people who share a love for this lifestyle. Lots of fond memories and a million stories!

See you soon,
Let us know what is happening in your lives. We love to hear from you.
Chuck and Chris

LOOPET 6

LAST LEG TO MOBILE BAY AND INTER-COASTAL ALONG THE NORTHERN GULF

GREETINGS to Friends and Family from Panama City, Florida, The weather report is a balmy 38 degrees with a freeze warning for the areas away from the Gulf. While we were doing laundry this evening a notice on the bulletin board read, "Water on the docks will be turned off when temperatures are predicted to fall below 32 degrees." We will be close.

On a walk through town, after devouring a shared "Super Trash Burger" (topped with animal crackers) at Joe's Bayou Cafe, I stopped at a sporting goods store and bought Chris a pair of *long underwear. It is definitely ear-muff weather if you know Chris!*

The last chapter of our journey on the rivers and now the Gulf Intercoastal Waterway (GICWW) has been a unique mixture of intrigue, adventure and caution. Our insurance carrier for the boat required that we not be south of the 32 degree parallel N before November 1 and we understand why. Since arriving in Mobile, Alabama we have been confronted with some cold fronts throwing their tantrums with windy unstable weather and warm fronts showering us with rain, to include hurricanes nearby.

We followed the company's instructions and leisurely meandered our way down the last miles of the Black Warrior-Tombigbee Waterway. With pleasant days and cold nights - short and tee-shirt weather during the day - we dodged our way through debris infested waters on our way to the Gulf. Storms up stream and work on the dams required a heavy release of water which caused the dislodging of stumps, trees and every kind of flotsam you can imagine, including refrigerators and vehicles. Many of the turns on the river did ninety degree switchbacks so we had to be especially careful not to sneak up on a large tug and tow creeping around the bend without notice, like a huge dinosaur ready to devour us. Many of the green cans or the red nun markers were either displaced, covered with floating trees and stumps or missing altogether so some special attention to the charts is required. One afternoon as we approached a highly eroded bend in the river, and while passing a boat traveling close to the bank; we heard a gunshot crack and a huge splash as a very large tree timbered into the river in front of the boat we were passing. It missed them but not by much. Later that day we saw other huge trees topple into the river from the bank adding to the raft of material on this aquatic obstacle course.

The mixture of: weather, scenery, people, wind, shallow water, tides, anchoring, finding docks, restaurants, phone service and anchor watches, thunder and lightning storms, walking and or borrowing cars to get food, stretching our fuel, worshipping when close to a church, animals, bridges and dams, locks and dark nights, looking for places to refill water tanks and fuel tanks, navigation challenges and oil changes en-route; to name only a few of the non emotional issues we deal with each day, is almost too hard to comprehend. It's hard work of the right kind and we wouldn't trade the opportunity for anything!

What a blessing to be given this chance of a lifetime and the health to do it. All the experiences we have had boating over the last 20 years have brought us to a point where we can enjoy this tremendous adventure.

Each leg of the journey has its own unique challenges. Since leaving St. Louis Missouri we had not been in a large city so when we rounded the bend at mile five mark and saw the few skyscrapers on the Mobile skyline and the water began to smell of the brackish scent of the ocean our boats were like steeds heading for the barn after a hard ride. Other than for brief encounters with Lake Union and Lake Washington Essi-Anna has been raised on a saltwater diet and hadn't had a good drink of it since leaving on that dry run across country from Olympia.

Mobile is a busy place where tugs, barges, cruise ships, pleasure boats, military ships, crane barges and ocean freighters all converge to dance the waltz of commerce, pleasure and security. It requires lots of communication on the radio as we pleasure boats give way to the wishes and instruction of our bigger brothers and sisters. Many are sisters, as Chris's five pages of names of those we have met can attest.

We docked in front of the convention center in Mobile, which is right downtown. It is a huge concrete wall with jumbo cleats that made our dock lines look like strands of thread. Due to the tides, which we will encounter for many months now, we had to tie our dwarfed little ships loosely to the wall so that when the water levels rise and fall our boats would not be left hanging in mid air on a leash. It was a free dock and no other pleasure craft took advantage of this primitive arrangement, but chose to find refuge in a spendy marina down the road. The Gulf only has two tides a day compared to our four and the tides are only "1.5 to 2.5" feet instead of the "10 – 15" foot ranges we were used to. None of the docks float and most of the time there isn't a dock. There are only pilings on both sides with a gang plank on one side which reminds one of the fantasies associated with being captured by pirates.

Mobile is a wonderful southern city. We had our first fresh seafood since leaving the Northwest. There are boulevards lined with huge live oaks laced abundantly with ferns and Spanish moss and some gorgeous, huge old southern, stone churches. We spent Sunday there and became Episcopalians for a day in a very old church built in the 1800's.

A highlight was a fabulous candy shop with all kinds of nuts and an old peanut roaster warming one corner of this landmark icon of a store.

When there is a bad weather warning for Mobile Bay one takes heed to listen before crossing to the eastern shore and that's where we were headed. Mobile Bay is very large and is exposed to heavy winds from N to S. It is also very shallow with an average depth of eight feet. (8 – 4 foot drafts = 4 feet) left to run in is how the math is done. If the tide is out and the wind is blowing 20 the water level can change dramatically as the water is actually blown out of the bay. This leaves less than four feet of water in the troughs - which is too skinny for our comfort. The day we crossed we had a comforting excess of four feet beneath our keels. This is a very strange situation for us Northwest boys who are used to deep water.

After crossing Mobile Bay at the right time and on a beautiful Sunday afternoon we stayed at a marina called Eastern Shore close to Fairhope, Alabama. The quaint little city is a like a mini Carmel, California - lots of Mercedes, BMW's and other expensive autos. A 2500 square foot ranch on a small creek with a little dock on the main drag in this hurricane alley area was $775,000.00. This area had been really hit hard by Ivan and the marina was still getting back on its feet. Ken and Doris, friends from our church in Vancouver who are doing mission work for six months rebuilding in New Orleans, came up and spent time with Bill and Gail and us. They shared unbelievable stories of suffering and re-establishing lives for people still recovering from Katrina. They had a truck so we crammed in it and Bill and I rode in the bed - out to dinner and exploring, donning earmuffs and stocking caps on what turned out to be a chilly evening.

After two days at rest we made preparations for our progress south to the GICWW which will take us along and inside the barrier islands of the Gulf of Mexico - protected except for the bays that connect the channels like large beads on a necklace. At each bay is a channel leading to and from the Gulf and cities like Pensacola or Panama City.

The islands that separate this inland passage are nothing more than huge sand dunes - some low, narrow, treeless and desolate; some wider, densely populated and highly developed connected to the mainland with numerous bridges. These are the infamous pieces of real estate of great debate and litigation following the numerous hurricanes which bombard this part of Florida and Alabama.

Our trip down Mobile Bay was uneventful but beautiful. The sun shone and the wind cooperated. Dolphins greeted us as we intersected the channel of the Florida inter-coastal waterway on the far southern end of the bay before heading east into the channel. The sky blue water and white sandy beaches only got better as we worked our way along the waterway. There were numerous condominium complexes and marinas, swampy areas and storybook homes each with their aerial lift dock and boat in the front yard.

Our settled weather window was brief and we knew we needed to find a place to tie down for two days. NOAA radio's electronic weather reporter warned of severe weather on its way which was to hit tomorrow with extreme winds, torrential rains, possible tornadoes and thunder and lightning. We had been through similar conditions on the Mississippi while at anchor with no other options but to ride it out on anchor; so when we saw a brand new marina close to a new shopping and restaurant complex, huge Ferris wheel, a movie theater and a Starbucks we decided to suffer out the storm there. The manager was getting ready to open this new facility called, "The Wharf". The electricity was not at the docks yet but the docks were new and solid and well connected to the shoreline – and empty. He wanted us to be safe and knew the marina we had planned to stay at was not as secure and further down the road with nothing close by; so he cut us a deal at $1.00 a foot. Many marinas in this area charge $2.00 a foot plus electricity at $5 - $10 a night.

Two days later, after two eggnog lattes and a couple of slabs of gingerbread cake - not to mention dinner out and two movies - we continued our journey east, saying goodbye to Orange. The storm did materialize, with winds that blew down a big palm in our area and lots of rain. We were blessed and spared the destructive forces that hit close by us.

We preferred to anchor out and the majority of time, where possible, we do. But when a storm like this is tracking down your path like a panther stalking its prey, it is best to take cover in a secure place. Even today as we approached Panama City on a very breezy day we couldn't help but notice a multi-multimillion dollar, three tiered yacht in the 120 plus foot range that had become stranded high and dry on an island near a shallow anchorage along the waterway. It looked like the whipped cream topping sitting high atop a hot fudge sundae. Ouch! This had happened during the storm we rode out several days earlier.

After four days at anchor in some fabulous places and a Sunday in Valparaiso, Florida where we attended church as Presbyterians; we arrived at Panama City around noon. The last two days have been very windy with waves around two to three feet - not unsafe for travel but challenging and a little bit of a bumpy ride. Not many of our fellow loopers were out there with us.

The first anchorage was in a special little bight almost a stone's throw from the Gulf. We walked the lonely white beaches and picked up tropical shells. Gail found a huge conch shell and we rescued a small octopus from the ravenous bill of a crane who was stalking it in a tide pool. Dolphins played around the boat at sunset and the water was so clear you could see the bottom at 15 feet.

The next evening we slid our way into a little city called Navarre along the Gulf Coast and on one of the barrier islands that was hit severely by Opal, Dennis and Ivan. Sustained winds of 130 miles an hour, which in Opal's case sat over this community and churned for many hours, left many homes demolished and the city under water. The land is owned by the government and the people who live there or lived there lease the land and pay ridiculous annual taxes. A 1/4 acre lot on the water is $750,000 with taxes on the land alone of $2000.00 a month.

There is so much snow white sand that is constantly blowing and mounding across the roads and into the yards and business parking lots that if you didn't know better you would think you were in the Arctic. There is a large dredged, sand barrier mound, rising 14 feet high which stretches the entire length of the city. This is supposed to slow down the hurricane storm surge "when" they get hit again. People use leaf blowers for the sand like we use them to blow leaves off our lawns in the fall. As Fred, the owner of the Sailor's Grill and Bakery told us, - "People really shouldn't be living here!" Even though he has been through three hurricanes with their business and has lost their home to Opal, he still calls it home.

The route getting into this free dock was unmarked so I scouted it out with the inflatable and Bill and Chris steered our respective boats safely into the spoon shaped indentation they call their harbor. The channel going in had two feet to spare on the depth with a pure sand bottom that could be seen from the bow watch.

The food, wine tasting and baked goods under this little palapa-roofed building made the effort well worth our while. In addition, we took our bike rides along the barren arctic-like landscape where even the scrawny palms had a hard time surviving and the landscaping of most of the homes that were still complete and inhabited adorned a mounded or drifted sand motif.

The beach combing was fabulous. The recent storm had washed countless shells of every imaginable type onto this little strip of somebody's paradise and another's hell. Our eyes sparkled as we edged our way along the beach, hunched over in anticipation of the next picture perfect specimen. Never had any of us seen such a display of what every person wishes they could find as they stroll along a beach looking for shells. We collected many of each type and sent them to our grandsons.

Leaving this place of beauty and destruction we headed east again to a huge bay called Choctawhatchee near Destin, Florida. We tucked into a tight little anchorage called Tom's Bayou where beautiful homes and yards well mixed with pines and palms come right to the water's edge. Each home has its dock and boat and there are fishing piers where locals try to catch their evening meal or just spend time catching up on each other's lives. It was Saturday night and some families were having backyard barbeque. It reminded us more of a freshwater lake than a saltwater bay. The other city close by was called "Niceville". We landed our dinghy on a sandy beach near the dock and walked the neighborhoods.

The next morning we all made a religious landing in the same spot and attended church up the street.

When church was over we got to the boats to find that the anticipated winds of twenty had hit earlier than expected. We had 20 miles to an anchorage that we had scouted on the charts earlier - a jumping off place to get to Panama City the next day. We had chosen the only nook which was deep enough and tucked behind a bridge causeway protected from the NE winds that were starting to howl. The depths on this bay are 12 - 18 feet so we knew we had the depth to travel even though we knew it would be bumpy and the water may be pushed out by the wind into the Gulf close by. We have traveled in much, much worse up north so there was no problem. But we wanted to be tucked into and anchored before dark, which comes at around 5:00 p.m. The whitecaps looked like a flock of sheep as we headed for the bridge three and a half hours away. After dodging crab pots and tacking to keep the waves from hitting us directly on the beam we passed under the bridge and poked our way half a mile N alongside the bridge until we were close to the land at the north end. The wind died down as we came in the lee of the causeway which was just what we had hoped.

We dropped our anchors as a freeze warning night blanketed our little place in the world. We were thankful for this peaceful, deep and quiet little sanctuary. We would share dinner with Bill and Gail, play some games and then retire for the night. Tomorrow is another day and we would make an early start to make Panama City by early afternoon. The wind on the other side of the bridge and out in the channel continues to stir the water and raise havoc on any travelers on the water this evening. With stocking hat on and four blankets on the bed, anchor light burning, we said our prayers, goodnight and laid our heads down and fell securely asleep.

Blessings to all,
Write us and let us know what is happening in your lives,
Happy Thanksgiving,
Say a prayer for my Uncle George who is recovering from open heart surgery if you would - much appreciated.
Chuck and Chris

Greetings to all our friends and family,
Greetings from Crystal River, Florida - home of 17% of the Manatees in this amazing state. They are those incredibly curious creatures that sailors mistook as mermaids. They have the nickname of "sea-cow." They are totally vegetarians and love contact with humans. Tomorrow at the crack of dawn we will attempt our first contact with these gentle giants. Weighing in at close to a thousand pounds, they give birth, after 13 months of gestation, to a single calf every two to four years and nurse their baby until it is two. Wow, that sounded almost like National Geographics. It is now the afternoon of the next day - more on Manatees later.

Trust this finds all of you well. We are anchored in a little bay 7.75 miles from the Gulf of Mexico, up the Crystal River. It is a very affluent area with as many boats as there are sand fleas on the beach and vacation homes and private residences that crowd the narrow canals which make up much of the water front property in "Snow Bird" country. There are two kinds of homes along this waterway - "The expensive" and "The horrendously expensive". Each property has its own dock and pool which is totally enclosed with screens and even garage doors with screens to keep the pesky, nasty, vicious, ravenous, blood sucking and itch causing - no-seeums out!!!! Our bodies have been pummeled by these miniature buzzards that sneak up on you in hoards, enter through chinks in our armor - inside or out - screens or no..... screens, spray or no spray. Their toxic effect is delayed by a day when what starts as a tiny insignificant red dot begins to welt up and show signs of a chicken pox like condition. We have found that an ammonia stick (After Bite - The Itch Eraser) or calamine lotion helps take away the itch. Once these little welts are scratched though, you will beg for several doses of Benadryl or other mind altering drugs. Other than that we are having a fabulous time.

When last I wrote we were close to Panama City and expecting cold and blustery weather. It did arrive. With Thanksgiving just a couple of days around the corner the streets and shops were beginning to take on the early appearance of Christmas. Windows were being painted and strings of lights adorned the palm trees and live oaks along the boulevards. The girls had been deprived of shopping for so long that they barely got the boats tied up to dock before they were off trying to find any bargains this little city could offer. Bill and I hit the sporting goods stores and the thrift shop which is all we could afford after Chris and Gail's rampage.

The city is close to an air force jet training station and also has a wonderful performing arts center. For the sake of culture and for some wonderful entertainment we went to the incredible performance of "STOMP" that evening, which is a percussion, high energy dance group that makes anything else you have ever seen look like a leisurely stroll in the park. They make music with everything from brooms, to fire extinguishers, to 55 gallon drums strapped to their feet. As they fly through the air on trapeze wires and stomp their way across the stage we all sat there disbelieving the rhythms they could produce.

Our goal for the next day was to make it just short of Apalachicola. I love that name. Try to say it fast many times. We would anchor in a little place called Saul Creek which is a well protected cypress swamp six miles from our Thanksgiving destination. It would be a long day through narrow cuts, a winding river and a very shallow lake with a cut just deep enough to pass right down the middle.

Some wives are referred to as, "Galley Slaves" - but not ours. Bill and I told them we were taking them out for Thanksgiving dinner and so we had a schedule to keep, in order to make good on our promise of turkey with all the trimmings.

On our way out of Panama City the air force gave us our own private "Blue Angels" show with awesome aerial acrobatics and fly-bys. The day was sunny and warm and we only skimmed the bottom once in the lake before arriving as planned at our destination.

Due to bad weather on the Gulf many boats had been held up at the Apalachicola Marina. They were waiting for a weather window to make the long crossing to Tarpon Springs or the semi-long crossing to Steinhatchee which would be our preferred route. Before leaving Panama City we called the marinas trying to find dock space but to no avail. So we figured in a pinch we would anchor in the river close to town and dinghy ashore for our Thanksgiving meal if necessary. We left Saul Creek early in the morning and arrived at Apalachicola to find the place deserted. The weather had broken and a flotilla of 15 boats had pulled out of this storybook town to make their assault on the Gulf. We took our choice of the sunniest spots on the dock, set up shop, unloaded the bikes and with a bottle of wine, cheese, crackers and turkey jerky peddled our way through this old historic, renovated Gulf shrimp fishing town which reminded us of La Conner, Washington.

First on the agenda was to find a place for dinner. "Carolines", on the river, was our ultimate choice and reservations were made for 6:00 p.m. Off we went for our peddle and picnic - building up an appetite for the feast to come. Dinner was wonderful. All had the traditional except me. I had to go for the seafood extravaganza with crème brulee to finish a fabulous evening. After pictures were taken to capture the moment, we took a peaceful walk back to the marina a half a mile away. We turned in for the evening with our prayers of thanks!

Morning brought another beautiful day with warm sunny weather which had been lacking in many of the previous days. On Thanksgiving all the quaint shops had been closed except for the restaurants but tonight would be different. This was the high-life night of Apalachicola. It would begin with Santa arriving on a shrimp boat at 4:30 and then a parade followed by all the Christmas lit and decorated shops hosting snacks and sales for the official beginning of the shopping season! Fun, fabulous and fortunate that we were there for this memorable evening in Florida's little Gulf seaside town. The timing was divine and the rest would prepare us for the crossing ahead.

We had been invited to skip Apalachicola and join some of our cruising family for a Thanksgiving celebration in Carrabelle just twenty-five miles down the road. This would be our next stop before the "Big Day" on the Gulf. But we chose to wait and enjoy our time in Apalachicola. After eating homemade chocolates from a little shop in town and putting a great Mexican dinner under our belts we headed for Carrabelle the next day. Some of the boats had left Apalachicola or Carrabelle for the overnight 150 mile, 20 to 25 hour direct jump to Tarpon Springs but we had decided to take the scenic, remote, backwoods, nature, big bend, armpit route to explore the special little towns along the way. This would mean some long days in and out of shallow waters, dodging strings of crab pots which were as thick as the bites on the back of my legs. But because we believed we would never pass this way again by boat and were on schedule for our Christmas departure from Madeira Beach we took the longer route.

On the Gulf there is a rule of thumb that for every mile out from shore you go there is one more foot in water depth - if you are lucky. We found that we had to go ten to twenty miles offshore and out of sight of land to get the comfortable, whooping ten feet of water to make a safe passage. For us Northwest boys who are used to several hundred feet this seemed absurd but having negotiated the Mississippi and its skinny water we had gotten use to it. There would be four stops for us from Carrabelle before hitting Tarpon Springs and we would be making long trips out of channels, runs along the Gulf several miles offshore and back in channels to get to rivers that would sport interesting towns we wanted to visit along the way. It was like playing "Marine Crochet" with the boat being the ball and the red and green markers being the wickets which would lead you in and out of these wild and remote, sparsely populated and interesting towns. With our draft being four feet we needed at least four and one half feet to enter and exit these channels. That is all we got in some places. One entrance into Cedar Keys (Keys = islands); we had little more than a foot from our keels and props to the bottom of usually harmless sand, for several miles. You learn to read the color of the water and trust your instincts.

Our jumping off place would be Carrabelle, which is home of many of the wintering butterflies we had seen heading south from Kentucky

Lake. So with water tanks full and the hopes of cheap fuel there so that we had an error of margin in our fuel tanks, we headed out on this minor, protected leg of the journey. The barrier Islands of Dog and St Joseph's would shield us from the Gulf for the last time before setting off for Tarpon Springs. St. Joseph's Island is very upscale with homes that are comparable to the mansions along the California coast. Dog Island is less upscale with access only by boat and much more exposed to the brunt of the Gulf's fury.

All exits and entrances are usually accompanied by dolphin escorts which approach the boats like nuclear torpedoes deflecting before contact and playing in the wake or bow waves of the boats.

Carrabelle - as the locals put it - is a, "Drinking Town with a Fishing Problem". We found the people very friendly, the real estate over priced and the fresh shrimp directly from the shrimp boats outstanding and cheap. For $15.00 I bought three pounds of tails that were huge and just caught by local fishermen. The wives sold the shrimp on ice as they nursed their little babies aboard well worn and rust laden net boats tied to rickety wooden piers.

We stayed at C-Quarters Marina on the Carrabelle River, where the men all congregate on the front porch and drink cheap beer and shuck and eat raw oysters which can be bought for $15.00 for a 60 lb. bag. They were very pleasant and helpful and even gave us rides to the small town nearby. Little kids scurried around the docks fishing and netting anything that moved and hung over the sides of docks like bats in the belfry. They wore no life jackets and had little supervision from the dads, who were spinning tales about their day's catch or the best lures to use for the next run of "redfish".

Fuel for the boats has been remarkably and pleasantly cheap compared to what we planned. Gas has run between $2.15 and $2.79 with diesel actually being a bit more expensive. The price of $2.55 was the going rate at C-Quarters so we filled up for the long run to Steinhatchee 75 miles away. That night we hosted a dinner of cheese- stuffed, bacon-wrapped and barbecued shrimp and sautéed shrimp Tequila. What a sleep we had. As my grandpa used to say, "You can't buy a meal like that!"

Leaving the river and marina the next morning, we staged ourselves a few miles away close to the Gulf where we could observe the weather and prepare ourselves and our boats for the next day. Just inside Dog Island and no more than an eye shot across the sand spit to the Gulf, we anchored in a turquoise - colored bay with a white sandy beach. A short dinghy ride to shore we walked endless miles of white sand picking up shells and wading in the water as the waves from the Gulf played their rhythm and beckoned us to join them. As the sun went down we returned to the boats for a wonderful dinner on JUWIKA. Since it was Sunday we listened to our sermons on tape and had a lively discussion. Then we turned in early in preparation for a pre-sunrise departure out the nearby channel on our way across our first "Big Water" of the trip. Before retiring each evening we listen religiously to NOAA for an up-to-date report on the weather, wind, wave and fog predictions. This evening would be no different. All sounded good and the day at the beach had been calm which should mean glassy seas in the morning. We had been joined by our friends in "Ariel" whom we had traveled with along the way and had first come to know in Pebble Isle. The night was clear with a million stars and the sound of the surf lulled us to sleep, calming our nervous excitement about what the morning could bring.

Loopet 7

Florida's Big Bend on the Gulf to Madeira Beach Florida

DEAR Family and Friends,

Anchors were pulled at 6:30 and as the sun came up we rounded the corner of Dog Island into the narrow channel leading us to the travel zone. Each of us had set our own courses on our chart plotters as we had seen fit, taking into account shallow areas well offshore. They would eventually lead us all to the same entrance buoys 75 miles away and based on individual speeds between 9 and 12 hours later. We would be out of sight of land for much of this time and out of sight of each other depending on our difference in travel speed. Essi-Anna is the fastest boat and has to travel a little faster based on hull design to optimize fuel and make the ride more comfortable. We stay in radio contact and monitor a dual station of 16 for Coast Guard and 18 for personal chatter. Should someone need help we would come to each other's rescue. Bill will stay with Ariel and we will go on ahead; each of us always prepared to help the other out should there be an unexpected problem.

The seas were a little bumpy as we rounded the last marker and into the open waters of the Gulf but the winds were calm and the weather report was for improving conditions. As we turned the corner and left the channel we encountered three foot rollers spaced at about eight seconds. They were not dangerous and since they were on the bow they were very manageable. We have had much worse conditions on the Straits of Juan De Fuca and Georgia Straits many times so this was nothing. As we passed the hour mark and were running in 19 feet of water several miles out, the wind started to come up and the waves became steeper. Within the next hour they had built to four to five feet and directionally were very confused, with the tops blowing off them, creating a field of blue green water topped with snow-cone white frosting which made them look like a flock of grazing sheep as far as the eye could see. To turn around was not an option since that would expose our beams to the seas, so for the next five hours we fought our way through this churning cauldron which yesterday had innocently played at our feet as we walked in the warm waves lapping on the shoreline of Dog Island.

There would be no relaxation and there was limited movement except to check that the dinghy was fast and that no cupboards had come open. Chris went below and duct taped a few things shut before the boat started wildly lurching in the building seas. I made a few checks on the engine room but the seas were wild and it was unsafe to move around too much. A call to JUWIKA startled us as Gail explained how the kayak had broken loose and Bill had wrestled it back aboard. Fortunately he was not hit by it as it swung from its perch along their fly bridge. At the same time their steering wheel had come loose and was working its way off the chain which required that they work fast to reposition it. The loss of steering in these seas would have been disastrous.

They worked together as a team and got it back in place. In addition the chain on the galley oil lamp broke and the lamp crashed to the floor spilling the kerosene all over and breaking the lamp. This would have to be dealt with at a calmer time. Before leaving Carrabelle I had checked our shaft set screws and keys since we had some issues with them coming loose. Sure enough there was some play in the keys and set screws so with some RTV, thread lock and Gorilla Tape from Bill I secured the keys and tightened the bolts so the shafts could not work their way out of the couplings. Some difficult and risky periodic checks to the engine room confirmed that all was OK and the fix was holding. Thank you, Lord!

As we approached the lee of the land six hours into the crossing the wind started to lay down, the water became a tranquil, translucent blue and the sun came out with all its warmth and promise. A large green sea turtle passed under our hull on its way to deeper water and the dolphins returned as our pilot escorts. During the rough part of the crossing we had said a prayer that all would be well and that we would be able to look back on this experience with adventure and excitement. We also prayed for guardian angels to watch over our little corks in this vast swimming pool. Two seagulls approached our boats just seconds later and stayed with us for quite some time. I don't ever remember seeing any angels in the children's Bible story books that looked like seagulls but I believe that while on the water they could not take on a better personage than these amazing acrobats. We radioed back to Bill and Gail and Dan and Kathy that there was calmer waters ahead to give them the hope they needed to continue the battle an hour or so behind us.

Chris made some lunch for us and then we each took turns taking naps in the sun like lizards dozing on a rock. The end to an amazing day came as we entered the Steinhatchee River and pulled into a dock at the Sea Hagg. A couple hours later JUWIKA and Ariel pulled in behind us. We had dinner ready as the sun was just setting and we greeted the men with a pirate mug and the women with a shell and bead necklace and a hug to commemorate a long day on the water. Dinner at our place was a reliving of each other's perspective on the experience and a word of congratulations and thanks as we prepared our tired bodies for a good night's rest.

Steinhatchee is a back-river community noted for sport fishing and the shrimp and crab industry. It is also the home of wintering pelicans - both white and brown. They surround our boat in the morning waiting for the fish carcasses from the previous night's fish cleaning at the Sea Hagg Tiki Bar and fish tale cleaning station. Upriver from the marina, comfortable cabins line the banks before the river turns to a more desolate place. A few more of our cruising family came in the next day. So eating snacks and spinning tales of the sea was the evening's entertainment before a nice dinner out at Roy's; one of the two local restaurants.

One of the couples we have met several times along the way, who are from Canada, had run aground on an oyster bed when leaving Steinhatchee. They tore up both props and one shaft. They had been stranded six hours. They waited for the tide to release them from their embarrassing and destructive mistake which captured them in a weak moment of inattentiveness. It can happen so quickly and when it does you have the piper to pay!

Morning came early. Our next stop along this nature route would terminate at Cedar Keys. This is an up and coming town. It can be reached by car over any of three bridges; or by boat through the narrow, shallow and infamous channel from the northwest; or the much longer trip through the southern channel which we would take going out. It is an artisan town which reminds one of Catalina Island. Golf carts are for rent and are a major form of transportation on the island. The docks there are in ill-repair having been destroyed several years ago in a hurricane and never rebuilt. They are unsafe to use for cruising boats, so anchoring out in the shallow, exposed bay of 10 feet depth was our only option. We were granted a calm night, great hike and bistro dinner. Most everything was closed, since we arrived late, the girls were disappointed that there would be no "shopping". Tomorrow would be another blustery day and we knew the anchorage would deteriorate and be unacceptable the following evening. Our plan was to leave early and play "Marine Crochet" out the south end, head south for a few miles on the Gulf some 10 miles out and then shoot through the many green and red wickets at the Withlacoochee River and head up stream to Yankeetown.

Yankeetown and the river leading to it are as Florida was years and years ago. The river is wild with no markers and lined with swamps, cypress forests, and huge snags upon which ospreys and vultures roost and build their gigantic stick nests. Alligators camouflage themselves under the overhanging tropical vegetation along the shores and fish, turtles, cormorants, gulls and eagles hold conventions at each and every turn. The river is deep and tannic, meandering its way to the delta through thick shoreline vegetation. At times, where the river is narrow enough that two boats would have a hard time passing, the palm trees hang over the water close enough to touch and wild pigs and deer rustle in the jungle like restless weather at night. Huge bullfrogs make their haunting fog horn chorus along the banks. Shrimp boats exit and enter each day, full of a day's catch, dolphins in tow, feeding on the heads of these delicacies as they are cleaned in route to the weigh station up river. It is a very remote place that mesmerized me; beckoning me to go further and further up river until Chris pleaded for a place to stay for the night. Bill and Gail had dropped the hook in a bend a few miles downstream near a gypsy camp of decaying shrimp boats inhabited by local characters who gathered around a small palm frond campfire on the shore, smoking something that looked like cigarettes. They eyed JUWIKA as pirates would view a Spanish Galleon loaded with the king's gold.

I talked Chris into a small nook – wide spot in the river a 1/2 mile upstream of JUWIKA. But as we backed down on the anchor to set it for the night she spied a seven foot alligator just off the swim platform. She told me if "I loved her" we should move downstream into a more populated area. I recognized fear and trembling in her voice and decided to honor her request. We found a little campground along the river which had a dock with no electricity. But it was a place where we could get the bikes off and explore. We rescued Bill and Gail from the clutches of the scallywags upstream and they rafted to us for the night. After a long bike ride through huge live oak trees heavy with Spanish moss we retired to the boats for dinner. After having been thoroughly chewed up by the no-seeums and after heavy application of the anti-itch stick we went to bed.

Morning arrived, bright like the spot light of the coast guard inflatable that had lit up the shoreline the night before as they canvassed the area along the Withlacoochee. Perhaps they were looking for alligators or checking homes that sat vacant and vulnerable to pirates' plundering. We paddled downstream, out the channel across two channels, avoiding rocks and dredge spoil areas, leading to a power plant and a barge canal. After another 23 miles we entered the mouth of our third river on the Big Bend.

This river leads us to the community of Crystal River on King's Bay. It is only 11 miles by car from our previous night's stay but many hours by boat and the slow buoy marked water route. Many of our friends had gathered here at an anchorage eight miles upstream for their personal encounter with nature's amazing and docile manatees. One of the couples had seen them the day before and others were out on the hunt when we pulled into the bay and found our place among the flotilla of boats anchored there.

This is where this letter began and the rest of the story is an experience that rates as one of our favorite. We did our research and checked out the area, walking into town and visiting the first "West Marine" store we had seen since leaving Portland. Walking is a way of life with many miles a day being logged on the pedometer. We reloaded on groceries and found a wonderful little wine bistro that would be hosting a live jazz band the next night. We returned to our dinghy which had been tied along a less than desirable wharf where crabs and cockroaches competed for any residual scraps that may have been missed by the gulls. We made a quick trip back to the boat across the windy bay in our little water taxi as the sun set and evening began. The water in this bay and river is very clean, clear and warm - 73 degrees. In certain places you can see 20 to 30 feet to the bottom as clearly as you can see through a glass of drinking water.

After dinner out with all the cruising boats and after many tales of the high seas we topped off the night with ice-cream cones and worked our ways back in the dark to our individual anchor lights which become as recognizable from the others as your own children become recognizable from the other kids on the block. Morning would come early and the experts told us that we would have to be to the manatee springs as the sun came up and before the raucous noise of the tour boats loaded with tourists disturbed the manatees so much that they planted themselves on the bottom, coming up only occasionally to take a breath every 20 minutes or so.

We got up at 6:30 and headed for a little bay about a mile away in the dinghy. The day was overcast but not raining. Throughout the manatee area there are no wake zones and areas around many of the islands that are safe havens for these remarkable creatures - places they can go where people are prohibited to enter. So if they get tired of us they go into a kind of manatee time-out area away from all the harassment, noise and excitement of us humans who can't quite get enough of their strangeness. It is interesting that they seek us out and want to communicate with us through touch and visual contact.

I got the snorkeling gear out and prepared the wet suits for the morning's adventure. Chris has a fear of putting her face in the water and was panicking at the thought of baptism by emersion, especially with a mask and snorkel on and a 1000 pound wild animal begging you for a belly rub. We were the second group on the scene as Chris donned the wet suit, fins mask and snorkel. One other family who is traveling with their boys on the Great Circle Loop was already in the water and had spotted a manatee close to our raft. I dropped our anchor and Chris, seeing the manatee close by, slipped into the water like a Navy Seal on a rescue mission in the Pacific. Before I knew it she was engaged with a big animal and with the mask on her face submerged herself under water to cherish this unforgettable encounter with one of earth's gentle giants. Before long a larger animal, covered with barnacles made its way toward her. It had just arrived back from the ocean where sharks are its only natural enemy. Boat propellers are the other. Chris handled herself like a professional diver as I watched from the dinghy several yards away.

Gail and Bill were observing the action from a viewing platform a short distance away. Eventually they tied alongside us and Gail put on a Farmer John wet suit I had and the fins and mask and went overboard as well. Quite a few other people had arrived by now and the animals started to spook. Chris, now tired from being in the water over half an hour, returned to the boat and I pulled her aboard. Then I slipped into the water with Gail. We tried to get in with a tour group of kids who were frantically thrashing about in the presence of a large animal who was becoming fed up with this party. The tour diver told them to back off and return to the boat as to not scare the manatee any more. Gail and I just hung out there and floated quietly hoping it would return to check us out. Before long a thick skinned, whiskered submarine surfaced in front of us and asked for a back rub. Then Barnacle Bill showed up and wanted some of the action. We swam with them for half an hour until they decided it was time to give us a rest and took sanctuary 10 feet below us. Gail - as excited as Chris - returned to the boat and I continued my search. Three more times I had close encounters; once with a mom and her baby. At $40.00 a person many had paid to have this experience on a guided tour. It is needless to say that money can't buy the exhilarating feeling of looking a manatee in the eye and having them slide by you under water like a seal in slow motion, or breathe with an odor akin to fermented grass in a lawnmower bag; as Bill and Gail experienced later in the day when they were drawn back to the manatee hot zone for one last look.

Later in the day I soloed up a narrow and shallow canal into the crystal springs themselves where water bubbles up out of the earth, clear and without distortion. Fish flourished there and the deep caverns that housed these aquifers were clearly visible, effervescing 20 to 30 feet below.

All the time I kept a watchful eye out for alligators who share these waters with the gentle manatees. It was like looking through an iceberg at the sun with only the gurgling of the spring's bubbles escaping into the air while being surrounded by lush tropical vegetation.

Our day ended with the last of our shrimp cooked coconut style and then a dinghy ride in the dark to shore. We had a long walk to town under a star lit sky where houses were decked with holiday lights and lawn decorations rang in the Christmas season. Our joy could not have been any higher. We enjoyed an evening of jazz at the wine bistro and sampled a few of their gourmet appetizers before reluctantly making our way in the dark back to the marina. The waiting dinghies were tied to a couple of pilings in the light of a half burned out gas pump sign. We slowly motored to our little sleepy hollows on the water. None of us wanted the day to end but it always does and there is always another that follows - with new challenges and adventures. We were grateful for our health which enabled us to experience the awesomeness of this day.

On the boats our heads hit the pillows and there wasn't a creature stirring - not even a mouse. The alarm was set with care for an early morning departure onto the Gulf for our last leg of open water. There would be 63 miles to Tarpon Springs and that much closer to our return to friends and family where we would hang the stockings with care and enjoy being land lubbers for a brief time.

Blessings to all of you. See you soon. We look forward to catching up on your lives and spending some time sharing the season of our Savior's birth with you.

Love and Fondly,
From Tarpon Springs, Florida
Chuck and Chris

Dear Family and Friends,

As we watch Christmas boats with all kinds of decorations and music playing cruise the waters of the inter-coastal waterway in Florida we can't help but think of our drifting on the Columbia River aboard Kimberlina with Bev and Paul as we enjoyed the Christmas boat parades. The only things missing here are the good friends and family we look forward to seeing soon. It has been unbelievable to have Bill and Gail to share this time with.

Bill and Gail's boat sports a lit Christmas tree in the window and a colorful string of lights in their galley. It reflects through the window into our little house when we are anchored together, heralding in the joyous season of Christ's birth, which we anticipate spending with friends and family.

As we travel from manatees to the Greek community of Tarpon Springs it is sometimes hard to absorb it all and to change gears as we reenter civilization and the densely populated cities of coastal Florida.

The first evening after coming in off the Gulf onto the Anclote River at Tarpon Springs we anchored in a small tributary off the river. As we negotiated the channel into the river we were passed by the Suntour boat carrying gamblers on the casino express fresh in off the Gulf where they are transported to and from a floating casino anchored offshore - a legal place where they can try their hand at lady luck. We passed them on our trip south as they were counting their winnings and walking the gang plank back onto the express that would return them to terra firma from several miles out.

The day of travel was one of beautiful turquoise water, bright blue skies, light winds and calm seas; not to mention hundreds of crab pots in the 15 feet of water we were powering through. The crabbing here is for Stone Crab claws. The fishermen pull the nets, tear off one claw (one is left on for the crab to use for defense and to gather necessary food), and throw back the crab which regenerates a new harvestable claw in three years. The claws are large and red with a black tip on the end. The shell is like stone and shatters when cracked. They are tasty but don't hold a candle to the luscious Dungeness crab we catch in the Northwest.

We are far enough south now that the weather is very warm and pleasant so it seems strange to see the palms decorated and the store windows with displays for the Christmas season. Still, the nights have been chilly and only lately have been warm enough that long sleeves are not needed.

Tarpon Springs is a very Greek community and the United States' natural sponge capital. At one time there were over a hundred sponge boats making their living off this ancient trade. Today there are five. It is also the home of baklava, tiramisu, gyros, dolmades and other Greek delicacies that one can eat at breakfast, lunch and dinner - and we did. We ate the goodies in and out, at Hellas, Mykonos and Opas. Pack it in and pack it on. We had been deprived of bakeries and made up for it the three days we stayed at dock, situated next to the sidewalk of main-street and the restaurants displaying these gastronomical delights.

Fortunately we had a schedule to meet and were forced to leave after three days. We really enjoyed this town and all it had to offer. We watched the movies of the sponge divers; very similar in vintage to watching the ancient film on the, "Sex Life of the Date", at Hadley's, Palm Springs. Never knew there was so much to learn about sponges.

One evening we even found ourselves at the "Biker Night" at one of the local marina restaurants where we rubbed handle bars with many of the finest citizens of the community.

There is a very excellent bike trail which extends from Tarpon Springs to St. Petersburg (approximately 45 miles) so we took advantage of some great weather and the protection of this safe passage trail to ride through this part of Florida and enjoy the countryside and back streets of the communities. Some of the trail goes along the water and there are many causeways that cross the inter-coastal to the barrier islands along the Gulf. The beaches of Clearwater and surrounding area are some of the best in the world and very beautiful with their white sands, fishing piers, surf shops, fishing opportunities, fancy resorts, marinas and cute boutique shops.

Condominium life is alive and well and for those who don't live in ultra fancy homes or condos there are always the ever popular mobile home parks. We have a much greater appreciation for the pictures we have seen on the news following hurricanes. The potential for destruction of these parks and marinas is inevitable, taking a heavy toll on the numerous manufactured homes.

Leaving Tarpon Springs with a pang of loss in our stomachs we made our way twenty miles south to a little Scottish community called Dunedin. We were expecting a significant wind storm and needed a place to tuck into for a few days. It was also within pedaling distance from baklava and tiramisu if we started to have withdrawals.

It just happened that the marina at Dunedin could accommodate our two boats for .90 cents a foot instead of the $2.00 a foot that Clearwater wanted just a few miles south. After landing and getting tied down for the blow we found that we had arrived on the eve of the big Christmas parade and Family Festival in the park at the end of our dock. The municipal workers were setting up barricades and the entertainment stage was visible and audible from our boats. Dunedin is also the home of some gourmet restaurants and more shopping!!! Not to mention a snow slide which magically appears for this annual event made with 300 blocks of ice and a wood chipper. It is probably the only snow some of these kids have ever seen. For a mere $2,800.00 this slide is created while the children of the town are fast asleep - dreaming of gliding down the slide on vibrantly colored saucers the next morning. Watching the faces in the line waiting for their 10 second descent from the 15 foot hill - including one slight mogul jump - was the high point of the festival's entertainment. Eyes bugged out and smiles on faces lit the day with such excitement that children probably were inspired to go onto becoming Olympic hopeful bobsledders in years to come. If Jamaica can have a team, why not Dunedin? Anyhow they were having a ball and parents grinned and snapped off copious pictures of this once a year event. Thanks to cold evenings there was still snow and a few kids who continued to enjoy the icy run until the wee hours of the morning.

After catching several strings of Christmas colored beads and candies from the floats making their way down the parade route, we retired for the evening. Sunday we worshipped at a local church and then headed for our final destination, Madeira Beach, where we would leave the boats for a month while we return home for Christmas.

Grand kids, kids, parents, friends and our church family are all on our minds as we pack up treasures found specifically for loved ones, soon to be put in packed Christmas stockings. The weather has turned warm and the rental car is in the parking lot ready for its journey to Orlando where we will catch our flights home.

Home is what hearts long for and ours are with all of you. We pray that you will have a wonderful and blessed Christmas. Enjoy every moment of this season as we reflect on everything good in our lives and the gift of Jesus Christ as our Savior. Pray for peace on earth and remember those who are not as fortunate as we or who will be unable to be with those they love because they have been called to serve others.

Until January when we resume our trip on the Great Circle this will be our last letter of progress. The boats have been put away with care. Visions of family are filling our heads and Chris has already settled down for her long winter's nap. We have put out the roach bait so that while we are gone there will be no creatures stirring. Out on the boat top I hear the clatter of seabirds on my freshly cleaned snow white fiberglass and know that after a month of vacancy the cousins of those same guardian seagulls that guided us across the Gulf will keep a watchful eye and creatively decorate Essi-Anna and JUWIKA as they celebrate their own Christmas and our absence.

God Bless and Merry Christmas to all of you and your families,
Fondly,
Chuck and Chris

LOOPET 8

Madeira Beach Florida to Stuart Florida (via Lake Okeechobee)

DEAR Family and Friends,
Greetings from Fort Meyer's Beach, Florida
I know it is a long ways past the New Year but how important it is to wish and pray for each of you that God will bless your year with peace and strength for whatever this world throws your way. Our prayer is that you and your families have a healthy and joy-filled 2007 but we're not in charge - only the "Good Lord" knows what the year holds in store for any of us. Much like the lessons learned on the loop - each day is special and wonderful - a gift to be cherished but a gift with its own unique challenges! We have been awestruck by the vastness and wrath of the Gulf as it dishes out a tropical storm and we have been mesmerized by the same waters and sky as it paints all the colors of the rainbow solely for our enjoyment. That is life! May yours be blessed!

My suitcase is packed for a quick trip home, a Northwest District Board meeting on January 26th and 27th. I will dinghy myself at 4:00 a.m., in the dark, half a mile up the inter-coastal waterway from our mooring buoy in the vast mooring field, south of Fort Myers Beach, to knock on JUWIKA's door. Bill will graciously leap into action from his deep sleep to drive me to the airport in a rental car, where I will catch a flight to Portland for a whirl-wind weekend.

Fort Myers Beach is a quaint little town on Estero Island about 2/3 of the way down Florida's West Gulf Coast. Shops line the only main street that runs down the spine of the narrow strip of land like a backbone runs down the body of a fish. The beaches are snow white with sand that reminds us of powdered sugar. The houses and buildings are painted with pastel colors of yellow, blue, green, orange and purple with coconut palms swaying in the front yards and along the boulevard. There are even fake palm trees that are lit like Christmas trees, flashing their artificial images to entice the tourists who roam this little piece of paradise to come and spend.

The sunsets on the Gulf draw people to the beaches in hoards. They stand like statues and gaze out across the turquoise waters as the crimson ball drops beyond the horizon like the New Year's ball in Time Square, leaving only the memory emblazoned in their mind - until tomorrow when the whole world will watch in awe again, each from their own little perch on this vast planet.

Nearby Sanibel Island is the shell collector's paradise with a treasure at every step. There is actually a name given to the posture one must take as they stoop over in search of the kinds of shells that most people only see for a handsome sum in shell stores.

Moorage rates in middle and southwestern Florida for a boat our size range from $70.00 to over $100.00 dollars a night. Some of the fancier marinas include spas, which cater to the lifestyles of the rich and famous would cost us $180.00 a night so... most of the time, not to break our banks, we try and find a little cove or duck behind an island for the night and drop the hook. We dinghy ashore to explore the islands and often times come upon quaint little tiki bars at the water's edge. We see pelicans dive bombing the water for a meal just offshore and dolphins playing in the wind waves or feeding their young in the shallows, feet from the sandy shore where we landed. We have grown quite accustomed to shallow water and anchoring in areas where to have more than three feet under our hulls at low tide is a real luxury.

We returned to the boat following a wonderful Christmas with friends and family in Vancouver. I did my elf-helper thing at one UPS Store owned by our kids and Chris watched the three "amigos" - Noah, Logan and Sawyer for two weeks so Esther could work with Steve and me. We stayed at Chris's folks and Esther and Steve's which gave us great family time in the evenings. One weekend Jeff and Anna honored us with a fabulous stay in Portland complete with the finest in French cuisine, a gorgeous hotel room and a night at the theater with them. What a relaxing and wonderful time.

The week before returning my son-in-law Steve and I went to Cabo San Lucas for a little male bonding time with my brother. While Steve took dive certification, Matt and I worked on tile floors and a swimming pool. Matt is excellent at those kinds of things and I am a very able-bodied assistant.

Upon return to the boat it was obvious she had weathered a couple of tropical storms. The burgee had blown off and the dinghy had lost a lot of its air so it was hanging like a wet rag on a clothesline off the transom of the boat but all in all Madeira Beach proved to be a great place to leave our floating homes. A brief two day stop in Orlando before seeing Essi-Anna and JUWIKA was wonderful fun - Epcot being the crown jewel for us.

With the boats washed and cleaned up and reassembled we still had the issues of a leaking water pump and a slipping shaft on the starboard side to deal with, so I made an appointment with a boatyard eight miles away to have things looked at and fixed. BOAT means "Bring Over Another Thousand" and that's what we left two days later at the boatyard, plus a little more for a job well done.

Bill and Gail waited at Madeira until we were finished and were ready to head south. We radioed them to give them advance notice that we would meet them along the waterway at red marker 30. Just as we were leaving our phone rang and Bill and Gail told us they would be a little late. They had run aground and were doing all the right things to free themselves from the sandy grave which claims many a weary sailor along the inter-coastal. With success and after much maneuvering and skillful use of the anchor they freed themselves and continued toward the rendezvous point. The channel we had taken to reach the marina at high tide was unmarked except for a sketch given to us by the marina. The morning we left to meet Bill and Gail the tide was a couple of feet lower and the wind was blowing stiffly from the east. Reading the water ahead as extremely shallow, we greased our way toward the inter-coastal when suddenly we found our bow aground. Putting the engines in reverse just stirred up the sand behind us so we decided to let the wind do the work and a few minutes later our depth sounder read positive again as we inched our way into the main channel. Just in front of us was a large boat that had not been so cautious and had run hard aground in his attempt to show everyone how fast he could pass them. There he sat stuck, and on the radio calling for a tow. The shallow water he was in prevented us from giving assistance so we motored south toward our next night's anchorage.

It would be several nights before we would be in Fort Myer's Beach. The weather had turned warm; in the 70's and 80's, and the waterway dished up large bays, narrow cuts, opulent homes and hotels, little pristine and remote islands and fancy private yacht clubs. We anchored out each night and enjoyed some wonderful stops that can only be described as storybook. During the playoff game between the Bears and the Saints we were anchored in a water cul-de-sac surrounded by very nice homes just off the main channel. Bev, one of our friends from church, was calling each time there was a score to let us know how her beloved Bears were doing. We told her that we could actually hear the cheers coming up from the homes around us but didn't know who they were cheering for until she would call. Eventually the boats turned on anchor enough so we could listen to the game on the radios. The delay was several seconds from the TV game that was going on around us so it was a kick to anticipate what was happening - anyway - for you Bev - GO BEARS!

Sarasota was a wonderful next stop! Bill and Gail and we have friends there so this would be a time of renewal of old relationships. The bay there is large with many living aboard their ill kept vessels. In some cases there were boats which had been neglected until only the mast protruded above the waterline or the hulls had become seabird rookeries with all the sights and sounds and smells associated with such. We fortunately were never downwind of one of these avian cesspools but can assure you that while looking for a place to anchor the stench coming from them cleared the nostrils like a dose of smelling salts.

Sarasota is the home of the Ringling Museum. Bill and Gail's friend took a day with us and showed us the sights. The museum and winter home of John and Mabel Ringling is fascinating. One of the museum buildings housed a 1/16th scale model of the entire circus which had been hand carved and assembled by one man over a fifty year period of time. It includes every detail from the trains that would bring the circus to town to the little boy eating cotton candy in the stands with his family and all the other families in the stands at any given performance.

Dan and Jo also showed us some amazing real estate - two of which he had built himself for several million dollars each. His golf course model home; complete with an elevator, lacked nothing and was the most beautiful home we had ever seen. Sarasota is a must see with a wonderful downtown, farmer's market, marina facilities and just the right mix of small urban city, culture and nightlife. Our friend, Linda, joined us for dinner on the boat. It was great to see her after 20 plus years.

The next stop was Venice Beach - not to be confused with Muscle Beach in California. There was an extreme red tide and as we motored toward the free city dock on a warm and sunny afternoon the smell of decaying fish and a pungent, caustic odor caused us to cough and breathe with difficulty. Hundreds and hundreds of dead fish clogged the waterway and lay amongst the mangrove roots along the water's edge like fallen bowling pins in a smoke-filled bowling alley. Hundreds of buzzards circled overhead and hopped along the shoreline devouring these stagnant entrees as if though they were dining on caviar. Needless to say we stayed only a day and were glad to find out that the red tide was local to that area.

The next evening we stopped at a world renowned little island called "Cabbage Cay". At 38 feet above sea level it is one of the highest islands along Florida's west coast. It was extremely windy with no place to tie up so we found what shelter we could behind a small forest of mangroves in 10 feet of water. The waves coming off the Gulf would not be dangerous but would make for an interesting night's sleep so I got in the dinghy and scouted out a channel leading through a coral reefed bottom into a seven foot deep bay that would give us more protection. Bill and Chris followed me into the bay like goslings following the mama goose in the safety of a park pond. We dropped the anchors and enjoyed the shelter this little bay provided. That night we crossed some very shallow water in the little boats. A mother dolphin was feeding her baby near the shoreline as we arrived at the only restaurant on the island. Cheeseburgers are the specialty so there we sat having "Cheeseburgers in Paradise" in an old tarpon fishing lodge surrounded by lush tropical vegetation. Behind the lodge a water tank sits high on stilts above the ground with a rickety staircase ascending. A climb to the top of the water tower provided an unbelievable view of the islands around us surrounded by the crystal clear waters.

Now here we sit at Fort Myers Beach surrounded by other boats tethered to mooring balls, bobbing up and down and doing our synchronized dance in the wind like the arcade ducklings one would pluck from the stream at the county fair in order to win the small stuffed animal or dice key chain. Sometimes our geometric paths come close to each other but all in all it is a nice little armada full of transients, live-aboards and abandoned vessels. The price is a bargain at a mere $13.00 a night which includes garbage drop and holding tank pump-outs by city sponsored pump out boats who will do the dirty deed for an unnecessary tip to the operator.

While I was in Portland, Chris stayed with Essi-Anna and tended to the needs of the boat. Bill and Gail had headed south to Naples with relatives who had flown in for some time on the boat with them. Each day she would start the dinghy and go to town by herself; walking the beach, shopping and meeting new friends. One couple she got close to was from Georgia, Paul and Stacy, later to become life-long friends. They sang karaoke together and visited each other's boat for meals. It was wonderful to have them close and protecting her from the scalley-wags that ply these waters. Paul was good enough to stay awake till 11:30 p.m. and help Chris pick me up at the end of one of the canals where the locals tie their flotilla of ragged landing craft. Along the shore mangroves grow down to the water's edge and the sand and rock is well packed from years of trampling. There is the usual debris littering the shore and even an old couch that is used for who knows what? Just steps away from this dark little site, is a seedy, waterfront bar attached to the back of a grocery store. It is very rustic and the home of Fort Myer's "Beer Drinking Society", as proclaimed by the message peeling off the sign painted on the outside of the building. There is also a crude laundromat attached to the bar so while the duds suds so do the buds.

I poked my head in there at 10:00 a.m. A goodly number of the society were already convened in a meeting. The discussion dealt with smoking something. I said good morning and exited before being inducted into the membership.

That day we left our little neighborhood amongst the mooring balls that had been home for five days and headed for Sanibel Island in search of shells at low tide early Wednesday morning. Danny and Linda Rude - Bill and Gail's kids' folks are with them. Being world travelers and adventurers they have shared some great stories and gotten us all thinking about what is next. The girls say such discussions detract from the present but the guys say it enhances it. It's the Venus/Mars thing. Anyway it is all in God's hands. We don't know the time or the moment when this part of our lives will be snatched away but for now we gave thanks for: health, joy, friendship, our faith our families and this incredible journey with Bill and Gail. We are very blessed and hope you are too!

At the time I am eating fresh coconut. I found the pod floating in the water on one of my forays into the swamps. I chopped the husk off with a huge knife I carry for filleting fish and then drained the milk into a glass and added a spot of rum to purify it. Gail, Bill and I took a few sips. One whack of the hammer produced this fresh delicacy - white, sweet and buttery! Wish you were all here to share it with us!

Dear Friends and Family,

What could be better than being anchored 200 yards from the, Miami in the water boat show, surrounded by waterfront skyscrapers, drawbridges adorned with colorful lights, cruise ships coming and going from exotic locations closer to the equator and the storybook colored seas of Florida surrounding us like a baby-blue cozy wrapped around a new born.

Well, I'll tell you; it could be sunny and the wind could stop blowing but who is complaining. We are very blessed to be here and have had a wonderful and safe adventure thus far.

We walk the docks, calculating what would have to happen in the stock market in order for us to be able to afford the down payment on one of them;, trying to imagine how common folks can afford them. Yesterday we spent the day in the Miami Beach Convention Center at the biggest boat show in the U.S. Bill and Gail's boat danced in the wind next to ours and from time to time we each reached the ends of our rodes, (lines and chains on the anchor) which snapped us back to attention, only to reverse our spin. We stayed on the radio to check each other's progress; the silence interrupted by all sorts of foreign languages as the crews on the gigantic and numerous cruise ships communicate their instructions for arrival and departure at the docks just minutes from our windy little anchorage. I think we will stay put amongst the skyscrapers which for the time are acting like a huge wind break.

When last we wrote we were leaving Fort Myers Beach to spend a day on Sanibel Island. We stayed at a unique little marina tucked into a tiny bay surrounded by multi-million dollar homes. The channel leading into the marina was very narrow so we had to hug the retaining wall for a high rise of condominiums on the starboard side to avoid grounding on the portside shoal.

Chris and I unloaded the bikes while Bill, Gail, Danny and Linda went exploring on foot. The island is a Mecca for shell searching and relaxing. Many people come here to get away from their fast paced lives and re-group. Low tide was in the morning so we decided to save all our energy for an early morning tidal walk tomorrow in search of the perfect shell. The girls wanted a head start so I loaded them in our dinghy and skirted the shoreline to where they wanted to be dropped. They had to wade a little to the shore but immediately went into a stooped posture, eyes glued to the sandy tide line as I returned to the boats for the guys. The reports of boundless bounty, which they had read about in the destination travel books, came up a little disappointing but there were a few nice specimens in their treasure bags when I picked them up several hours later. After a slice of key-lime pie at a local hangout and a wonderful bike ride on this gorgeous barrier island, we said good bye to the Gulf of Mexico with sadness in our hearts and headed east.

The next stop would be several miles up-river to Fort Myers, not to be confused with Fort Myers Beach. Most of these Gulf cities have a beach section that is called "beach" which is totally different from the older part of the city away from the pristine waters of the Gulf which bears the same name minus beach. The approach to this city is a tricky one. It has very shallow water just outside the channel waiting to ensnare any mariners who take their eyes off of their charts in a lapse of concentration, if only for a second.

Fort Myers is the home of Edison's winter home and lab and Ford's winter estate. Both of these are along the river and next door to each other as both men were friends and often spent time collaborating. Along with Harvey Firestone, these friends partnered their intellect, building America one invention at a time. Edison had the phenomenal record of having an invention a year for sixty-five consecutive years. His lab, located in Fort Myers, was used primarily to experiment on a process to make rubber from different plants. Using genetic and agricultural genius he produced natural latex which Ford and Firestone thought would solve the issue of rubber shortages for their products. It eventually became evident that it would be too expensive and the idea was put to rest. We toured the homes, the lab, gardens and museum; struck with awe at the genius of men who changed the course of history.

We spent two nights at Fort Myers on the dock since there was heavy weather building north of us. The wind was howling and the reports on the radio and TV spoke of destruction and death not too many miles away. The swath we had traveled earlier had been hit by a tornado and eighteen people had died, leaving in its wake massive loss of property as well. We only felt the shirt tails of the storm and all was well. We gave thanks to God for continued protection and safe travel.

Some friends from church, who were in the Tampa area, rendezvoused with us the evening before Danny and Linda left; so we had a dock party and enjoyed an evening of "fellowship" at Joe's Crab Shack, swapping stories and sharing experiences.

Morning broke with the sky black and overcast but the wind much calmer. I had changed the engine oil the day before and Essi-Anna was ready for the trip across the state to the Atlantic. There are two ways to make the transit. One is around the Keys and the other is across Lake Okeechobee. We chose the lake route which meant traversing Florida on a river system, crossing the lake and then descending on the St. Lucie River to the Atlantic at Stuart. It would take us several days and depending on the weather we might get held up on the west side of the lake. Lake Okeechobee can pack a mean punch if the wind is up since it is the second largest fresh water lake entirely within the U.S., some 30 miles wide and long. The term "fresh water" will be clarified later as our crossing was more like playing in a big mud puddle.

The Caloosahatchee River led us through the middle of Florida's agricultural area. Cattle ranching and sugar cane are big business in this region. Herds of long horns browse the grasslands next to the waterway. Several locks step you up to the lake level with towns few and far between. We felt like we were on our old friend "The Upper Mississippi" again and were glad to be out of the heavily populated areas along the Gulf Coast. Manatees played in front of the boat and in one instance we heard the fish and game people talking about a manatee that had been hit by a boat and was being pushed into safe water by its companion. We had just come through that area and in spite of slow signs a large boat had stormed through the manatee habitat and passed us creating quite a wake and perhaps had been the culprit.

Night time was falling and there was little space on the narrow river so we tied Essi-Anna between two large pilings on the side of the river just yards from the bank but out of the channel. JUWIKA tied alongside us and there we sat tethered between these two big poles, called dolphins, like trapeze artists walking the tight rope, in the middle of Florida's heartland. This method was a first but worked out well and was very secure and safe.

In the morning we took our leashes off and continued upstream toward the lake. It was a windy day and as we navigated our way through fields of sugar cane we mentioned how lucky we were that they weren't burning that day. The fields are burned before they are harvested to make the process easier and rid the area of anything that may be lurking in the canes. No sooner had we talked to Bill and Gail on the radio about our good fortune when what appeared to be a mushroom cloud billowed up and loomed in the distance. The wind was blowing our way and before long we could see several fires burning on both sides of the river. They were some distance from us but as we got closer the ash and smoke drifted over our boats like a foggy, black, snow storm. It was a very strange sensation; the smell of smoke filled the air for several miles. Other than a little residue from the ash falling from the air we suffered no harm and made our way toward the lake. This area would not be our choice for retirement. Talk about second hand smoke; the people in this area live with this constant inconvenience which can't be too good for one's health either.

Coming out of the last lock on the Caloosahatchee we entered another world of strange and eerie vegetation. The trees were naked and eagles roosted in the branches while the waterway itself turned dark brown;

lined with levies on one side and heavy marshlands on the other. We were virtually alone on this stretch of the trip with the exception of a few bass boats that raced by us toward their favorite fishing holes. One minute they were there and the next minute they were gone. To actually eat fish from these waters you should either have an iron stomach or be a major stock holder in Pepto-Bismol. I never saw a fish come out of the water but I would venture to say they may have been born with three eyes or two dorsal fins. The passage toward Clewiston on the west side of the lake's edge and our next stop for the night, was a few miles off and there was no place to anchor that would be safely out of the channel. We did spot a couple of poles that might work as a landing spot but a huge, half-sunken derelict fishing vessel lay on its side in the midst of them.

The lake was now visible on our port side and it was kicking up some pretty good waves. We would cross another day.

The city of Clewiston is located behind a lock that leads into an irrigation canal, impossible to boat traffic our size. As the water fluctuates on the lake there are times when you must lock through to get into the dead end channel which allows boaters access to the town. The gates were open since the water level on the lake and at the town were at the same height so we motored through the lock and narrow canal that terminated at Martin's Marina and Tiki Bar. The docks were being wrangled by none other than "Little Man", the legendary dock-master who demonstrated his rodeo rope tricks as he lassoed us to the cleats of the rickety wharf which took up half the channel and was dwarfed by the huge stilt-like tiki deck just feet from our fly bridge. Little Man produced a magazine article which heralded his prowess as the best dock-master in Florida.

We could actually sit on our fly bridge and watch TV directly across from us in the open air, roofed bar. Bill and Gail pulled in a few minutes later. We exchanged glances as if to say we had entered into a surreal new world.

It was "Super Bowl" weekend so this would be home for a couple of days while we waited for a weather window to cross Okeechobee. It was the only option we had and literally the end of the road. The price was $1.75 a foot. That night a sixty-five foot metal conversion scow entered our Waterworld and squeaked by us with a foot or so to spare on our flanks to join our odd flotilla of boats waiting in this strange but friendly place.

Well, as you know the Colts won and our good friend Bev was saddened by the loss taken by the Bears. We sat in the bar and watched the game amongst people we had met minutes earlier and commented how nice it was to watch the Super Bowl with friends!

All in all it was a unique and relaxing stay. Great thrift stores, an excellent cafe, a nice ship's store, a great Hispanic super market and a vintage hotel with a beautiful mural in the bar. I also met a fun guy named Skinner who was a master barbecuer operating a man-sized rib and chicken grill on the front lawn outside the marina. He cooked up some awesome ribs with a special citrus barbecue sauce that was second only to my son-in-law Steve's NFL ribs recipe.

The next day we backed out of our little refuge and exited the open doors of the lock on our way to the lake and another step closer to the Atlantic. Chris waved goodbye to "Little Man", the legend, who had taken quite a liking to her and had managed to give her a peck on the cheek when I wasn't looking. I had to look into her eyes to see if this little red-headed, "marinized" cowboy had stolen her heart. She assured me that we were still good so off we went, our marriage having been tested.

The wind was supposed to build in the afternoon to 15 knots so we felt we had enough time to make the four hour crossing without getting beat up. Leaving early, there were two other power boats several miles ahead of us that had also spent time in Clewiston. The lake is quite shallow; less than 20 feet and there are many shoals and rocks to avoid on the route. It is like crossing a mini ocean with the other side invisible from the starting point. The water is a disgrace, black and polluted from agriculture and the problems associated with drainage and fresh water runoff. Certain areas just outside the channel are extremely shallow with no room for error.

The wind came up quicker than expected about an hour and a half into the crossing but too late to turn back. The waves built to between three and four feet smashing their muddy crests against our hulls and across our decks. Sea birds followed in our wake hoping we would churn up a dinner, making it visible in the quagmire blended by our props. We were glad when we entered the lock on the other side. Our boats were filthy with the proof of our crossing - having played rough in the murky waters of Okeechobee. Leaving the lake we were very careful as we passed through the lock leading us to the river. One man we had talked to in Sanibel had hit something in the lock and there had been other reports of boats being damaged. Some speculated that perhaps it was a huge alligator and others said perhaps there was a deadhead or piling lying just below the surface. The word was out so we steered clear of this trouble spot.

It was a long day from Clewiston until we finally dropped anchor in Stuart, Florida. We were within earshot of the Atlantic and the girls were already talking about the possibilities of searching for shells along another shoreline. I had a meeting in St. Louis in two days so we rented a car from our favorite car place; Enterprise, and readied for my departure in a day. We had anchored near another mooring field but there were no buoys for us so we tucked ourselves into a little nook off the shoreline and got permission to use the dinghy dock, trash disposal, water-fill station and head pump-out from the dock-master. This enabled us to get to shore and explore and it afforded us all the necessities including a place to park the car. It was a great spot – Bill, Gail and Chris would wait there, at anchor until I returned. In order to make my journey to the arched city we had passed months prior, I needed to dinghy to shore, drive an hour and a half to Fort Lauderdale, turn in the rental car and fly to St. Louis only to repeat the process in reverse in two days.

My flight took me over parts of the Mississippi we had traveled on earlier in the fall. It was now frozen over and river traffic had come to a halt.

The beaches along the Atlantic are a different blue than those of the Gulf yet very gorgeous and very warm. They host a myriad of shells so the girls spent a lot of time scouring the shoreline for the biggest, most beautiful and most perfect specimens - which they found. It took a little wading and a little running in and out of the surf to grab those that hadn't come ashore yet, but at the end of a good day they had a collection to be proud of. The beaches were also littered with jellyfish. Some were still floating in the water, sails extended like navy blue, floating crescent rolls. These marine wonders have the potential to give a nasty sting dead or alive from the tentacles that extend from their transparent bodies. We avoided stepping on them or having one bump us as they sailed ashore in the surf.

While I was gone the three musketeers attended the Stuart Art Festival which was a few blocks away in the old town. They kept a watchful eye for the water sheriff's patrol that had stopped us earlier and asked to see our life jackets. He also wanted to know why our dinghy wasn't registered which I explained according to federal law and Washington State law wasn't necessary. He didn't like it but let us go without a ticket knowing we were legal.

Early into the dark morning hours shortly after midnight, in some heavy wind, Bill and Gail's dinghy came untied and drifted away. We use our cell phones for emergency calls so ours rang around 1:00 a.m. announcing his horrific problem. I jumped out of bed and went to Bill's boat in our dinghy to pick him up. We estimated the drift of the boat according to the wind and began the search with our spot lights, like looking for "Where's Waldo in the entire world". Fortunately the wind was blowing toward a shoreline a quarter of a mile away where we eventually spotted the lost lamb. It had grounded itself near the bank, amongst the mangroves. We had to get out of the boat and wade in the shallow water to retrieve it - taking precaution that no snake or alligator was lurking in the coal black darkness or had found its way into the dinghy while unattended.

Saying goodbye to Stuart we headed a few miles east on the intercoastal until it turned north or south. Our plan B instead of going to the Bahamas, should the wind not cooperate (and it didn't), was to head for the Miami Boat Show and then proceed further south to the Florida Keys. Some of our friends on the loop had emailed us and said they had waited three weeks to get a day to cross to the islands across the Gulf Stream. The Gulf Stream flows north and when the wind blows toward the south the Atlantic between Florida and the Bahamas stands up like a flat top with butch wax. The waves build to ten feet very quickly and many a boat has found itself in trouble. The same wait can happen on the way back so we abandoned that idea, not having the time to get caught in inclement weather. Besides it takes a couple of days for checking in and out and the entry fee for our boat would be $350.00 so we executed our plan B.

We had spent six days in Stuart - attended worship at a wonderful LCMS church where the pastor actually stood out in the entrance to the parking lot and greeted people as they came to church. In preparation for the next leg we filled with water, and emptied our holding tanks. Little did we know that the next stretch of water we would traverse would be one of the most affluent areas we had ever seen.

Loopet 9

Stuart Florida to the Florida Keys

Dear Family and Friends,

On our way to Miami our route intersected names like: Fort Lauderdale, Delray Beach, Boca Raton, Hollywood, and other sections of Florida that looked like, smelled like and sounded like money. It is an area of more "Keeping up with the Joneses" than one could imagine. Neighbor upon neighbor upon neighbor had homes many, many, many of which were only surpassed by the likes of the Hurst Castle. Some of these gargantuan palaces were on pieces of real estate that faced both the Atlantic and the inter-coastal. In front of each were yachts that stretched the entire width of the property and in some cases literally blocked the view of the house. Horizon pools bedecked the backyards and large bronze statues and fountains graced the palatial landscapes. Not one or two or three but hundreds of these architectural wonders left our eyeballs popping and our mouths gaping.

Small lots on the water were going for $2,000,000.00 so these homes had to be in the $10,000,000.00 range with the yachts being equally expensive. Our saying for this stretch was one that we borrowed from Jerry McGuire; none other than, "Show me the money!!!!"

In the evening we would actually nestle ourselves into these ritzy neighborhoods' aqua cul-de-sacs and throw out the anchor. From our boats we enjoy watching their big screen TVs and listening to their parrots mimic their masters while the soothing gurgle of their fountains doze us off to sleep – all for free.

We also made a few stops to check out local bakeries and on a few occasions found some public access to the beaches where the girls resumed their shell game. Gail really got into it on one beach where the water was 73 degrees and before long she was wet to the waist. With a smile on her face she displayed her pristine shells - well worth the effort and the soaking. I followed suit and added some beauties to Chris's collection.

On the waterway between Stuart and Miami there are numerous bridges that cross from the mainland to the barrier islands. Some are very tall and others are called bascule bridges which must be raised to allow passage of boats. Our boats, at the highest points of our radar arches, are 18 feet off the water so we were able to squeeze under those that measured 19 feet to 25 feet. There is actually a substantial fine for not lowering your antenna or asking a bridge to open unnecessarily since this often holds up traffic on these busy roads. Many operate on a schedule so to time them in sequence is a feat of coordination. The inter-coastal in most areas has a speed zone which diminishes the wake and reduces erosion of the precious soils that support the homes lining the waterway. Several bridges measured 10 - 15 feet according to the charts and the scale on the side of the bridge so we had to time our trip to be at these bridges when they were scheduled to open. The times of openings are part of the cruising guide information which we found to be inaccurate so radio calls to the bridge tenders confirmed actual times for passage. It was a safe and interesting trip and then we were on the doorsteps of Miami.

And that is where we began this little chapter of adventure. We are anchored in the Florida Keys tonight but that will be a different letter. Sorry for the delay in writing - I won't wait so long next time. We are all well and send our love and greetings to all.

There is a lot more to share but it is time to turn in. The night is so calm that the boats appear to be sitting on dry ground. It is a nice relief from being at anchor and spinning in the wind like a top. With hundreds and hundreds and hundreds of times at anchor we have learned to trust the safety of our great claw anchor, joined to Essi-Anna's bow by lots of chain.

When last you heard from us it was mid February and we were

anchored amongst the skyscrapers of Miami attending the largest boat show in the United States. It was a wonderful event and although the wind howled and the boats jerked at the end of their leashes we enjoyed our stay and didn't do anything irrational - like buy a new boat.

We left Miami under gorgeous, sunny skies and headed south into Biscayne Bay and the northern part of the Florida Keys. Having been at anchor for three days and having traveled south for the previous three days without filling our water tanks we were getting scarcely low and our holding tanks were in need of pumping out too. Florida has some very strict laws about discharge and we feel strongly about being good stewards of the waterways, so we look for pump-out stations whenever we can find one. There are even traveling pump-out boats that ply the waterways and do the dirty deed for free - courtesy of the taxpayers of the cities or counties you are in. This makes it very convenient. These little traveling septic tanks are reminiscent of our own Northwest pumper in Roche Harbor of the San Juan Islands whose name is the, "Fecal Freak" and whose motto is, "We take Crap from Any One". Enough of that!

As we traveled further south the water became an amazing and mystifying blue color and visibility to the bottom was as clear as if you were looking through a plate glass window. Reading the depths has to do with the color of the water. Where there is sand and the water is shallow it appears a light bluish white, where there is coral or sea grass or sponges the water changes to a darker color (which can mean shallow), and where it is blue it usually is deeper and a good place to travel. When in doubt entering and exiting anchorages or channels leading to marinas, Chris stands on the bow of the boat and reads the bottom visually to tell me how deep it is. That along with the depth sounder gives us the assurance of running in safe water.

The first night we landed in a little place called Black Pointe Marina. Ninety-four cents a foot - what a deal! We followed a narrow and shallow channel which was well marked and buoyed deep into the mainland side of Florida. Here we restocked and watered up, preparing the boats for time at anchor in the Keys. Surprisingly the marina was well maintained - mostly used by locals and run by an ex-navy guy named Ken - whose favorite saying was, "Roger that!". He is quite the character who reminds us of a loving drill sergeant. He warned us not to swim in the marina water since it was inhabited by a 14 foot alligator named Sebastian. He compared Sebastian floating by to watching the state of Rhode Island drift through the marina. He assured us that Sebastian would take off a leg or two should you try to play Captain Hook.

We rode bikes into town and checked out the local real estate. It is very expensive, even for tract homes which although large, with pools and many of the superficial luxuries, are poorly made and in the $800,000 to 1.2 million dollar range. We sat under the palapa-roofed restaurant and ate conch fritters, fresh shrimp and drank the local Key West Ale in preparation for our launch into the alluring, Jimmy Buffet world of the Florida Keys.

As the sun crested the eastern horizon, we reviewed our tide charts to determine high water and then slid out of the channel on our way to Elliott Key. It is strange to drop your hook in such clear water and watch your anchor hit the bottom twenty feet below and then gaze upon your chain as it unwinds itself along the bottom like a galvanized linked snake slithering along the sea bottom. The anchorage was gorgeous and about a mile from the shoreline of mangroves on the barrier island separating us from the Atlantic. A dinghy ride to shore and the white sandy beach was a treat as small tropical fish scurried below us and a five foot shark slid by under our keel in search of an evening meal. The wind was nonexistent. Bill and Gail had rafted to us for the evening. They launched their kayak for the first real paddling adventure of the trip and glided out into the bay like two Seminole Indians in search of a lobster dinner.

The night was very peaceful with little more than a whisper of wind. The next day was to be the same so we determined we should exit the protection of the inside waters and venture out onto the Atlantic in search of bluer water, coral reefs and a tropical adventure on the high seas. We found a little passage called Ceasar Creek which lead us into the ocean. We wanted to traverse it on a rising tide since its entrance was only a foot more than our draft. Having entered the channel we battled a tidal current in deeper water for a few miles until a vista of the Atlantic opened up, revealing all its beauty on a day when a pair of shorts was all that needed to be worn. We were on our way to an area known for diving and snorkeling with many reefs lining the coastline at a distance of three to six miles from the eastern shore. The Atlantic was like a pond with even more aquarium like water reflecting the color of the powder blue sky. The bottom was undistorted and visible at over 30 feet as we cruised for four hours south - mouths agape in awe of this magnificent passage. Turtles, Manta rays, fish and dolphins played in our wake and swam below our boat. The sun glistened on the water and the only breeze was the warmth of the air caressing our faces as the boats made their way south. At times we set the auto pilot and went forward to the bow to catch glimpses of the wonders below. It was truly magical.

As late afternoon approached we entered a channel on Key Largo's eastern shore and meandered our way through a mangrove chocked river which entered an everglade like sanctuary known as John Pennekamp State Park. People come from all over the world to this place to enjoy what I have just described to you. We picked up a couple of mooring buoys in a little lake nearby and planned our next day, which would include going offshore to a reef and actually getting into God's great aquarium. Key Largo is a long island at the north end of the Keys. We were about halfway south on this key and having a wonderful time.

The next day we took Essi-Anna out the river and headed to a reef called the Cannon Balls several miles offshore. It is a smaller reef that doesn't get a lot of traffic from tourists. When we arrived there we found a mooring buoy so we tied off to it some 200 feet from the reef. Some of the reefs have these buoys so that people don't have to disturb the ocean floor with their anchors. It was an unbelievable day and the ocean cooperated with minimal wind and crystal clear visibility. Bill and I led off and swam to the reef which was packed with all kinds and colors and sizes of tropical fish, sponges, sea cucumbers and corals. I had a large barracuda swim by me and turn to check me out! It was like being in an underwater garden maze where leaving a trail of bread crumbs was impossible and useless for finding your way out. We looked like Lloyd Bridges on "Seahunt". A quick glance above the surface oriented us to the boat's location and the trail leading back to our wives who were waiting their turn.

Bill and I returned to the boat and I took Chris and Gail, in the dinghy to the edge of the reef and dropped them off. They each swam a short distance into the reef wearing wet suits and snorkel gear. They were great sports and made a valiant effort, enjoyed what they saw but soon signaled they wanted to be picked up. I positioned the dinghy near the edge of the reef again and they approached the sides and held on, tired and a little nervous. I asked them if they wanted to get into the inflatable - which they did - but hoisting these tired explorers over the gunwales of the dinghy would be a different story. They flutter kicked and I grabbed their wetsuits and hauled them over the side. They were half in with their legs dragging in the water like a couple of human outriggers. They looked like a couple of seals trying to get up on a rock in the surf. We all laughed so hard as I drug them back to the boat where they could climb the ladder onto the deck. Bill and I were very proud of their efforts and they added hilarity to the day and mental photographs that will last a lifetime. Fresh water showers on the swim step several miles out in the ocean after such beautiful scenery, we made our way back to our anchorage as the sun set in the warm, crimson sky to the west. The gentle breeze of the boat moving through the water dried us quickly – soothing our bodies and minds like a Swedish massage after a great meal.

The following day we made our way out the channel and headed for Pumpkin Key which would require us to travel on the Atlantic again and make passage through Angelfish Channel back inside the barrier islands. We anchored off the private Key; complete with its own dock, beautiful home, golf cart cars and gorgeous sandy beach surrounded by swaying palms; paradise at its best.

Our time in the Keys would come to an end the next day as we traveled back toward Miami to spend a night in Hurricane Harbor. It is another one of these special places where beautiful homes line the shoreline and huge boats line the docks in front of them. Manatees played in the bay and a 100 plus footer made its way through the narrow entrance to its home in the harbor. It looked like a battleship in a bathtub and almost toy-like as the captain worked his precision trade, maneuvering the yacht into place with a shoehorn.

We would have to retrace our steps heading north through some of the same country we had passed heading south but vowed to stop at different places to experience the beautiful parts of Florida we had bypassed. We spent two nights in Fort Lauderdale and enjoyed a seven mile walk that wound along the beach, into wonderful shopping areas and beside the many canals that make up the city. From our boat we gazed upon hundreds of millions of dollars in yachts and homes. Hard to believe there is that much money in one place. Captains and their crews, landscapers and maintenance people scurried around keeping these vessels and homes in ship shape.

Florida is a diverse place with as many ethnic groups, animals and plant life as any place in the world. It is amazing to drive along a road and see signs marking alligator, panther, tortoise and key deer crossings. The bird life is a potpourri of: eagles, cranes, egrets, geese, pelican, parrots, eagles, cormorants, gulls and every kind of song bird.

Chameleons and small lizards like the ones we use to buy at the state fair scamper about your feet on any walk and although we haven't seen any there are tons of snakes. Florida has lots of alligators and even freshwater crocodiles. We even spotted several large iguanas basking in the sunshine on the wooden structures near one of the many bridges along the inter-coastal. We surmised they must have escaped from a pet owner and populated this little area since it was our only sighting.

There is every kind of insect; one of them being our resident boat spider who has traveled with us for a couple of months and had made his home in a little hole behind a piece of molding near the back door. He comes out at night and spins his web; catching insects and being the messy eater that he is, he deposits a little waste on the fiberglass wall outside his lair each evening. He was a little guy - about the size of my little fingernail. I have loathed spiders in the past to the point of it being a phobia but this little guy captured my heart. This last week I haven't been greeted by him or her in the morning. Perhaps - like Charlotte - my little friend has left this earth or perhaps he or she joined us unaware, on our snorkeling adventure and now, like Jonah, is in the belly of a big fish.

We are back in Stuart now, where we started this east coast Florida adventuring. We will be heading north soon. Life is good and we are blessed. The next part of the journey will be without our wives as they have gone home to take care of some urgent family matters and see the grandchildren. Bill and I will paddle north once his boat is back in the water (bottom paint) and our wives will meet back up with us in a week or so. Until then we will eat out of cans and drink out of the big bottles in the fridge to save on water and doing dishes. Pray for our safe travel and their safe return.

I will send a batch of pictures which will include some of the yachts and homes - kind of like a mini home and boat show of the rich and probably famous but we don't have the names to go along with them so you will just have to use your imaginations.

Let us know what is going on in your life. Trust all is well with you and your families. We miss you and our church family.

Blessings to all from the loop
Chuck and Chris

Loopet 10

Stuart Florida to Fernandina Beach Florida (Solo)

DEAR Family and Friends,
Greetings from Daytona Beach – Home of the Daytona 500 and from Fernandina Beach.

Having returned to our starting point before heading south to the Keys we have had an unbelievable journey along the inter-coastal of Florida. Heading north back to Stuart we have explored cities we missed on our way south. We have held up in different little anchorages with the exception of a few favorites. We spent a couple of our days in Fort Lauderdale nestled amongst the mega yachts of this extremely affluent coastal city. Hundreds of millions of dollars of boats line the docks; double and triple and quadruple-deckers complete with landing craft and aircraft which can transport their owners to and from their mansions on the water.

It has been the decision of our wives to go home for a couple of weeks while Bill and I take the boats to Daytona Beach where we will rent another car and make the mad dash back to Fort Lauderdale to meet them at the airport. Our wives have done remarkably well in staving off their grandmotherly instincts and not abandoning ship earlier. Christmas whet their appetites to be with family as it did ours. But someone has to stay with the boats; and since they are often times referred to as our mistresses, we have been chosen to remain on the water and work our way north without the girls, in order to stay on schedule.

When the girls left us we were anchored up in a little bay called Manatee Pocket just east of Stuart. JUWIKA needed to have her bottom painted, which will take a couple of days, and was scheduled to be pulled out of the water this afternoon. Bill and Gail are sleeping aboard Essi-Anna tonight. The rental car is tucked into a little neighborhood close by. Bill and I will take the girls ashore early in the morning, leaving the dinghy tied to a nearby dock waiting for our return, and deliver them to the airport at Fort Lauderdale for an early morning departure.

The process to get to and from airports when we are anchored out has become a routine one with lots of coordination from the rental car company – always "Enterprise". We should be the poster children for their ads. They truly are amazing and accommodating. Service is written on the smiles of every young and educated person we have dealt with. We couldn't have done it without them.

It is strange to make a dash at 60 or 70 miles an hour by vehicle through the same number of miles that has taken us a month to do on the boat at eight knots. No waiting for bridges or no wake zones on the heavily traveled interstate. If given our choice the slow and methodical pace of the boats is our preference to contending with road construction and traffic jams.

Cities like Boca Raton, Fort Lauderdale and Palm Beach whiz by as we crisscross the waterway we absorbed into our souls just a few days before.

We gave a kiss goodbye and a wave as we pulled away from the terminal in the dark, ready to return to Stuart; but then it struck us. We were no longer constrained by our slow rate of progress on the water. It was still early and Bill had never been to Key West. A nod from Bill confirmed that a few hundred miles south was the end of the road south and another adventure waiting. We made a quick u-turn and headed for the Keys.

Ariel, a boat we had traveled with on the Gulf and Tenn-Tom, was there at anchor and there was wind that a boat show was taking place that day. We called Dan and Kathy and they said that we could hang out with them and stay overnight on their boat if we wanted to. Our goal was to return late that evening to Essi-Anna since the weather report was for heavy winds around midnight. Even though our anchor was securely set and we had no worries of moving it is prudent to ride out bad weather aboard.

As the sun came up we passed our mark at Key Largo and continued south along the narrow strip of land and bridges that connect the string of pearl-like islands that make up the Keys and separate the Gulf from the Atlantic. The water here is some of the most beautiful in the world. The channels winding their way through the Gulf are marked and unforgiving should you stray from them without local knowledge.

Just before noon we pulled into Key West. It has its own culture and atmosphere – an attitude of its own with a mixture of old buildings and residences crowding each other to gain a foothold in this desirable Mecca of the sun where people come to lose themselves in the world of historic taverns; like the "Green Parrot Saloon" and a "ville" that reminded me of a Mexican drink. Here key lime pie, rooftop bands and open air markets share space with the tourist trinket shops lining the wharf and streets. A rooster crows in someone's backyard, another scrambles under your table at a local restaurant and tales are spun over beers about the way things are and use to be when Ernest Hemingway called "Key West" home.

Bill and I connected with Dan and Kathy until sunset, invested in a jar of lime jelly and watched as the sun started to dip low in the sky before we said our goodbyes to the deep warmth of the southern sun. To the sound of "Wasting Away in Margaritaville" we turned the rental car key, our heads and the pint size economy car north for a five hour dash back to Stuart. The wind was already starting to come up and the traffic up the coast would increase as we approached Miami. The old deserted and dilapidated bridges next to the new ones that connect islands to each other now were wall to wall along the rails with fishermen looking for their dinner or just burning time. Make shift shelters had been erected by some for overnight stays. In one place the low, narrow road is the only barrier that keeps the Gulf and Atlantic waters from mingling.

Night came speedily as we worked our way back to Essi-Anna and JUWIKA. Two traffic jams and one accident later, with a delay of more than an hour brought us tired and satisfied to our resting place. In the dark we made our way back to the boat to find everything as we had left it.

Tomorrow I will change the oil and fuel and oil filters in preparation for a departure the next day. Over five hundred miles in one day – the distance that we would cover in the next two weeks, spinning in our heads we laid them down and didn't stir until the warm Florida sun streamed through the windows.

With breakfast aboard and a day of work getting JUWIKA back in the water; Cuban sandwiches for lunch and dinner aboard our own vessels, another day was coming to a close. We talked strategy and safety as we made plans to solo until Chris and Gail rejoined us. Our goal was to continue anchoring out as much as possible and rafting when we had settled weather. This stretch of the trip would be totally inside with a variety of stops, some of which would require pulling off the inter-coastal water highway and parking on the shoulder in the lee of bridges and causeways.

Essi-Anna is equipped with a power windlass with 100% chain that can be easily deployed from the bridge or the bow. JUWIKA does not have a power windlass so we decided that Essi-Anna would drop anchor and JUWIKA would raft up to her when possible. We would travel with fenders out as to not have to re-rig every evening. JUWIKA would also travel with lines attached to be deployed when rafting.

In the morning we would release lines and Juwika would pull away first. Then I would bump Essi-Anna forward as I retrieved the anchor from the bridge or bow depending on the currents and wind. Wash down of the chain and anchor would be impossible in windy conditions since I would have to power forward and retrieve the anchor using the bridge controls.

On a few occasions we would pick up mooring buoys and raft in the same order or anchor independently. Docking would also have its special routine with prep work done before approaching the dock.

Since this stretch of water is fairly narrow and busy with boat traffic we would prepare lunch before pulling anchor and take a small bucket to the bridge as well, should we have to relieve ourselves en-route. Stopping along the way and just drifting with no one at the wheel while making a quick dash downstairs would be both dangerous and difficult.

Day one without our mates we motored out of Manatee Pocket and said goodbye to Stuart. We made the left hand turn to port heading north. The day was calm and the sun glistened on the water just inside the channel leading to the Atlantic.

Chris arrived home and had been to visit her mom and dad who live in the small condo we bought for them five years prior. It is located within a couple of miles from our home. They are grateful to be there and always say it is the best move they ever made. When you are in your 80's life takes on a whole different meaning and perspective. The question of when is your next doctor's appointment takes precedence over discussion about the weather and politics, and a coupon to Applebee's for "two for one early bird specials" is something to be cherished.

Chris's mom had been poorly and had suffered a couple of setbacks with her heart. Due to her diabetes she also has kidney problems and when these two are combined with each other it is a battle to see which is most necessary to treat. Low blood pressure doesn't feed the kidneys adequately, weakening them and the medications and methods for helping out the heart can damage the kidneys. It is a lose/lose situation. She had not been doing as well as we had hoped according to our daughter's regular reports so Chris would not only spend time with the grandsons but also assess the needs of her mom and dad. Her trip home will be more of a mission of mercy and ministry than it will be one of relaxation and renewal.

On March 7th our goal was to reach Vero Beach and spend a couple of days on a mooring ball while Bill waited for another fuel pump. The one he had installed in Stuart had been giving him some problems. The mechanic was honorable and made the trip to Vero to take care of business. This mooring field is tucked behind a little island in the inter-coastal and the entrance is straightforward after passing under a bridge which connects the barrier islands to the Atlantic side. The field is usually crowded and the marina requires rafting on their mooring balls while charging each boat as if it were by its lonesome. Bill and I explored the area on foot and by dinghy, taking in a Little League game at a close by ball field visible from the boats. We also shuttled our bikes ashore and rode to the beach which is only a mile or so away.

Picking up a mooring buoy while soloing is an interesting process and takes some preplanning, fancy foot work and knowing your boat as well as calculating the wind direction carefully. I was assigned the task and Bill tied along Essi-Anna after an uneventful landing. Even though we usually give each other a hard time – radioing each other with a jab that, "Friends don't let friends cruise with their fenders on;" Bill and I decided that so long as we were in protected water and not getting sloshed around too much we would travel with our fenders out to save time and give us quicker response time in case someone needed to anchor and or tie alongside in a normal rafting situation or in case of an emergency. It worked well. Later in the trip we would find that while transiting the Erie and Trent Canals we traveled with our locking fenders fully displayed on both sides of the boat routinely to save time and always be prepared for the rapidly advancing locks.

On March 10 we slipped away from Vero Beach under sunny skies and calm winds heading north to another anchorage at Melbourne Bridge. This little wide spot in the road is close to another one of the many bridges that connect the mainland to the islands like tendons joining important joints to each other. We each dropped our anchors in and around some crab pots which dot this area but well out of the swing range that the boats would dance during the night. The weather was to become unsettled so we felt that being on our own anchors would be safer. With an electric windlass, which can be deployed from the deck or the bridge it was easy to find a spot, drop and then back down on the anchor from the bridge, to set it securely while watching a fixed point on land to make sure you are hooked well. With the proper scope, the right anchor and a good bottom there has never been a problem in over a thousand nights at anchor.

I dropped our inflatable, which is deployed from the transom with an electric winch, and went to Bill's for dinner. The first two days had been perfect, long and lonely yet a new experience and challenge for both of us. As we sat on the deck of JUWIKA we could see the lit launch pad at Cape Canaveral in the distance. We gave thanks for another free and restful spot for the night.

Retrieving the anchors in the morning under calm winds I inadvertently drifted over a crab pot marker. Fortunately Bill saw it happen and radioed me before I engaged the transmissions. I quickly dropped the anchor again in a lunch hook fashion and fished for the small strand of nylon line with the extended boat hook from the swim platform of the boat while Bill held his position. I soon had the line in hand, pulled the pot, which looked like it had been abandoned and quickly pulled forward out of the danger zone. One bullet dodged, we were quickly on our way.

The weather report, which we religiously listen to each evening and morning, was calling for strong winds coming from the north. Our destination was to anchor in the lee of a bridge and causeway which would give us some protection just south of Titusville, Florida. We dropped anchors independently just off the channel as the wind started to howl. The little bite is shallow and just off a small public beach where people come to hangout. In order to get any protection we had to be just far enough off the channel to get out of the wind tunnel under the bridge and not too far to starboard to be out of the protection of the high spot in the road and the beach buildings on the east side of the bridge. Our anchors bit well – we sat on our boats talking over the radio while we checked our positions to each other and to the stationary points we had chosen on the land.

After half an hour we decided we were hooked well and decided to dinghy ashore at a marina some half mile up the channel where we would go ashore for dinner. I picked up Bill. As we rounded the abutment of the bridge and back into the channel the wind sent spray over the front of our little water taxi. We were thankful for safe sanctuary where we would rest peacefully for the evening.

Titusville is a less than exciting place, with minimal restaurants – thus we chose Kentucky Fried Chicken. We picked up a few groceries at the local market which made us pay for bags to carry them in and a local resident, I trust jokingly, told me that I couldn't buy deep fried pork skins because I was Jewish? Go figure!

We splashed our way back to the boats, having seen a couple of alligators in the local kid's park pond and were glad when we rounded the corner of the bridge to find the boats resting in the calm we had chosen for them. Tomorrow we will call the bridge for an opening time before pulling anchor since we are within shouting range of the tender. Goodnight Titusville!

New Smyrna Beach at anchor was our next great rest stop. The wind was calm and the weather was supposed to hold so we rafted up. We enjoyed the evening on the boats and decided to explore in the morning. The town is extremely quaint with a wonderful waterfront monument honoring its original forefathers. The main street is dotted with friendly shops and a drugstore which sports a soda fountain style café where the locals come to fill up on daily specials served by gals with aprons who have fun joisting with visitors and town gossipers alike.

There had been a major motorcycle rally, just a few days prior; Florida's version of Sturgis in Daytona Beach, which would be our next stop. We had seen many of the riders the night before in Titusville. There remained a remnant of them still in New Smyrna.

By this time we had gotten into the rhythm of traveling solo. It is lonely but a great time to reflect on how much you really love that other person who usually occupies the seat next to you. To share this experience with someone who loves it and you as much as you do it and them and is as adept at living the life of a looper is something that will fill our conversations and add a sparkle to our hearts and eyes; even when our bodies are no longer able to make such a voyage or even to walk down the hall of a retirement home without a stumble.

How could you ask for anything greater than to have a partner for your entire adult life who contrasts and compliments you like my wife and best friend. I was looking forward to her return but a phone call from her that evening told me that she wouldn't be returning with Gail on the flight to Fort Lauderdale in another day. She needed more time and wouldn't be coming back until March 20th. I understood, yet the loneliness of solo cruising along the loop crept into my heart.

Bill and I would travel on to Daytona Beach the next day where we tied up at Halifax Harbor Marina, rented another Enterprise car and made the dash south to retrieve Gail, returning like a yoyo to Daytona Beach. The boats were in need of fuel and water as well as a good bath and a hull waxing. This was the first big city since we had left the Stuart area. Being the home of the infamous Daytona 500 we had high expectations. After solo landings for fuel and then the slips assigned to us for the two night stay, we had dinner aboard and retired for the evening after a long day.

The rental car awaited our early morning departure for a long return trip to Fort Lauderdale. Since airline tickets require roundtrips to return to the same airport you leave from, we had to pick Gail up there. Chris would have to lose her half of the return ticket and would purchase a one-way in order to return to Jacksonville, close to where the boats would be in another week.

Of all our stops we saw little of Daytona Beach and spent the entire time taking advantage of the dock and driving. We'll have to return by car there someday. With Gail aboard JUWIKA and glad to be back, our next evening would be at anchor again at mile post 809 - the Cement Plant Canal - and then onto the crown jewel of this part of the loop – St. Augustine.

This was one stop Chris sacrificed for family. It was a place she dearly wanted to see but would have to put aside. There are two anchorages on the inter-coastal near the city. One is on the south side of the bridge near the marina and the other is past the bridge and in the shadow of the historic fort.

We chose the former and with heavy winds forecasted anchored separately amongst a potpourri of transients and local scows of every size and description. This anchorage is notorious for heavy currents and dragging anchors so each of us set our hooks as usual with some extra rode in anticipation of the need for more scope should the wind continue to build. After our usual due diligence, watching our swing and set, we each dropped our inflatables, paid our $5.00 landing fees at the marina and went ashore for a walkabout in this very old, well preserved and historic town.

The old church, fort and walled streets make it a wonderful spot to take in history and explore the many shops which duplicated another era. We sat in a medieval looking pub and drank a draught of beer and then took in our fill of fragrances in a spice shop where you would be senseless if you left empty handed. We ate dinner out and then we returned to the boats.

The anchorage had some newcomers since we had left but everyone looked in order and the wind was still at about 10. Evening came and the pillow finally found my head about 11:00 p.m. With the anchor light burning I retired to our aft cabin and quickly fell asleep.

About 3:00 a.m. as usual, I awoke and decided after a trip to the head to take a walk around the decks of boat. I could tell the wind had come up. My location and set hadn't changed. Essi-Anna was still pulling on the anchor in the same direction and a glance at the chain from the bow pulpit assured me I wasn't straining my set. All appeared well so I returned to bed.

No more than 30 minutes later I was awakened by a horrific bang on the starboard side of the boat. I leapt from bed and scrambled out the back cabin door into the cockpit. There, lying alongside me, at mid ships was a small, ill-kept sailboat in the 25 to 30 foot range manned by a middle-aged unshaven gentleman who was yelling something at the top of his lungs about me dragging and running into him. In the light of the city I could make out other boats around us and knew that with the wind and the current pushing us we would soon have a whole clutter of boats entangled unless I did something quickly.

Knowing that one or both of us were no longer securely anchored I ran back inside, started the engines and raced up the stairs to the bridge – spotlight in hand. I motored forward stopping the progress of our drift and at the same time started to bring up my anchor – all the while shining my spotlight on JUWIKA's aft cabin window and yelling Bill's name above the howl of the wind. After all he did owe me one since I had been awakened late one evening to wade in the Florida swamps in search of his lost dinghy.

The wind was blowing heavily and over the side I yelled to the sailboat's captain to fend off while I motored forward and tried to untangle our anchors. About the time my light and voice were ready to give out I spotted Bill's weary body climbing into his dinghy and heading my way. He tied off on the back of Essi-Anna and came to the rescue.

The anchors were up and intertwined - my Claw anchor being badly bent. Bill bent over the bow pulpit and worked out the tangled mess of chain and metal anchors. We released the sailboat from our side and yelled that we would see him in the morning. His anchor dropped back down and seemed to be holding his drift. I was concerned there was a hole in Essi-Anna's side and that with any kind of lapping of waves we could take on water and flounder in this awkward place. With Bill aboard; cold and both of us shaken, we steered our way through some foul ground with only the streetlights of St. Augustine reflecting light on the water, toward the fuel dock which was empty at the time.

The night dock attendant met us and helped us tie off. We told him of the ordeal and he replied that this happens all the time here. We quickly inspected the starboard side and to our amazement could find no damage at all – not even a scratch. It was late and we were tired and shaking from the cold night and adrenaline. In the dim light there was no more we could do except wait for morning.

Tied to the dock securely with the permission of the dock-master to stay until daybreak when I could make arrangements for the next night across the inter-coastal, I fell asleep, with prayers of thanks that everyone was safe and that no major damage had been done. My dreams were streamed through the thousand times plus we had been at anchor without a mishap and questioned who did what and whose anchor had let go.

In the morning I inquired about space at the dock next to downtown St. Augustine and was told as I had been the night before that they were full.

I called across the canal. They had space and said that I could come any time. It was still early and Bill and Gail had not come ashore yet. Bill had taken a good chilling during the ordeal; not having on a sweatshirt or coat.

I left my name and cell number at the marina office in case the sailboat skipper wanted to get a hold of me before I paid him a visit and then moved to the opposite marina. Anchoring was not an option as our trusty claw's shank was bent at a 30 degree angle. Before pulling lines I checked Essi-Anna's starboard side again and to my utter surprise there wasn't more than a rub mark just below the rub rail. Not even a spider web crack or dent or scratch. Praise God!

After landing at the other marina and getting settled in I dropped the dinghy for a trip to the sailboat when my cell phone rang. It was the local police who wanted to know about the incident. Apparently the skipper had called them and said I had run into him and that I had done major damage to his boat. I told them I was on my way to pay him a visit and where my boat was located. I also told him that I really wasn't sure who had run into who but that I had anchored extensively and in much more hazardous conditions. I told him also that I would check out the damage that had been reported and call him back. He thanked me and told me that they did not respond to such calls on the water and had no means to but wanted the right thing to take place. I agreed.

A short hop across the channel and a knock on the side of a very rustic and dilapidated sailboat aroused the skipper who poked his head out of the make shift door of the cabin. This was obviously a live aboard situation and he wasn't even the owner but lived in these primitive, tight and poorly maintained quarters with his girlfriend who was very sick inside and needed an operation for a major illness. A couple of cats also poked their scrutinizing noses out of a port hole window or maybe it was for a breath of fresh air.

He came topside with a limp, one leg obviously badly damaged from a previous knee injury. It was very swollen and appeared to be extremely painful. It appeared that they had little means for cleaning up aboard. Immediately he started his accusations, which included telling me about his conversation with the police. I assured him I had also talked with them and would be calling the officer back when I was done assessing the damage he had reported.

When he showed me a couple of lifeline rails and stanchions which were bent and pulled loose from the deck I commented that for such recent damage they were extremely rusty and that the screws and holes had obviously been missing or loose for much longer than a night. I was glad to see that his rub rail was wood which had saved me some nasty fiberglass repairs.

After my comments I told him I really couldn't say for sure who hit who but that there appeared to be no damage to my boat except for the anchor which would cost me a couple hundred dollars. I also told him that I was sorry no matter what had actually happened and that I could see he and his girlfriend needed money – basically being homeless on the water except for the boat they called their shelter.

We talked more and he told me he was from Tacoma, Washington, had run into hard times and needed help. I told him we were from Washington too, and soon things lightened up.

At the end of our conversation, which terminated in a handshake, I tucked $100.00 into his palm; he smiled and wished me the best as I did him.

We parted friends and I felt good our paths had crossed since they were obviously in need of help.

As promised, I called the officer and explained what the condition of his boat was and what had transpired. I also told him I was on a schedule heading north and would be pulling out of town the next morning unless he needed me to stay. He assured me his part was done and thanked me for the way I had handled the situation.

Bill showed up a few minutes after I landed back at the boat and I relived the last hour with him as he assured me that my anchoring skills were rock solid and there was no question in his mind as to how the chain of events the night before had unfolded.

My next task at hand was to research the possibilities for another claw anchor. My inquiries produced a West Marine some five miles away which I assured myself I could make on foot if they had one in stock. After a quick cell call I was in business with a 30 pounder which was what JUWIKA sported on her bow and which would be minimal for Essi-Anna. To carry one back to the boat would be a different story but I had them hold it for me. I figured that if I became uncomfortable with this size anchor I could always switch it out with a large fortress I carried as my back-up spare.

Two hours later I returned to the boat by cab with the claw and readily attached it to the chain rode which I had unraveled onto the dock. With that job done and the anchor looking a wee bit puny to handle the job I jumped in the dinghy and headed for my rendezvous point with Bill and Gail for a little sight-seeing at the fort.

I would spend the night on the dock, radio Bill and Gail in the morning and continue our journey north to pick up Chris a few days later in Fernandina Beach – our last stop in Florida.

St. Augustine had dished out more than I had bargained for but all in all everything worked out well and new lessons had been learned. Our next stop would be at mile marker 744 Pablo Creek, alongside the intercoastal. The current here runs fairly swift but we would probably be the only ones there and the wind was supposed to be calm. The day shone bright and the water was calm as we worked our way in that direction in hopes of a peaceful night in a much less populated area.

It will be nice to have Chris back aboard soon. I was beginning to miss her and greatly appreciate all she does to make my life complete and this journey one that should only be done if it can be shared now and in reflection. The new anchor works well and after a peaceful night's rest we are on our way again, heading north and soon to leave this exciting state of Florida.

The northern part of Florida along the inter-coastal is much less populated which suits me just fine. We were heading north toward a place called St. George Creek where there was supposed to be a temporary dock from which we could explore a plantation museum along the waterway. The approach is shallow and the river called St. George's Creek is narrow. The dock ended up being a place to land our inflatables so we anchored as close as we could to the center of the river in hopes that the slight current and wind would keep us from swinging into the shoreline, which was a muddy banked, grassy swamp like area.

After our usual wait and location checks we went ashore to the plantation which is still well preserved and a haunting reminder of extreme civil rights abuses and human atrocities. The master's home was open for inspection and the grounds were filled with large oaks and cleared areas that had been worked by the many slaves in the early 1800s. One section of the property was neatly lined with perimeter foundations and some better preserved adobe cabin style shelters made from a mixture of ground up clam shells which created a rustic kind of cement. These had been constructed by the slaves for their living quarters – some 25 units. The ones that were more complete had an indoor fireplace that was used for cooking.

As we stared at these remnants of a shameful part of our history, we could almost hear the singing of spirituals as these people, who in spite of their lot in life, showed joy and care for each other as they met in the evening around a crackling wood fire after a hard day's work on the plantation.

The grounds are also inhabited by burrowing tortoises, which sit at their earthen den entrances to catch the rays of the sun that casts its heat upon the grassy knolls they have dug with their powerfully clawed front legs.

We returned to the boats bewildered at the whole slavery issue and how one person could own another to include their life, freedom, family and future.

After checking that we were holding well and the tide hadn't changed direction or height to put the boats at risk on the bank, we decided to scoot down the narrow cut toward the ocean, which was connected by a very shallow and meandering lead toward the east. The tide floods and ebbs through this narrow channel, which could only be navigated in the small boats and that with the possibility of running aground due to the sandy spits, which extend their reach well into the passage.

Fifteen minutes later we ran the dinghy up onto the sandy beach, exposed to about half ebb tide and attached the line of the small navy anchor I carry in a 50 quart cooler, used as a seat, to the painter on the front of raft. Being buried deep in the sand up the beach, I pushed the little boat back out into deeper water so that it wouldn't be high and dry when we returned.

There was no path to the beach but we knew it was someplace over the dunes which were peppered with a low growing ground cover cactus with sharp and spiny darts which penetrated my rubber boat shoe soles just enough to add excitement to the trek. Before long we could see the Atlantic – a beach worth suffering a few pricks for and strewn with the shells we had come for.

Returning to the raft by a different route, which had fewer cacti, we picked out the thorns from our shoes, pushed the dinghy off the beach into deeper water and meandered our way back to the boats.

The boats had changed direction in the ebbing tide and in the process JUWIKA had swung her stern into the muddy bank. Essi-Anna was not in the mud yet but closer than comfort would allow. We decided this would not be a good place to spend the night, as the river was just too narrow for peaceful sleeping. Bill pulled in a little rode as I gave JUWIKA a budge with the dinghy and she swung free.

Pulling in rode on Essi-Anna put her closer to mid channel and with a day's exploration done we weighed anchors and headed north through a savannah type grassland surroundings on this desolate part of Florida's northern inter-coastal. Our destination for the evening would be Alligator Creek just a short distance south of Fernandina Beach, our destination for the next day, so we would be staged up to meet Chris in Jacksonville.

Alligator Creek is a beautiful pond like setting surrounded by golden, waving grasslands and flat enough so that looking to the west we could capture and enjoy the setting of the glorious sun we had so enjoyed in our almost four months since entering Florida on the Gulf. What beauty and diversity we had seen and experienced in this awesome state.

The loop has thrown us into every emotion since we first cast our eyes on the crystal blue waters of Florida. We have traveled her entire length and have crossed her middle. We have driven her roads and lived her history. We have been soothed by her warm ocean breezes and have gazed beneath her waters into reefs blooming with coral. Our anchors have been dropped in the cul-de-sacs of the rich and famous where mega yachts and palatial homes are commonplace. We have traveled her rivers into small fishing towns and been at the mercy of her storms.

Shells lay on pristine beaches; butterflies and dolphins played in our shadows, and manatees breathed in our faces as we silently waited their rising from the bottom of their sanctuaries on Crystal River. What more could we have asked for and what would be its equal on this journey through the Loop?

Chris would return tomorrow and my life would be complete again. She would return gratefully and yet reluctantly knowing her mom was more fragile than when we had left on the trip in August. Life is full of twists and turns much like the loop. Sometimes the water is shallow and sometimes it is deep. Both have their challenges and their dangers. They both must be navigated with care.

Sometimes life is lonely and sometimes it is full of people excited to make their mark in the world and the lives of others.

There are times when you sit silent over a fresh cup of coffee, eyes closed while the warmth of the morning sun crests the horizon and evaporates the dew on the well traveled boats and then there are times when the challenge that only the wind and waves can muster reveals another side of life, which when the battle is over renews your adventurous spirit, allowing you to give sincere thanks only after you are tied securely to a dock in a safe haven harbor.

This time without Chris had been like that for me and for her and so our reunion would be an end to this chapter on the loop at home and in Florida and the beginning of another page of our journey in life and on the loop.

Morning came like another storybook beginning and Alligator Creek became a memory. We arrived at Fernandina Beach before noon. The anchorage here is broad and well out of the channel so with anchors well set and another city to explore and a rental car to pick up we headed for town.

The marina where we landed was virtually vacant and sits in the lee of an artificial breakwater adjacent to a paper mill. The docks had been invaded by sea birds and the smell is pungent enough to drown out the odor of the mill – droppings everywhere. The town is just across the railroad tracks and the main street is well preserved and typical of a beach resort destination. Thank goodness for a free, secure and fresh smelling anchorage.

We have a trip to Jacksonville to make. Trusty Enterprise will deliver our chariot soon and I will be in search of a larger anchor, which will give me the security we need as we travel up the Atlantic coast.

Chris is coming home!

Blessings from Fernandina Beach,
I'm excited to see my first and only mate!

LOOPET 11

GEORGIA AND THE CAROLINAS

DEAR Friends and Family!
Happy Easter to all - it is supposed to be spring even though it feels more like winter here in Georgetown, South Carolina. Today we walked the streets of this quaint, southern city after a fine lunch of shrimp and grits, topped off with fresh New Orleans beignets and coffee. We saw a little girl tuck under her grandma's long, wool trench coat to get out of the frigid wind; only her little nose and eyes were exposed as they walked down the main street looking like some, weird two-headed lady out of some strange circus sideshow.

We are safely tied to a dock at Hazzard's Marina with the wind gusting thirty plus and the waves entering through the opening into our little working marina are slamming like kettle drums against our hull. Tonight the wind is suppose to be stronger still and the temperature is projected to dip into the 20's - record cold for the Carolinas around Easter. In spite of this chill we managed to have ice-cream cones for desert yesterday, after a lunch of fried shrimp; from which we gleaned the tails to feed the alligator waiting for his easy pickins under the deck where we ate.

On the twentieth of March we picked Chris up in Jacksonville, Florida. She had to change her return point to Jacksonville in order to accommodate our progress further north. She had spent an extra week making sure her mom was OK and would be there when we ended our trip in August. There were no guarantees, but both her parents knew we would be home in an instant should they need us.

Our boats are anchored off a little town called Fernandina Beach - the last port of call and northern most city in the state of Florida where we have enjoyed eternal summer for the last four months! Before returning the car to Enterprise we explored the beach in hopes of one last shell souvenir. A beach by the name of "American Beach" was the last beach we would walk on in Florida. It was at one time the only section of sand along the Atlantic in this area that Black people were allowed to use. There are several historic markers that show what the area used to be like. Most of the old buildings are in dire need of repair, with hopes of restoration and revitalization. It is a testament to a pain which plagued our country; one of ignorance and hate and prejudice which still live today in the hearts and minds and actions of some.

A short way north from Fernandina and a hard port turn and then five miles up the St. Mary's River we entered into Georgia with some sadness in our hearts, many months in Florida behind us, but ready for another state and a new adventure! We had called ahead to the only dock in this little border town of St. Mary's and made arrangements to spend the night in this out of the way berg. Nat, the dock master is an older black gentleman and was gone when we landed. So the tour boat coming and going from Cumberland Island responded to our hail on the radio and told us to take any open space on the dock. Nat eventually showed up and confirmed our arrival, helping us with electrical hook ups and information about the town. Just off the dock in the middle of the river was a huge marker which delineated the border between Florida and Georgia. We attached the new plow anchor, which was all we could find and which had come highly recommended by the manager of the West Marine in Jacksonville where we had purchased it. We repainted our depth markers on the 200 feet of chain we laid out on the dock. Then we went for a walk around this little town heavily endowed with huge live oaks heavily laden with gypsy moss. There are some very pristine vintage homes and an old church which had been refurbished to its original graceful stateliness. It is a beautiful place and the weather was perfect.

Chris and I checked out some of the local shops of which there were a few and happened along a cigar store with the "Cigar Store Indian" beckoning us to come in. Cigars and pipe tobacco always smell so good, creating a temptation to novices to see if they taste like the magical aroma they produce when smoked. More practically, these rolls of tobacco, when smoldering in the mouth or in the hand act as a great insect repellent. The mental picture of us smoking them while carelessly strolling the southern streets under a full moon, with a warm spring breeze blowing in our faces off the ocean was just too hard to resist. We bought four stogies for that evening after dinner- two petite flavored ones for the girls and two "Robustos" for Bill and me.

    The last time I smoked a cigar was in college and the time before that was when my brother Matt and I found a virgin "White Owl" laying on the side of the road while doing our paper routes one Saturday morning in the British Properties of Vancouver, B.C. Helping each other on Saturdays was our usual routine. We cut it in half and after the ceremonial licking, smoked it down by the creek. Our folks were gone to the U.S. to look for a home, as they were planning on moving back to the states after living in Canada for the last ten years. Needless to say, Matt and I didn't find much pleasure in the long hours that followed.

    Having not learned my lesson from prior experiences, I showed off my prowess by blowing smoke out my nose and making "OOOOOs" so Chris could see how macho I was, as the four of us sauntered the tranquil, evening streets of St. Mary's. To say the least, without going into all the details of how the sweats began and the excess saliva began to milk up in my mouth and the strange feeling at the joint of my jaw just in front of my ears commenced. I wobbled a line back to the boat in the hand of my good wife. The response of my little, shaking body took me back to the paper route morning long ago and the infamous "White Owl". The last 100 yards to the dock and to the boat were ones wrought with difficulty; trying to hide the ensuing agony and eruption that would soon take place. The shades of green, which adorned my face, were hidden by the night. A gasping, undetected goodnight to Bill and Gail and I was back in the shelter of Essi-Anna.

    Rather than interrupt Chris's sleep I spent the night on the couch hugging one of those large, disposable plastic bowls and calling out the name of my mom, while the others slept soundly with dreamy rings of aromatic smoke encircling their heads. When morning broke I was grateful to be back among the living and have vowed that I will never be enticed to smoke another cigar as long as I live.

We headed down stream and across one of the many inlets that takes you to the Atlantic. This particular inlet is a passageway for large navy ships and submarines. There are restrictions for pleasure craft and at times when navy vessels are in transit, pleasure boats must wait until the military ships have cleared the channel. The day before that we had seen them and heard them offshore doing maneuvers and transporting goods with large helicopters, cargo net slings dangling and swinging beneath them. Our passage was safe without any military encounters.

In a few miles we were anchoring in the lee of Cumberland Island, Georgia - a historic federal park which at one time was the island paradise for the Thomas Carnegie family and the Coke family. During the time of the Spanish exploration the conquistadors left some of their horses behind, which under the protection of the Carnegies have multiplied and now roam the island in small herds. As we set our hook for the night three of them grazed down the beach next to our boat. This is a tourist area but left un-commercialized with only a campground and a few historic remains of an era of great affluence by one of America's wealthy "new money" immigrant families. The island was the summer home of the Carnegies. In all its glory "Dungeness" was their huge mansion retreat with manicured gardens and pristine beaches. The Carnegies were not allowed to join the old money millionaire club on Jekyll Island not far north so they created their own on Cumberland. Today the ruins remaining from a fire in the 1950's are all that is left. They are inhabited by snakes, wild horses and armadillos. There are no paved roads on the island and the only way to the island is by foot ferry from St. Mary's or private boat. Walking several miles and tracing their steps amongst the huge trees and tropical vegetation, we could hear the voices of those who had made this estate one of the most opulent places in the world.

Winding north on the river we crossed several other inlets on our way to Jekyll Island - the home of the Millionaire Club which included names like Rockefeller and Ogelthorpe. There is a wonderful little marina along the river and in the route path of our trip north so for the sake of exploration by bike and the ease of landing we tied up for the night.

There are bike paths circling the island and the sand is so fine and well packed that for the first time in our lives we rode our bikes on the beach. Shells, jellyfish and manta rays littered the shoreline and the mast of a sunken ship poked its finger out of the sand like the "X marks the spot" on some ancient pirate map. The village, with its shops and vintage hotel are encircled by well kept summer homes where yachts delivered America's wealthy industrialist and entrepreneurs for vacations and "deal making" as they "rubbed shoulders" during drinks on the veranda or a game of golf, planning their futures in the realm of high society. Chris and I rode around the island, sat in the shade of massive oaks on wooden pastel painted Adirondacks, sipping mint juleps and reminiscing about all we had experienced, while a game of crochet was being played on the lawn out front, as it had been done for ages. The azaleas in every shade of red and white blossomed along the walks and the spire of the exquisite age-old hotel reached to the sky above the porch where modern day, not so rich guests like us lazied the sunny day away in rocking chairs fit for kings and queens.

Leaving the dock after a lot of exercise and a peaceful evening, we headed for St. Simon Island - vacation central - for Georgians. We anchored in a dead end channel near a marina. Chris and I took our bikes ashore in our inflatable and rode the island to the little town. The south end of the island is a quaint village with shops and a light house which is manned by the coast guard station at its foot. The channel to the island was rough and scattered with sandbars so we had to go far out into the entrance at the mouth of the ocean, only to make a sharp port turn to work our way back into safer and calmer waters and our anchorage. On the turn to come back in we spotted a large Loggerhead turtle some two feet across. Turtles, when approached by boats tend to dart under the boat so you have to be very cautious that these endangered animals don't get hit by your props. At the north end of the island is Christ Church, founded by John and Charles Wesley who came from England in the 1700's. The church today is very old and very active, with a membership of over a 1000. In the cemetery of the church is the tomb of Eugenia Price who is a famous author from this island. She wrote about the history of the Civil War, plantation life and the south in and around St. Simons. Fort Fredrica is just a cannon shot from the church and was the last stronghold of the British troops who ran off the Spanish in an invasion that they made to the south. Georgia was used as a buffer zone between the Spanish held territories and the British Carolinas.

These three island hops quickly put Georgia on the top of our list for interesting and beautiful places on our trip. We had had enough goofing off. We readied ourselves for a long 67 mile day to an anchorage in the middle of the swamps and back country of Georgia named Cane Patch Creek. The wind was whistling through the marsh grass across the deep water, which leads off the inter-coastal. The channel winds like a bag of twisted pretzels dumped out in random order in front of us. We saw very few signs of civilization and that night chose one of the pretzels to call home as we dropped anchor for the evening. The wind was coming from the NE so we found shelter in 15 feet of water tucked behind a little island in the swamp that had managed to support one of the few stands of trees in the area. We rafted up and gave our new anchor the first major pull test since its installation at St. Mary's. Visions of Savannah filled our dreams that evening. We would get an early start. As the magical moon rose over our quiet and desolate little anchorage we said good night to our neighbors and fell quickly to sleep. The wind died to a whisper and the sound of Georgian silence was deafening.

The Savannah River was about thirty miles away and eight miles inland from the ocean is the wonderful city of Savannah, full of southern charm and hospitality. We planned to spend two days at the dock only a boardwalk away from the heart of River Street and the historic district. Savannah boasts the third busiest seaport in the U.S. with huge freighters traversing this narrow waterway just yards from our boats. Powerful, droning tugs stand at ready 24/7 to assist any that may go astray or need a little shove here or there. The city itself is ancient by American standards; dating back to the late 1600's and early 1700's. It is the home of the Cotton Exchange Building which was an extremely important part of the commerce of the south during the time of slavery. Houses and churches are so well preserved that you would think them modern replicas and not the real thing. Horse drawn carriages vied for their place on cobblestone streets now accompanied by cars and city transportation. Huge warehouses, which at one time had been part of the cotton plantation way of life now housed touristy shops on the main level and apartment dwellings above. Wiring and plumbing looked out of place as it hung to the exteriors of buildings that had been constructed 100's of years before such things were thought of. Live oaks mixed with palms, wisteria, orange blossoms, dogwoods, camellias, irises, azaleas and hanging baskets of every shade and color line the boulevards like rainbows, amongst the gypsy moss that still adds its haunting look to the revolutionary and civil war cemeteries that dot the cityscape.

The churches here are magnificent and remind us of the cathedrals in Europe. As strange as it seems in the south, where you would think the Baptist Church would be the oldest, we were astonished to learn that none other than the Lutherans were the first to build their church in this city and were some of the first worshippers as early as 1731. Go Lutes! They had come to work the cotton fields and were considered some of the hardest workers, thus delaying the need for slaves in this area.

We also happened to be in Savannah during a huge music festival so we took in the quarter finals of the vocal soloists featuring American composers and song writers, and a wonderful hour of concert piano by a German pianist.

An evening carriage ride, a pre-dinner drink at the Alligator Spirit and dinner at The Pink House, which dates to the early 18th century, topped off our stay in Savannah. The cozy, tavern with a low ceiling below the restaurant had a rustic wooden floor and a fireplace at each end with lantern lights and cozy well worn and closely clustered chairs which allowed intimate conversation. The voices of life in another time whispered throughout this place of meeting, where our presidents and military generals had dined and drank. What a splendid time and what a historic city to explore. Having walked the parks, which are central to each block in the historic district, and a bike ride through streets that truly came out of a fairy tale, we left the city where the girl scouts had their beginning and headed down the river to a cut that would take us further north on the loop.

Hilton Head was our next stop - the place to be seen and to see how the upper crust lives. There is a section of this exclusive resort island that is off limits to common folk and no bikes are allowed, so we rode the island on the other bike paths that took us to beach resort hotels and public areas. A friend would meet us here in a couple of days and travel north to Georgetown with us. Glenn would be our first stowaway of the trip. The weather turned ugly with some high winds so we found a dock away from the Ritz and paid our $1.50 a foot instead of the several dollars a foot in the circular harbor of the rich folks. We paid a quick visit to one of the beaches, which had a blue carpet leading you to the ocean. The people vacationing there were hunkered down in their fox holes with sand drifting around them like the dunes at the Oregon coast. People trying to lay down in this sand blast storm were soon buried alive with their bodies exfoliated by the grit flying through the air like 440 sandpaper.

I had a diver change out our shafts, trim tabs and transom zincs and clean off the scum line that had formed from all the tannic water we have traveled through. There is a real mixture of brackish, fresh and salt water, which along with the varying temperatures allows all kinds of things to grow on the hull. Keeping it clean makes the boat much more efficient; and at a gallon a mile we need all the help we can get.

In addition to the work done on the zincs, the rear holding tank sprang a leak so I had to bury my head in the bilge to repair the trickle of septic honey coming from a broken pipe. Two hours and several rolls of paper towels later I had reconnected the internal sewer pipe from the back head and we were back in business ... so to speak!

Glenn arrived in time to join us at anchor just off the docks we had stayed on for two days. Small ferries and foot passenger tour boats travel this channel and often times gave us the brush pitch just to let us know they own this stretch of water, even though we were in an approved anchoring spot. We just waved and blew kisses.

Beaufort - pronounced B -YOU -FORT! - was our next port of call, with a beautiful anchorage just off the city waterfront and a wonderful public dock to land our dinghies on. There were several other boats on the hook here and we gave them wide berth when we set our anchor. Even so, one gentleman some 100 yards away asked us to move because he thought we were too close. We assured him we were not and told him we would kept an eye on things and move if we thought there was going to be a problem. When you anchor a good rule of thumb in calm weather is a 3/1 or 4/1 scope with chain. We anticipated a light wind and had set our scope at 5/1. The worrier had set his at over 7/1, which in a crowded anchorage is way too much. Beaufort - this mini version of Savannah - was a delightful town with unique shops, old inns and churches dating to the middle 1770's. Chris had purchased a marina guide and chart kit for me six years ago at the marina here; it was the first information I had received on the inter-coastal between Miami and Norfolk. It was the spark that lit the fire to do this trip.

We celebrated our 34th anniversary by taking everyone out for dinner in an old plantation home called the Beaufort Inn. After an outstanding meal, complete with chocolate lava cake, on the house, we returned to the boats and called it a night. As we got ready to go to bed a small sailboat arrived between us and the worry wart. There was a small light on in the cabin but no one was stirring. As the boats swung the little sailboat got closer than one should so I took out my spot light and shined it in his window hoping to raise someone. Eventually a head popped out of the hatch and we greeted each other with courtesy. Bill and I informed him that he was too close for sleeping comfort. He hinted that perhaps we had moved. We informed him that we had been there for a day and had not moved and that the worry wart would flip out if he could see where he was. Rules of the road dictate that if someone encroaches on your space after you are anchored, it is up to them to move. We asked him what he planned to do and finally he pulled anchor and exited - stage left!

Sundays on the water are interesting because you never know which church is going to be within walking distance of the marina you are staying at or where we are anchored. We have found ourselves walking great distances to worship and have changed our allegiance, based on proximity rather than brand name. At St. Simon we were Methodists on bicycles, experiencing a full blown Easter extravaganza worship with full orchestra and professional soloists. As Baptists in Beaufort on Palm Sunday we again happened upon another awesome and soul inspiring musical with orchestra, military horn players and a superb choir and narrative done by a man who sounded like Sean Connery. Beaufort is close to a huge Marine training base on Paris Island, so many of the talented young men and women were from the base. We have been

Episcopalians, Lutherans and other community church Christians as well.

After leaving Beaufort and a day on the water we wound our way up another of the desolate creeks hidden from sight except for a narrow entrance that's hidden in the tall waving grass until you are upon it. This 150 foot wide, tannic tea water estuary which is the home of: dolphins, alligators, osprey, owls, song birds, insects and fish of all kinds would be our resting spot for the night. Many of these streams and creeks are deep to the edge and deeper than the dredged channels we travel on during the day. Golden marsh grasses that go on forever like the savannahs in Africa make you feel like a hippo or a giraffe should surface or come sauntering by any minute. Many of these little havens of peace and serenity are virtually untraveled and uninhabited so when the sun goes down and the bugs come out the stars shine brighter than the one that shone over Bethlehem long ago. This one was called Tom's Creek. We never met Tom, but slept soundly as the boats swung upstream and downstream with the ebb and flow of the tide from the ocean nearby; the boat almost touching each side of the creek as it changed position in the night.

Charleston was our journey's goal for the next day. We rose early, untied JUWIKA and then pulled anchor; descending downstream to the inlet that would lead us to our next adventure. Charleston is the crème de la crème of historic cities in the south. It is considered one of the most historic of all the cities and has been preserved even more deliciously than Savannah. It is a city more than 300 years old and was the center for the slave trade, rice plantations, exquisite heritage homes, historic forts, open markets, and palatial churches - with cemeteries, the first chamber of commerce in the U.S., the first municipal university, cobblestone streets and gardens behind, in front of and between each and every building. These gardens are as individualized as the ginger bread and lattice iron work that adorn the houses and buildings throughout the old part of town. Huge trees line the streets and parks, filtering the sun's rays in the thick canopy above.

This is also the home of pralines, one of the south's most delightful sweets, in my estimation. Barkers at all the candy stores dole out samples of this brown sugary pecan treat. I get my fill as I eat both Chris's sample and my own at every shop we pass.

We anchored just off a marina on the river close to the heart of downtown. For a nominal fee the marina allowed us to land our dinghies and dump our garbage. There were a few mega yachts on the dock and several other boats like ours spending time in this magnificent city.

Many of the old homes had plaques with circa (date) on them to show how old they were. Interestingly, the city was the birthplace for many of the insurance companies that insured these homes. Each company had its own fire department and each home that was insured had a seal by the front door showing who they were insured with. Some homes were insured by more than one company. When a home caught fire all the fire departments would respond but only those whose plaques were displayed would fight the fire. Some of the homes also displayed wooden rope-like trim around the front door which was the symbol for a merchant. The larger the braid in the rope around the door the more prosperous the merchant was. Charleston was also where Bank of America began its business; in a small brick, two story building no larger than a matchbox. One famous street called "Rainbow Row" has some of the most expensive real estate in the area. These antique homes are two stories on the street and painted pastel colors, with wrought iron gates, shutters, gardens in the back, planter boxes, ornate hardware, woodwork and character that would make Lucille Ball seem like an ordinary woman. The whole city is almost an overload of beauty, charm and Americana.

Chris and I have friends just outside Charleston in a suburb called Summerville. It was originally a place inland where residents of Charleston could get away from the bugs and malaria carried by mosquitoes closer to the water during the hot season. Today it is a growing city of its own just beyond the byway that is home to some of the south's oldest and most auspicious plantations. Owen and Julie and one of their three sons, Matthew, would be our tour guides for the next couple of days. In true southern grace they drove miles for us, toured us around the city, took us to their home, made southern food gift baskets for each of us and served us an awesome meal of chicken and sausage gumbo, potato salad and bread pudding with bourbon sauce. They also took us to the Middleton Plantation. The Middletons were prosperous rice growers with over 600 slaves on 26 plantations. (You were considered quite well to do if you had 50 slaves.) The gardens surrounding the home reminded us of Versailles, with fountains, statues, butterfly ponds and manicured grounds. Rice was a huge cash crop in "The South" and took much more labor to grow and harvest than cotton. Alligators cruise the ponds and azalea and camellia gardens grow beneath the gigantic oaks. One wing of the home is still intact and very much as it was in the days the Middletons farmed this plantation. Two wings, which were not attached, were burned in the Civil War and the remainder of the ruins came down in an earthquake in the mid 1800's.

Inside the house we viewed a hand written note, signed by President Abraham Lincoln, giving safe passage through the enemy Union Lines, to one of the Middleton girls who needed to attend a funeral. They must have been a very prominent southern family to have such influence during this time in our history..

The wind came up so for the last night in Charleston so we moved to the docks. Owen and I changed out all our screens to a smaller mess to keep out the no-seeums which had been regularly taking blood without asking. We cooked dinner for everyone that night on the boat and made arrangements for Chris to stay with Julie for a couple more nights while Owen flew his Delta airplane to Haiti. Matthew was on spring break so I suggested that he (13) and friend Jared (15) travel north with Glenn and me to Georgetown, two days away by boat and only an hour by car. Chris and Julie would make the trip by car in a couple of days and pick up the boys and Glenn, who needed to return to Charleston to make travel connections. So on Thursday, under Glenn's and my supervision, the two boys, with all their electronic gadgets, junk food and sleeping bags boarded the boat on an adventure. The girls waved goodbye from the dock with smiles on their faces. But that is another story and another day. All went as planned and we had a fabulous time with the boys.

We have now come ashore in the golf capital of the United States - Myrtle Beach! It is the day after the Masters and there is always a huge charity game there the next day. This year was no exception. As we traveled north from Georgetown yesterday our senses were confused by the changing seasons. We had left Florida and Georgia in what we perceived to be summer and now we were entering into what felt like a crisp spring day. Our latitude is equal to where we were in late fall as we traveled down the Tenn-Tom waterway to Mobile. The vegetation has gone from tropical marshy grassland to Bald Cypress swamps. The water has gone from blue to brown and the pollen in the chilly air reminds us spring is near and that winter still has a grip on some of the areas just north of us Hurricane season for this area is just a month and a half away so mustn't linger too long but we mustn't rush to meet old man winter either as he spins his last efforts to make us put three blankets back on the bed.

God's Blessings,
We pray for you often!
Pray for safe passage for us!
He is risen!
Fondly and Love,
Chuck and Chris

LOOPET 12

GEORGETOWN, SOUTH CAROLINA TO THE DISMAL SWAMP IN NORTH CAROLINA

DEAR Friends and Family,
It is a most glorious morning as we cruise at a snail's pace down one of America's most historic canals, which connects Albermarle Sound to the Chesapeake - North Carolina to Virginia - The Dismal Swamp! It is anything but dismal just as Desolation Sound in British Columbia is anything but desolate. The forest forms a canopy of pines, vine maples, dogwoods and cottonwoods in every color of green overhead. A carpet of vines, lily pads and poison ivy reaches out from the water's edge like the hands and feet of a million goblins trying to grab us at every turn. The sun filters through the vegetation to create shadows in the tannic, tea brown water that flows gently through this unique forest. The mirror-like images that reflect reality from the glassy canal create a surreal feeling of vertigo as the sky, water and trees blend together to make a painting that looks like something out of a troll fairytale. The feeling is like floating through a dream world where all your cares are absorbed by the beauty of the moment.

The birds are singing their melodious songs to each other and to us and the insects hover above the water, dancing their ballets as they dart back and forth looking for whatever insects look for. The night air is also filled with the sounds of rigid wings and legs of un-seen, armor-coated exoskeletons grinding out their shrill sounding harmony in a metallic symphony. If you look close enough or listen hard enough you may see a snake or otter dip beneath the surface or you may hear the cry of a bobcat, growl of a bear or the hoot of an owl. It is truly a unique place in the world.

The canal was started in the 1700's and hand dug by Negro slaves as a waterway of commerce and transport for all kinds of goods, to include timber which was logged off along the canal. This waterway was initially funded by a group of investors which included George Washington. Today the canal is run and operated by the Army Corp of Engineers.

The water is the color of espresso coffee in the sunlight, but because of the tannic acid created by the cypress, cedar and pine trees, which border the rivers in thick stands, the water is extremely pure and very drinkable. No bacteria can grow in it. In fact it was considered as water that could be sent on space flights because of its capacities for staying fresh. I did not stick my head overboard and take a big slurp. I'll take their word for it.

Our home last evening was a rest stop and visitor's center; complete with bikes you can use to ride on a paved and shady bike trail into a little one gas station/ice cream freezer town nearby. The rest stop is also used by cars traveling along the interstate highway. Many of those stopping along the auto route walk down to the free docks to stare at the boats tied alongside the canal.

The Dismal Swamp Canal and connecting rivers run for some fifty miles and have America's oldest lock at each end which lifts you up at the south end and lets you down at the north end. If you were to traverse this waterway at night you might see eerie, fire like flashes in the woods. These were not ghosts of the past as some suspected, which remained from the time when this route was used as part of the freedom underground railroad prior to the abolishment of slavery; but methane gas escaping and igniting in the peat bogs which surround the canal. Needless to say this part of our journey was very scenic and wonderfully peaceful.

When last I wrote you we had just left Charleston S.C. with Glenn and me chaperoning two teenage boys - Matthew and Jared. It was anything but peaceful but a whole bunch of fun. It has been many years since coaching junior high boy's wrestling teams so this was an awakening for both Glenn and me. We traveled for two days as we made our way toward Georgetown where Julie would deliver Chris back to the boat, pick up the boys and take Glenn back to Charleston for a transportation connection.

Boys, and for that matter guys, can be ready to go at a moment's notice with very few clothes, a sleeping bag and tooth brush; which may or may not get used. They also had a stash of junk food to go along with a couple of all time favorite goofy videos they had seen several times in the last month and which belonged to their personal collections. Matthew and Jared were no different.

The first night we anchored in Five Fathom Creek and the boys emptied a five gallon tank of fuel racing up and down the remote passages; doing donuts and cookies as they took the dinghy to the extreme limits under the distant scrutiny of Glenn's and my surrogate parental observation. During one check in pass they yelled to us that they had seen a large snake some six feet long and four inches in diameter slithering toward the swamp grasses. I went with them to have a look and it was gone!

The following day we arrived at Georgetown S.C., home of the legendary "Swamp Fox", where the boys again burned through another tank of mix while agitating the water of the once peaceful Georgetown Bay. The marina we stayed at wasn't called "Hazzard" for nothing!

Glenn treated us all to a lunch at an outdoor patio pub - minors allowed - where the boys fed an alligator lurking under the deck. Boys will be boys and the alligator got a taste of a shrimp laced with wasabi mustard, unbeknown to Glenn and me. This made him slide into the shade of the dock to quench his or her thirst in privacy.

With a touch football game, lots of unhealthy food, funny stories, the boys playing receivers in the dinghy and Glenn and me quarterbacking from the boat and being chased by a pelican down the dock, we made some special memories with the boys and invited them back for another round in the summer. They were great and kept Glenn and me in stitches.

Georgetown is another one of South Carolina's jewels with homes and churches dating back to the 1700's and old commercial buildings of the same era restored to pristine and authentic condition. Bill and Gail's nephew, John, joined us for Easter, as we Lutes became Episcopalians and attended a spirit-filled service in a 1730's church. The seating was an arrangement of not pews, but boxes, where each family sat in a square, some facing forward and others facing toward the back. I had the unique privilege of facing most of the congregation during the service, so I was able to see who was really listening and who was meditating on the sermon's finer points with eyes tightly closed to weed out any distractions.

Our stay, complete with a meal of shrimp and grits, spicy sausage and a dollop of butter to add some color and a little more cholesterol, we paddled north to a little remote anchorage nestled in the back country of South Carolina's bald cypress swamps. We were heading north into spring as the pollen dusted the boats with yellow flour and the trees showed signs of new life in their limbs. We had left palm trees and tropical vegetation and now the latitude was changing and the surroundings were starting to remind us more of what we had experienced coming south along the Tenn-Tom in the fall. It appeared we were going from summer to spring, which was in the wrong order. The temperature dipped overnight. It would be necessary to layer on the blankets once again until summer had made her move to catch up with us. Little Bucksport amongst the Barbie doll house, floating fish cabins was where we dropped the hook and laid our heads.

The following day we rose early and motored north to Myrtle Beach, the "Golf Capital of the U.S.", where we started this chapter. It is located on a narrow stretch of water so if we wanted to stay in the area a marina would be our only option. Years prior there had been a free dock along the banks of North Myrtle Beach which now had been replaced with a $1.00 a foot a night dock. Barefoot Marina paralleled the waterway and was skirted by a wonderful mall built on a huge lake. The popular rock group, Alabama, has a Branson-like concert hall there and there is a great Blues restaurant with live music. A private party where the band "Hootie and the Blow Fish" was performing displayed a sign outside the concert warning people of a huge fine and even imprisonment for taking guns into the concert - OK then! There is also an alligator adventure farm, shops of all kinds and a system of bike paths which winds down to the beach and along the Atlantic. We even had a fireworks show at our doorsteps on the lakes in front of the boats and Greg Norman's Grill sent tantalizing barbeque smoke over our boat as we sat out on the decks enjoying the boat traffic as it went north and south on the inter-coastal.

As is prudent we always listen to the weather report to see what we can expect for winds and so we can plan our anchorages for the most protection and calmest evenings. The long range forecast was for heavy winds and some extreme weather conditions that were shaping up to be what they were calling; the worst storm in twenty years. Tornadoes, high winds, thunder and lightning and some rain were predicted in a few days, so we started calculating our strategy.

The next few days would be travel days leaving fairly early and making some miles up for the time we had spent lingering in the fabulous cities of Georgia and South Carolina. The days were very windy and fortunately we were provided some wonderfully protected anchorages at Southport, Wrightsville Beach and TopSail Sound. These places have good holding ground and we could dinghy to shore and get in some leg work. We had also crossed the border into North Carolina and other than the scenery along the waterway with only a sliver of land separating us from the Atlantic. There were no major cities of historic importance and no real sightseeing opportunities. The contrast from where we had been was dramatic.

The weather continued to build and the distant forecast, which was now on our door steps, was expected to hit in the afternoon of the next day. Marinas had also been scarce so we decided we must secure a spot immediately and get in early to be ready for whatever mother-nature might unleash. Our marina of choice, because there were no others, ended up being a small working boatyard on the New River. It is rustic and had been badly damaged in previous hurricanes but it had sturdy docks that floated and the price point at a dollar a foot fit the pocketbook. They also had a courtesy car we could use - the first one we had run into since we left Alabama and Mississippi. The entrance to this safe little artificial harbor was shoaled badly with only a foot to spare but there was adequate water inside the marina. We were the only two transient boats in this little safe haven until we were joined by a 30 foot Nonesuch which had passed this way several times and was on its way back to New Jersey. We shared meals with Jane and Mac. He was an ex-fighter pilot and they were both seasoned Latin American travelers. We enjoyed their company as we swapped stories of adventure on the high seas.

The storm did hit with a vengeance. Consistent, shifting winds howled at 35 with gusts to 50. The boats tugged at their storm ties like a dog trying to take its master for a walk. Waves rolled through the entrance of the little marina and slammed up against those boats that sat near the opening. The halyards on sailboats clanged their rhythmic cadence heralding the waxing and waning of the wind like personal audio weathermen. Tornado warnings came and went as we monitored our radios, with reports of others in nearby areas being hit harder than we - yet always the threat of a direct hit loomed with each gust.

We were safe. The docks held well, the rains came and the water level rose. The marina bathrooms and laundry became a huge mud puddle which we sloshed through to get to the washers and dryers but we were safe. The courtesy car, the first we had seen in months of travel, gave us an opportunity to get to the beach, go out for dinner and make the best of the three days in Snead's Ferry/Swan Point!

One excursion took us to a beach where we anticipated finding a plethora of pristine shells washed up by the storm. The sand blew in sheets, licking at our faces and sifting its way into every nook and cranny of our clothing, hair, ears and eyes. Walking with our backs to the wind was fine but to make the return trip we had to walk backwards to keep from having our teeth whitened by the pulverizing, shifting dunes. I did meet a couple of boys and their dad who showed me how to look for small prehistoric shark's teeth, so I began sifting through the sand and gathered a small sack for Noah, our grandson.

Sleep is never better than when you know that you are safe no matter how loud the raucous of the storm outside. We had weathered the storm and now it was time to move on. There were places to go and after three days we were antsy to be on the road again.

The day broke bright and the wind continued to get in its licks even though the forecast was for calmer weather by that evening. We had a couple of large bodies of water ahead of us, Pamlico Sound and Albermarle Sound, both of which can deal you a nasty blow if the weather chooses to change. We also would pass through an army base called Camp LeJuene which could be practicing live fire so we had to do our homework to see if we could make passage that day.

With clearance from the military and the sun shining we paddled north to Spooner's Creek - a little protected bay amongst some nice homes. Well protected we spent the night and I even found a barber shop where I took off about five pounds of hair. Chris says that if they were still stuffing car seats with hair I could make a fortune supplying the major auto manufacturers with an ever ready and never ending supply. A little dock at the head of the bay gave us access to WalMart and Lowes just a few blocks away.

The next day we passed by Moreshead, North Carolina, and headed for Oriental, North Carolina. This city is named Oriental because when it was founded and before it was named, someone found a placard from a sailing ship on the beach with Oriental written on it. A bird in the hand is worth two in the bush. The sign was put up and the city was named - "Oriental".

It was quaint with an M&M restaurant and some "chic" shops. It also sported a great marine store and had loaner bikes, which looked like they had been donated by the local wrecking yard. Bill and I rattled our way through town with plastic bags over the torn, water soaked sponge rubber seats to keep our pants dry.

We had anchored in the small bay near the marina and rafted to save space in this little nook. A couple times Bill and I had checked on the boats - they were where we had left them. There is a free city dock but it was full. The wind was slight and so we were comfortable that all was well. We have done this hundreds of times before.

After catching up with the girls we decided to take one last peek out to the boats before walking a different route into town. At a glance we could see that the wind had come up drastically in the few minutes from our last check and had shifted to an opposite direction where there was nothing to break its impact. The boats were dragging the anchor and fortunately heading for deeper water at the entrance of the harbor. I broke into a sprint and launched our dinghy toward the boats, leaving Bill, Gail and Chris to follow in theirs. My plan was to get to the boats, start our engine and control the drift until Bill arrived at which time we would release him, pull our anchor and find a more protected spot.

All worked well and our guardian angels watched over us again with no damage or problems from this uncommon occurrence. We tucked into a nearby bay on the lee side of Oriental in six feet of water and had a most peaceful evening of great food and a lesson in Bridge.

The next morning Pamlico Sound was covered with another flock of sheep, which is a nice way of saying the wind was blowing and white caps on top of messy three footers were the predominant water feature. The wind was supposed to kick up even more in the afternoon so we left early and sloshed our way through the snotty 30 miles that lay ahead. Fortunately, they were on our bow, so other than getting salty and wet we had a relatively comfortable ride with an occasional splash reaching our windshield thirteen feet above the surface. Bill and Gail drove inside to keep from getting soaked and also reported that their decks were awash a few times. Our destination was Belhaven, North Carolina, a sleepy little town where the only place to eat is a miniature burger, hush puppy, catfish and shrimp place called Farm Boys, where you "order in" from a group of southern ladies with heavy accents and take your food out to picnic tables where the inexpensive fare can be devoured on the main street of one of America's least progressive small burgs. A walk through the back streets gave us insights into this little town. One of the residents told us that when there is a storm of significance, the river floods and the water runs under the homes one way; then when the tide goes out the water returns from the other direction to complete the full flush. FEMA had actually paid to have all the homes jacked up on foundations several feet off the ground so that the water can ebb and flow under them without damage to the residences.

There is also a very old mansion in the city which was reminiscent of the Munster's home. It had gone with the wind and was in poor repair but we were able to look inside and talk with an elderly woman who ran the front desk of what is now a B&B.

The primary tree now is the pine. Gone are the palms. In fact they have been gone for some time even though an occasional new development plants them as a deceptive lure for northerners looking for their little piece of warmth and paradise in the south. The birds are also on their journey north. Pairs of Canadian geese are nesting in this area and the Pelicans are less frequently seen even though on occasion flocks of them can be seen heading toward areas on the Mississippi. Every available marker and snag is populated with a large stick nest where mother and father falcon are raising their new little brood of hatchlings. The other day we were actually chased from a mother goose by her lifetime mate as he hissed and flapped at us, protecting her and the eggs which will soon hatch into their little gaggle of goslings. Eagles are seen from time to time and the ever present sea gulls do their acrobatics in the spring winds.

With hopes that North Carolina could redeem itself having not come close to the measurement set by the rest of the trip, we motored toward the last bastion of civilization before heading for Virginia and the Chesapeake. We would have to slide lazily down the Pungo River Canal, crash through murky, tannic wind waves of the Alligator River and traverse Albemarle Sound to arrive at Elizabeth City, the "Harbor Of Hospitality". Our stop the night before our arrival would be a small bay tucked far back into a winding labyrinth of a river flowing through a series of awash mud flats and shoals that made it appear that there was deep water all around. Not to be tricked by this illusion of depth we made our way using the electronic charts which had been and continue to be very accurate and trustworthy. They delivered us successfully to our anchorage for the night. There were a million stars out in this remote spot just a glide from where the Wright Brothers made their infamous first flight and not too far from one of the most treacherous capes on the east coast - Cape Hatteras.

Albermarle Sound was like a pond as we made our way toward Elizabeth City. The predictions for calm winds and calm seas allowed us to make the five hour trip in complete comfort - even making it possible for Chris to cook a nice breakfast in route and for me to eat it instead of wearing it. The opposite is the usual here.

Elizabeth City got its reputation from a tradition started in the 1984 when two men, Fred and Joe, started meeting and greeting boaters at the free city docks. Every afternoon at four-thirty, when there are more than four boats in the harbor, Fred (93) brings down wine, beer, cheese and crackers for a little dockside gathering and welcome to the town. Fred arrives as he always has, in his golf cart that he drives around the town. He also brings his rose clippers and snips off a rose or bud from the waterside rose garden for each first mate - thus the name "Rose Buddies". It has become a tradition that has put Elizabeth City on the nautical map, having been written up in most of the yachting journals and travel guides.

We left some dollars in this little town at the local grocery store called Whiteys, bought fresh shrimp at a local seafood market, were lucky enough to get last minute tickets to "The Odd Couple" at their local live theater, went to their new museum which houses the history of the sound, and rode bikes along the river where the grand homes are surrounded with gardens blossoming and manicured with dogwoods, camellias, azaleas and flowers of all kinds.

Fred invited me out for coffee at Muddy's, a local haunt which use to be a gas station on a place called the "Corner" where the town's people meet and catch up on the daily local gossip and scuttlebutt. Fred is the unofficial mayor of the town and is allowed to drive his golf cart down the one way streets the wrong way. He invited us over his home and his parents' home which is just in front of the converted garage he calls home, for a tour of his antiques and relics which date back to the beginnings of this town where he was born. He has several out buildings; one of which is a make shift library, stuffed with books and periodicals with an old over-stuffed chair centered in the middle of this tiny shed wide enough only for one person to sit under the stark light bulb and while away the hours lost in some imaginative world. The other sheds are filled with priceless hand carved decoys, baskets, carved wooden bowls and artifacts collected over a lifetime on a mail route that use to fill his work days.

Visitors to the docks include: lovers, the homeless, and picnickers consuming large quantities of fast food chicken from Hardees, a man who rides a bike and brings his parrot "Pickles" down to meet the boaters, Jehovah Witness disciples trying to hand off tracts and their female counterparts trying to evangelize the boaters. Then there are the dog walkers and the baby strollers, the couples who are thinking of doing a boating adventure and those who have finished one in their previous lives and are still reliving the fond memories. And of course there are the coffee drinkers who have just visited the bakery down the street and who are starting their day basking in the morning sunshine, on the park benches overlooking the river, while catching up on the daily news.

The docks themselves are monitored by an unofficial, official dock master named Sam who barks out orders on channel 16 even though it is supposed to be used exclusively for hailing and distress; in spite of the fact that Elizabeth City is the home of the largest Coast Guard base in the country. At close to 80, Sam must have a special relationship with the base commander because I never heard a reprimand over my radio for Sam using this exclusive channel to beckon boaters onto his docks.

We went to church on Sunday as Methodists. Then with a rental car from Enterprise on Monday we went exploring down the coastline to Kittyhawk, Roanoke and Cape Hatteras. Kitty Hawk was amazing and the story of these two preacher's sons who converted bike knowledge into the first manned flight is a miraculous one.

We "didn't see" the Lost Colony of Roanoke but watched a film about the first settlement in America dating some 35 years before Jamestown. To wrap up a perfect day we climbed the 279 stairs to the top of the Cape Hatteras lighthouse. It was ingeniously moved from its former location a half a mile away where the ocean tried to claim it like it had so many of the ships that were lost in what is called the Atlantic's graveyard.

We returned back to the boats late, after stopping at our favorite shopping center - WalMart Super Stores. The groceries unpacked and stowed, we said our prayers of thanks for a wonderful day and stay at Elizabeth City. We had missed the four-thirty gathering that day which is almost an unforgivable sin but knew that our dreams would still be filled with unforgettable visions of this most hospitable little town in North Carolina. Our faith had been restored in the northern sister to South Carolina and now the Dismal Swamp lay ahead of us - another adventure for another day. We would leave at 10:00 am to make one of the few openings of the lock going into the swamp. If the swamp was to nature what Elizabeth City was to hospitality we would have to give North Carolina a standing ovation for fond and exciting, lifelong memories.

As I finish this, Chris is defrosting the fridge with her hairdryer in a little marina in Portsmouth, Virginia. We are packing a few clothes and our good friend Owen has secured us standby tickets for a quick trip to Cabo San Lucas, Mexico. Bill and Gail will explore Jamestown, Williamsburg and Yorktown which we did by land last year with our friends Glenn and Sharon. We will rendezvous with them in a week or so and continue our journey through the Chesapeake and all points north.

We trust you are all well. Keep us in your prayers as we keep you in ours. Let us know what is happening in your lives. Until we see you - blessings, peace and joy.

Fondly and Love,
Chuck and Chris

LOOPET 13

VIRGINIA AND THE CHESAPEAKE TO CHESAPEAKE CITY, MARYLAND

GREETINGS to Friends and Family,
Chesapeake City is a hoping little town that sits on the border between Maryland and a mile from Delaware along the C&D Canal (Chesapeake and Delaware Canal) - a narrow 12 mile long canal which spans the land between the Delaware River and the Chesapeake. The canal is 450 feet wide and 35 feet deep which allows ships up to 866 feet long to transit this shortcut. Military ships, car carriers, freighters, huge tugs and barges dwarf the miniature recreational boats that share this manmade cut.

As I write this, the little harbor, which is just a bubble off the side of this cargo canal, is filled with anchored, docked and rafted recreational boats. It is lined by restaurants, parks, a public free dock and a quaint boardwalk. Michael Jackson's, "Billy Jean" is echoing across the water as a Saturday night band entertains guests from the surrounding areas of Pennsylvania, Maryland and Delaware; while a bride and groom say their "I Dos" complete with horse and buggy, flanking our port side in the park above.

Much has happened since we left Portsmouth, Virginia to take a breather and do some work at our home in Mexico. We left you off after a wonderful journey through North Carolina and the "Dismal Swamp" on our way to Portsmouth, Virginia and Norfolk and then onto the majestic and history packed Chesapeake.

Portsmouth and the surrounding areas are where America's Navy really shines. The docks along the Elizabeth River are crowded with behemoth military vessels of all kinds and in all states of repair and refit; an array of aircraft carriers and destroyers, battleships and patrol boats, inflatables and landing craft. Norfolk is also the home of the USS Wisconsin which is open and free to the public, but still an operational battleship which could be re-commissioned if necessary. Tourists scramble about its decks like fleas on a dog as retired and active duty navy men stand watch and share their knowledge of this massive naval workhorse. The river itself is a hub of activity with large freighters and military craft sharing their waterway with us little guys.

Chris and I decided that since we had explored Jamestown, Williamsburg and Yorktown last year with our good friends, Glenn and Sharon, we would take a little break from our floating home and head for Cabo to check out the hard work and progress Mateo, my brother, had made. He has spent numerous hours finishing the house and adding a pool along with fighting CC&R regulations to protect our privacy from the development behind our house. Thank goodness he was there and monitoring the progress, holding them accountable for a nice privacy wall and removal of some non-conforming patios and landscaping. Nice job brother.

A friend of ours, who is a Delta pilot and who was our part of the Choate family who hosted us in Charleston got us standby tickets. So seated in first class with the warm towelettes, a glass of wine and a great movie we left Essi-Anna at Scott's Creek in Portsmouth and headed for twelve wonderful days in one of the best climates in the world - Cabo San Lucas! Matt and Marsha greeted us at the airport and we had a wonderful time with them.

We returned to the boat on the 9th of May after Matt out-fished me on the Pedregal Beach. We had many days of excellent food, Cinco de Mayo celebrations, a neighborhood potluck and party at Janet and Ernie's, time at the beach and a little bit of work. Essi-Anna had been through a couple of wind storms. Bill and Gail were 150 miles north of us on the Chesapeake traveling with some friends, Paul and Stacy, whom we had met in Fort Meyer's Beach. They had explored the southern Chesapeake and experienced the rich history of the revolutionary war and the 400th anniversary of Jamestown and were now lazily making their way toward areas like Solomon's Island, Annapolis and Baltimore.

We needed to get back on the water and put some miles under our keel so we could resume our journey together. Thursday morning, after getting in at 11:00 p.m. the night before; we washed the boat, fueled up and let the lines go at around noon. There was no wind and the sky was clear until we rounded the corner 5 miles from Scott's Creek and saw the fog rolling in from the Atlantic.

Navy patrol boats scurried around the Elizabeth River, like a nest of hornets, with blue lights flashing. The chatter on the radio was full of talk about the fog on the Chesapeake. Warships were giving directions to commercial vessels near the channel leading to the Atlantic just a few miles away. Pleasure craft were ducking into marinas like kids playing hide and seek and the fog continued to thicken as we made our way down the channel to Chesapeake Bay. We had a contingency anchorage just a few miles away should the fog go to zero visibility and the wind come up. We had to exercise the option as the fog thickened, only to have it lift just as we got ready to set the hook in the protected water we had chosen out of harm's way. So we decided, with everyone else off the water, except the big guys out there who would look like mountains on our radar, we would head back out and float the necessary miles to catch Bill and Gail who were a couple of days north.

Just as we made our way back out the channel into the pea soup visibility, the silence on the radio broke with a demanding call from a battleship somewhere out in the fog. It instructed a pleasure craft who was within the 500 yard restriction zone around any military vessel, to immediately change course. There was no answer. The radio man's voice broke the white, blinding silence again demanding the same action but with an additional warning that if the boat did not respond immediately they would be considered hostile. There was no response.

Chris, nervous at the tone of the voice demanding the pleasure craft to change course and questioning our position in the fog wanted me to reassure her that they were not talking about us. Based on our speed and the location given we were not that pleasure craft. Silence! Finally the demand became very strong and very precise. The pleasure craft was told to change course immediately and slow down or they would be fired upon!!! Brutal! We hoped the guy had his radio on and that he responded to the navy vessel. We never heard another call and don't know what happened in the end.

Fog adds a new dimension to travel on the water. As we cleared the mouth of the Elizabeth River into the less traveled waters north of there, we saw the distorted, ghostly image of the towers on the huge, gray battleship pass behind us. Then the curtain dropped again and we were surrounded with white - the GPS, compass and radar our only life lines to the anchorage we were headed for some 20 miles up the Chesapeake.

That evening we settled in on a little creek well off the main body of the Chesapeake. The late afternoon sun burned away the blinding, snow white blankness that we had traveled in and we sat on the deck and enjoyed the serenity of our peaceful place of rest.

The next morning we made an early start. We were headed north past the York River and Yorktown to a little berg called Reedville - named after Elijah Reed. It was founded as a fishing town on the Chesapeake where a huge net fleet of gigantic seiners had plied these waters for some 150 years in search of menhaden which were rendered for their oil and used as protein and omega oils. There were some amazing turn of the century homes and Cockrell Creek provided a peaceful night's rest. We staged ourselves for the next day's leg to Solomon's Island where we would catch up with Bill and Gail after three long days of travel on the water.

With another glorious crimson sunrise and calm water, the shades were pulled to greet the sun. Hoards of bugs had been attracted by our anchor light in the wee hours of a windless night. These menaces had secreted their green jujube juice all over the boat. Mixed with the dew of the morning Essi-Anna looked like she had been decorated for an early morning Easter egg hunt. The bugs had died in their own juices and the boat was a mess. A sponge bath was the first order of the day and fortunately the sun bleached out her strange looking polka-dotted complexion before the day was over. I don't know why God created those crazy bugs.

That afternoon, after a fabulous day enjoying the scenery of the land and water along the colonially historic Chesapeake, we arrived at Solomon's Island. It is a resort and fishing town, which has become one of the most popular boating areas on this part of the Chesapeake. Bill and Gail were held up here having some repairs done on their transmission and would also rendezvous with Gail's sister and her husband Mark who were coming into Washington, D.C. from Seattle. When we rounded the corner of the harbor on our way to an anchorage at the head of a little creek, well protected from the expected wind that evening, there was JUWIKA at dock and Bill and Gail waving as we passed by.

This little town is a short shot from the nation's capital and the mighty Potomac. We spent two days there and re-provisioned at a great organic specialty grocery store located just behind the Holiday Inn. It was a short distance from where Essi-Anna lay at rest amongst some wonderful cottages and homes that lined our little, almost private harbor.

It was "Mother's Day" weekend so we partied vicariously (except for our calls to our own moms) with our unknowing surrogate families having a barbeque on shore. Relatives came and went in pristine, vintage mahogany day boats and classic cars alike. We were also visited by the infamous swan that makes its rounds begging for handouts and a mother and father mallard with their gaggle of cotton puff little ones in tow.

Bill and Gail made the trek to Washington, D.C. to pick up Mark and Judy and Chris and I hung out and relaxed. That night everyone came to our boat for dinner and we planned our strategy to depart early the next morning on our way to Annapolis - home of America's great Naval Academy.

On the way out of the harbor the next morning Bill and Gail, who were ahead of us, called and said they were having overheating problems. They edged their way into the semi deep water off the channel and dropped their anchor out of the flow of fishing boat traffic heading out for a day's catch. We discussed possibilities on the problem and surmised that it had to be related to the recent work done on JUWIKA. We offered to tow them back to the boat yard and wait with them or take Judy and Mark with us not knowing what the problem was and how long it would take to fix. Bill contacted the yard and they said they would be out with a tow boat and get right on the problem. We decided it would be best to go on and meet them up the road. Mark and Judy decided to stay in spite of the fact that the weather was turning to windy and the ride north to Annapolis could be bumpy and lumpy later in the day - to put it mildly.

The Chesapeake is a huge body of water with the potential to whip up 4 to 6 foot waves in a jiffy. If the wind is coming up and down the bay you can drive into or away from them with some discomfort. But if the wind comes off the land or the ocean the beam seas can make the passage up and down the bay a sideways roller-coaster that you wish you never had boarded.

Bill and Gail would have to be back on the water quickly that day to make the miles to Annapolis or spend the night back in Solomon. This ended up being the case. The forecast was for wind the next day so they would make an early start to get off the water before battling mother-nature. At 5 to 6 miles an hour though, 50 miles can turn into 10 hours on the water. If the current is running against you and the wind is creating a washing machine action, which has just put you on spin cycle, the journey can be less than a pleasant one - though safe enough. You are very grateful for a finished passage and a calm anchorage out of wind and waves. Such was the following day's passage to Annapolis for them.

The problem had been a set of plugs that should have been removed from a newly installed heat exchanger which cools the engine. The engine was getting no water. So the cooling impeller disintegrated and distributed rubber fragments throughout the cooling system. The entire heat exchange system had to be dismantled and reassembled at no cost to them, other than a day wasted on the dock and a rough ride north the next day.

Chris and I had a sunny calm day and pulled into Annapolis on schedule. This historic naval city was founded in 1649 and at one time the nation's capital. We arrived under overcast skies to find our friends Stacy and Paul on a buoy in the mooring field just in front of the naval academy. We picked one up too and settled in for the night. The skyline of Annapolis is amazing with the greenish dome of the cathedral at the academy, the massive, ornate, stone French style dormitories where all 4000 plus students live, the largest wooden constructed dome of the state house or capital building, and many church spires decorating the skyline.

From our vantage point, which was no more than a half a block over water to the main street of the town, we could see old buildings and store fronts from the 1700's. They are well maintained and full of the character; transporting us back in time to the revolutionary war.

Annapolis is one of the few places we said we could call home. The streets were lined with cobblestone and brick. The row houses of brick and wood, sometimes no more than one room wide and three stories tall were lined up like colorful dominoes along tree and flower lined streets. The roofs were often times made of tile or slate or painted tin, which had protected their inhabitants from rain for over three centuries. There were wrought iron gates and fences, tight little alleys, porches that looked like something out of a fairytale. Planter boxes filled with blossoming beauties, rockers and benches and bells and metal knockers in the center of wreathes of every kind gave insight into the people who lived behind these inviting portals.

We walked the streets in awe as we passed by multimillion dollar homes no bigger than a dollhouse and gazed at historic homes where Washington and many signers of the Declaration of Independence had lived or visited during the fight for independence. One such home was that of the band director at the academy who wrote, "Anchors Away".

Paul and Stacy took us to breakfast the next morning at a quaint and historic cafe called, "Ruth and Chicks" where at 8:00 a.m. all those present stand and face a large flag over the counter and sing, "God Bless America". It was very moving and the place is always packed.

We toured the state house where George Washington resigned after the Treaty of Paris ended the war. On display were original oils of the great revolutionary general valued at over 20 million dollars and a copy of Washington's resignation note roughly written out which had been handed down through generations from a spectator who was present at Washington's speech. Washington had promised Martha that he would be home for Christmas and she had promised him his favorite dish which was stuffed pigeon inside stuffed duck inside stuffed goose, inside stuffed turkey. I think I got that straight and if not you get the idea. The original speech, written by George Washington, is now property of the state and will be displayed in a special case being made as I write this note to you. It had remained in the hands of the original family until just a few years ago.

The portraits, which hung in this historic chamber, were painted by Peale who had been unsuccessful in his saddle making trade and decided he could make lots of money painting dignitaries and the wealthy upper class. Some of the portraits display only the bust and others the whole body. He charged by the number of body parts in the painting, thus the saying, "costing an arm or a leg".

Bill and Gail pulled in the next day after being beat up on the Chesapeake and we directed them to a quieter little mooring field behind the bridge where we had moved. The wind in the first mooring field had created a nasty wave action, which rocked and rolled the boat all night long like a mechanical bucking bull, which on many occasions came close to throwing us out of bed. This made the wakes of the B.C. ferries and cruise ships feel like a mother gently rocking her new born to sleep. It was by far the roughest night we have ever spent on the boat.

The following day the "Plebes", or first year cadets and the entire academy would gather on the parade field for a display of colors and a wonderful ceremony in full dress uniforms. Sabers and rifles, Scottish bagpipers and marching bands, cannons and strict adherence to military protocol in front of proud parents and spectators made this a special event for us. These young people, who are considered some of the best and brightest in our nation, both academically and athletically, were a sight to behold as they displayed their pomp on the field in front of the beautiful buildings of the academy, which created an amazing backdrop. Admirals and generals were there to review the parade and give their salute of respect and approval as the entire academy passed in front of them.

We toured the grounds later under the expert instruction of our guide and visited places like the Athletic Hall of Fame, Cathedral and the Crypt of John Paul Jones who was one of America's greatest military naval heroes during the revolutionary war. He had been buried a pauper in France and after 113 years of obscurity, his body was found under the streets of Paris and brought to this resting place under the Annapolis Naval Academy Chapel - enshrined in a crypt that rivals that of Napoleon Bonaparte. He was a Scotsman and I am told a patriarch of our clan. The generals and admirals present must not have recognized his resemblance in me for they awarded me no special privileges during our visit.

That evening we happened upon the Washington Symphonic Brass concert at the grand old St. Anne's Parish, founded in 1696 and the home congregation of Francis Scott Key, who wrote the "Star Spangled Banner" during the War of 1812. All said, Annapolis is a keeper and a place that everyone should take time to visit if the opportunity affords.

The following day after a most interesting and historic stay, we moseyed north to Baltimore where we hoped the only "Red, White and Blue" navigational marker in the world would greet us just off the shore of Fort McHenry. Francis Scott Key wrote what is now our national anthem while watching the battle as a captive aboard a British ship in the river off the upper Chesapeake near this location.

Baltimore was another one of those historic treasures along our route. We docked at a rustic little marina having not been to a dock in over a week and went exploring in the old section of Baltimore; where wooden trade, privateer and war ships had been built from the 1600s until the 19th century. It was a rough part of town where the British said pirates, raiders and scallywags hung out. Old taverns - like "The Cat's Eye" lined the streets and the row houses here have stone thresholds that have been worn down by centuries of wear. This is where "Sleepless in Seattle" was filmed. These Baltimore row houses in the Fell's Point district capture your eye and imagination as you try to recreate all the legal and illegal activity that has been part of this now restored section of Baltimore.

The downtown harbor was a hubbub of activity with a great national aquarium, the USS Constellation, the USS Chesapeake and other tall ships on display to the public. The old warehouse buildings have been converted into unique shops and restaurants. The city was alive with activity and the fact that the Preakness was going to be run the next day threw the doors to party and celebrate wide open. We walked home late that night after a full day in another unforgettable city we put high on our list.

Sleep came sweet and morning came early. It would be a long day on the water to the C&D Canal and Chesapeake City where we started this chapter. We would say goodbye to Virginia and Maryland and the Chesapeake which had stolen our hearts and captured our historic imaginations. We had walked where the men and women of the revolution had fought for our freedom and gained a new appreciation for another area of our fabulous country along the Great Circle Loop.

Good morning from New York City. Like the immigrants that have traversed these waters in hope of a new life we enter through this amazing national portal with the same enthusiasm after traveling thousands of miles by water to start on this new leg of our journey. The adventure along the Delaware and Jersey Coast to the "Big Apple" will have to wait for another day. Off to Central Park for a parade.

Later!

Love and Blessings to all,
Let us know what you are doing. We love to hear from you.
Chuck and Chris

LOOPET 14

CHESAPEAKE CITY TO NEW YORK CITY

GREETINGS Friends and Family,
Where do I begin on this leg of an unbelievable adventure? So many experiences, new faces, lifelong friendships and memories that two lifetimes would be hard to pack it all into, not to mention a few more chapters.

Our last run up the outside on the Atlantic to New York City, the Erie Canal ahead of us and a myriad of other stops and bumps and rain drops and scenery make this journey unbelievable, exhilarating and challenging, so that when your head hits the pillow and the lights go out only a dream could make this whole experience seem like reality.

As I write this we are tied to an old concrete wall just west of Lock #11 on the historic Erie Canal which was built following the War of 1812. It connects the Hudson River, some 160 miles northwest of New York City to Lake Ontario via the shorter Oswego Canal and a series of rivers and lakes. This passes through the land of the Mohawk Indians and the Douglases (like Kurt Douglas) and the Fondas (like Henry and Jane and the gang).

The scenery from New York City to our present position - the little berg of Amsterdam - is one that reminds you of a mini Columbia River Gorge. There are high bluffs of gray basalt topped with heavy evergreen and deciduous vegetation in all shades of green. Small waterfalls cascade down the slopes into cleaner, clearer fresh water as we travel further north and west. Gigantic cottonwood trees line the shoreline with groves of littler cottonwoods - releasing showers of puffy, white seed pods in such quantities that the air is filled with flurries of snow so thick that it appears you are in a blizzard. The water is also coated with a blanket of this downy fuzz, as soft as the new plumage of the little goslings, which scurry across the river under their parents' watchful eyes.

But where were we when we last wrote? I believe we were just leaving Chesapeake City and heading into Delaware along the C&D Canal. After a wonderful and free stay on the docks in Chesapeake City we set our sights on the jumping off spot of Cape May, New Jersey, which is at the eastern end of the expansive and weather torn Delaware Bay. When the wind blows off the ocean into the bay and the 2 to 3 knot current is ebbing, the waves can stand up like soldiers at attention with bayonets raised. When the directions of these elements are reversed the same is true. When it blows from either side of the bay you take a beating on the beam. The day called for light winds, which is the clear ticket to a comfortable passage, but when we cleared the canal and headed onto the Delaware Bay it was evident that the wind would be more like moderate and we would be getting a push from the rear. This means you have a long day of heavy steering ahead to keep the boat on course and the stern where it should be. It would be four or five hours of rock and roll before entering Cape May through the backdoor on the Cape May Canal just shy of the Atlantic Ocean. We blew through Delaware without a stop. After dodging row upon row of crab pot lines and commercial fishing boats we finally left the white caps on the water behind us, gave a large ferry boat right- of -way and slid into the calm water of the canal. Bill and Gail would do battle for another hour before they could take a well deserved rest and Paul and Stacy, having tried another route to maximize the current, pulled in just behind us.

That evening we anchored just offshore from the Coast Guard station and assembled our little flotilla to prepare our minds and bodies and spirits for three days on the ocean which would land us in front of the Statue of Liberty. We had made the right decision to hold up in Chesapeake City, battle Delaware Bay and stage ourselves in Cape May for what the weather radios were calling five to ten mile an hour winds on the Atlantic for the next three days. Divine intervention would allow us to motor out of the inlet just around the corner and travel on a calm ocean to Atlantic City, which would be our next stop. Usually early mornings are less windy than afternoons. The sun heats up the land and starts its thermal wind tunnel, which usually equates to larger waves and a bumpier ride. We turned in early in anticipation of an early departure just as the sun showed us its first rays of light in the east.

The crimson globe shone its fiery glow over the waters as we pulled anchor and porpoised our way through the gentle and evenly spaced rollers of the Cape May Inlet. Once we cleared the shallower water we turned to port or left for those of you who don't boat, and made our way in comfortable seas up the coast, staying some three miles offshore. The water was an unforgettable blue and the forecast held true. The reflection of this day's new sun created sheens of blazing mirror glass on the surface demanding us to pull the brims of our hats down over our eyes to create only a tiny slit through which the light could pass.

The shoreline was dotted with beach resorts and hotels, wind generators and amusement parks which sported ancient, wooden serpentine roller-coasters, and Ferris-wheels that beckoned us from the ocean to come and ride.

Forty-five miles later we caught a glimpse of the high rise casinos of Atlantic City. This is the home of the infamous Atlantic City boardwalk which stretches like a wooden pedestrian highway between the ocean and a thousand funnel cake vendors, pizza peddlers, souvenir shops, amusement arcades, restaurants, massage parlors and casinos.

We made our way through the reds and greens into the harbor and with the guidance of a guardian angel, who heard us talking on the radio about an anchorage, shared his local knowledge on the best way to work our boats into a safe haven lake that on our charts showed no access. Dockage here is spendy, so a free place to drop the hook was greatly appreciated.

We took the dinghies across the channel and walked the old, wooden boardwalk. Sections of it are in terrible repair and other parts have been restored and are open for business as the merchants pick the pockets of locals and visitors alike. Casinos and hotels like, Caesars Palace and Bally's beckoned walkers to come and try their luck. Tourists and locals gamble away paychecks and street entertainers ply their gigs in hopes of making enough for that night's meal.

If you tire of the eight mile walk roundtrip you can hire a wicker basket three wheeled buggy to deliver you to your next destination, much like they had done when this unique, ocean-side resort area was frequented by those who escaped the burning sun on a blanket with their baby under the boardwalk.

Atlantic City is unfortunately a place where you don't venture past the strip located near the boardwalk. We were warned by locals and our research that one should only venture off the strip and into the city if you are carrying a gun and willing to use it.

We had planned to make a longer run up the Atlantic the next day to a small town, called Manasquan which had a decent inlet some 65 miles away. The problem with the other inlets between Atlantic City and New York, i.e.: Little Egg and Big Egg Harbor are that each Atlantic storm silts in the entrance and the channels change dramatically, causing one to need local knowledge to know where the deep water is. Shallow water in the inlets and heavy winds with opposing currents cause breakers to form. This can make passage very dangerous. Running aground in an inlet under such conditions creates a dangerous situation so we went to bed with ocean on our minds. We would leave at sun up to reduce the chance of late afternoon winds but 65 miles at six to eight miles an hour would mean eight to ten hours on the ocean and a long day.

As is our usual routine when making these passages, I wake up around 4:30 to listen to the weather, have devotions, and say a prayer for a safe day on the water. The weather forecast had changed from the night before and the wind was supposed to pick up earlier than expected. So near our departure time of 5:15 the three boats discussed our options. We decided to take the inland route, which is 11 miles longer through some very, very, very shallow and winding waters. Our timing for this route was not optimum because we needed to have as much water under us as possible and we were close to slack low which would have been the best time to exit the Atlantic City inlet and approach the Manasquan channel. But ten hours on a rough ocean was our second choice with no options except to battle the weather once we committed ourselves.

We left the neon lights of the casinos and hotels behind us as well as

$5.00 Chris left for Mr. Trump and headed into the skinniest part of the eastern inter-coastal. Our time spent on the Gulf of Mexico in shallow water had given us some experience with the security of minimal depths under our keels but the charts recorded certain areas of this route to be only equal to our drafts at low tide which was within the hour.

I volunteered to put our inflatable in the water and run in front of the boats with my depth sounder on to find the deepest part of the channel and verify that we had enough water to skim through safely. Four and a half feet would be the magic number and if I got a reading of less than that I would relay the message to Chris via walkie-talkie and she would share the information with Paul and Bill. We would have to hold up and drop anchors in the channel to wait for the tide to give us a little more water. Several times the depth sounder bounced briefly between four and five feet but everyone continued to follow in step with my wake. After several miles of nail biting anticipation of grounding we were safely in 15 feet of water and I returned to the comfort of the mother ship. The day was long; peppered with bridges, channels, low water, windy bays and populated communities but we passed the test; Bill only bumping the muddy bottom once. We all arrived at our destination 11 hours later. Sleep would come early and be very sweet.

We set the anchors for the night in a river five miles from the inlet to the Atlantic and searched the shoreline for a place to land the dinghy for a long awaited walk on terra firma. We also needed some groceries since we had not re-provisioned since being in Solomon's Island some ten days prior and the stores were getting scant. A gentleman was working on his boat tethered to a private mooring buoy and when we inquired as to where we might find a small grocery store he offered to drive us to one and let us use his dock to land. We assured him we needed the walk but took him up on the offer to park for an hour or so. A mile away we discovered a wonderful meat market and deli as well as produce stand where Bill and I talked to the owner and learned some new four letter words while the girls did a little shopping.

The next morning we would make the last leg of our Atlantic Ocean voyage on the way to the Narrows and New York Harbor. There is no other option but to run the 35 miles outside so we were hoping the wind would cooperate or we would have to wait for a weather window. The channel leading from our anchorage was narrow and the current runs like a freight train through this manmade trough skirted by homes as it drains the inland waterway through the Manasquan Inlet into the ocean. So we made ready for this Nantucket sleigh ride and headed for the opening. Just before rounding the corner and into the ocean there are two bridges; one of which has a five foot vertical clearance and is used for passenger trains which infrequently bring tourists to the area. The chart books say that it is usually open and closes occasionally. I had just talked to Paul and Stacy on the radio about a man from our club who had traveled the Swinomish Channel near LaConner, Washington, for many years and who had passed by a similar bridge a myriad of times. The swing railroad bridge was never closed and in all our years of boating there, the bridge has never been closed except the time this gentleman and his wife were driving from their lower helm station and took it for granted that it would be open. By the time he noticed it was not, the current had taken him under the bridge, ripping the top off his 32 foot Grand Banks. The moral of the story is to always anticipate that it could be closed. Bill was in front of us and had just passed the bridge with us close behind him and SeaSea behind us when the bridge started to drop with almost no notice. Chris was driving and quickly threw both engines in reverse in time to stop our race to the ocean and make the turn to a safe spot behind the bridge as a train thundered by. Ten minutes later we proceeded through the open bridge, glad we had been on our toes and ready for the unexpected.

The forecast was ideal, with winds at five knots, but the residual waves from higher winds the day before sent swells into the channel. We bobbed fore and aft out onto the ocean past the heavily guarded jetties and made the turn to port in these rollers. The day broke glorious with dolphins on our bow and the sun peeking over the horizon to the east, greeting us and seeming to say, "Welcome"! We replied with a sincere "Thank You"! What a day to be on the ocean and what a pleasure it would be to enter into New York Harbor under such ideal conditions. Four hours later we saw the skyline of New York and in another hour we had made the turn around Sandy Hook headed for the Hudson River.

Since 9/11 the security measures and police presence in the city and around all bridges, buildings, monuments and military vessels and installations has been greatly increased. Police boats circle around all the bridge abutments and there is a restriction that all pleasure craft stay at least 25 yards away from all bridge supports. There are safety and security zones that are off limits and when transiting any waterway with military vessels you must stand off a minimum of 500 yards which in some cases is hard or impossible to do.

New York harbor is one of the busiest in the world with tugs and barges, ferries and tour boats, navy ships and huge ocean going freighters sharing a limited amount of space with pleasure craft that come last on the pecking order. You monitor 13 and 16 on the radio and stay out of everybody's way and everything will be just fine. The water is constantly being churned by propellers and hulls of all kinds, and the wakes from everyone going in every direction, creates a less than desirable situation to leave the wheel and snap a quick picture of this awe inspiring moment. All this, while the Statue of Liberty, Ellis Island, the Empire State Building and the high rises of New York City loom above you puts you into a sensory overload. It is an experience that can only be compared third to getting married and watching the birth of your children and grandchildren. The awesomeness of the city and fact that we had traveled some 4500 miles and 8 months to get here made us feel like New York was home. Our landing spot would be the 79th Street Boat Basin on Manhattan Island 7 miles up the Hudson River. After our spirits returned to our bodies and we had taken every photo opportunity possible in front of the "Grand Lady of Liberty", while dodging heavy tourist and commercial boat traffic, we headed up the Hudson against the current. We were leaving salt water for the last time on our journey and entering a new phase of navigation.

Our daughter Anna, and son-in-law Jeff, were also in New York City so we were elated that the weather had allowed us safe passage and time to spend with them. Bill and Gail and Stacy and Paul would meet up with us at the basin where we had secured mooring buoys for five nights at $30.00 a night in the heart of the action and only a short dinghy ride to a nearby secured and gated municipal dock. What a bargain when dock space would run us several dollars a foot per night and hotel rooms in New York City would range from $200 to $500 a night. The mooring buoys were exposed heavily to the wake of all the passing traffic up and down the river during the day. Fortunately we would be out exploring during that time but at night the water calmed down and the sleeping was peaceful. When we returned to the boat after a full day in New York City we would put the books back on the shelf and rearrange a few things that had been jostled in our absence. We were securely planted within a short walk to the subway and some wonderful inner city markets. In the morning we could watch the passing of bike riders, joggers and strollers along the park path which was less than 100 yards from our moorage and kayakers paddled around our boats in rented kayaks, inquiring about our trip and welcoming us to New York City. The people of New York City were wonderful and very friendly. They were helpful to us and each other and never did we feel overwhelmed or apprehensive.

The weather was outstanding with temperatures in the 80's and people were out in hordes enjoying the official start of summer and the Memorial Day weekend. I could write a whole book on our time in the city alone but with all due respect New York City surprised me with its: friendliness, cleanliness, awesome restaurants - some 4500, Broadway shows - we saw "Jersey Boys"; the story of the Four Seasons; and Central Park which is huge and magical and diverse and wonderful. It has a fabulous transportation system and we had a general feeling of safety. In addition the bakeries were wonderful and the fruits and vegetables we bought in the compact community markets were the best we have ever eaten. We attended a street celebration in Little Italy. We picnicked and played Frisbee in Central Park, while listening to an African music concert. We ate pizza. We attended a huge street fair near our little harbor and visited Grand Central, the United Nations and the Metropolitan Museum of Art. We had ice-cream from one of the many vendor trucks that station themselves conveniently around the city and we spent time with the kids exploring the city and sampling the best of the best foods. Jeff and Anna took us out for breakfast to a remarkable hotel where they were staying. They only do breakfast and celebrities frequent the place because of the unique fair and exceptional quality and service. They also took us to a Thai place in another section of town and then we grazed our way around New York City sampling the Cuban, Italian, Japanese and Irish Pub fare. There is a lifetime of eating here without ever repeating a restaurant.

On Sunday evening we attended a church service near the boats. The introductory music was jazz Christian and the worship service was wonderful. The church was packed with young people. Never in our lives had we been so elated to see so many young Christians worshipping together. We were by far the oldest people there.

A solemn visit to ground zero ended our stay in the city. A cross made from the metal girders of the twin towers stands as a monument to the lives lost and coins thrown through the peek holes into the new construction zone are a testament to the memory of this horrific day and the lives lost. Not too far from the site is "Fire Station 8"; first responders to the scene, who lost many in their brave and sacrificial rescue efforts. Thank you to all who put their lives on the line for others.

We said good-bye to Jeff and Anna after experiencing an unbelievable and memorable time with them. They had made our stay exceptional and our time with them will be treasured for a lifetime

That night we moved the boat to the dock in the dark and filled with water in anticipation of an early start. We were headed up the Hudson on another of the many adventures awaiting us. The Erie Canal waited ahead of us. The Great Lakes were calling our names and the journey would continue - our minds filled with so many awesome memories that "grateful" can't even come close to describing how fortunate we are.

We went to bed after returning to our little mooring ball in the shadows of the skyscrapers of Manhattan. The night air was calm and cool, and the sounds and images of New York City danced in our heads. Good night!

Good morning! The trip up the Hudson into upstate New York will have to wait for another day. So much to share and so little time to write and read!

Blessings to all,
Let us know what is new in your lives,
Love,
Chuck and Chris

LOOPET 15

NEW YORK CITY THROUGH THE ERIE AND OSWEGO CANALS

DEAR Friends and Family,
   Leaving New York City we meandered our way up the Hudson River. The tidal effect from the Atlantic on the Hudson reaches some 150 miles north to the city of Troy, New York, close to where the Erie Canal starts, so we had to plan our exit strategy as to not buck the current all day. Tides and currents aren't always in sync so we waited until the boats started facing upstream then sadly waved so-long to one of America's greatest cities.

   The Hudson is a huge river, dotted with little towns along its banks much like any large water transportation route. The trains - both cargo and high speed passenger linking people with New York City, skirt the shoreline; so wherever you anchor along the Hudson you are sure to contend with train noise. Sometimes they are so close you can almost count the freckles on the faces of the business men and women staring out the windows at our little armada as they commute to the city each and every day from up state.

   The river is deep to the shoreline and well marked so that navigation is simple with only an occasional challenge. The scenery rises more steeply than what we have been accustomed to along the Atlantic seaboard. This was the first time we had been out of saltwater since leaving the Tenn-Tom at Mobile, Alabama.

Pollepel Island was our first stop some 40 miles upstream and yes it would be close to a train tunnel which meant heavy blasts on the horn day and night as passengers stared out the windows into our little river world. Who knows what they were thinking as they caught a glimpse of us at anchor 200 feet away.

The island is abandoned and hosts a huge deserted medieval looking castle built by an arms salesman who developed the island into a private retreat and arsenal. It is a place that could have been the inspiration of Edgar Allen Poe's writings and even though the island was off limits we took the dinghy around the shoreline and investigated this haunted looking, dilapidated old fortress from a short distance. We went to sleep that night in its silhouette clearly visible in the golden moonlight - safe at anchor along the Hudson. We also left behind the stone fortress city of "WestPoint" which is no longer available as a stop since 9/11; its ramparts perched on a curtain of granite at the river's edge. A visit to the army's elite officer training university would have to be for another day.

Breakfast on the run is the norm so after an engine room check, anchors were pulled and we worked our way out of the narrow slit of deep water that had led us to our castle. Freighters passed in the channel as we entered the main stream of the river and the sun warmed our spirits as we prepared ourselves for another day on the Hudson. Current would continue to be a factor so we timed our departure to get the best and longest push possible. We were headed for Catskill in the heart of the forested Catskill Mountains which are not to be mistaken for our definition of, "the mountains of the west", but still very beautiful. There would be free docks waiting which was part of a restaurant that caters to boaters and allows free moorage if you have dinner with them - so we did. The main street of this little riverside town is lined with uniquely decorated, large papier-mâché cats of every kind, texture and persuasion representing different sponsoring individuals and businesses, much like the cows and horses and salmon statues which have shown up in other cities across the United States.

The Hudson River has many small tributaries that add to its volume and at the confluence of the larger ones as well as at tricky bends and shoal areas along the river stand numerous lighthouses to warn mariners and guide river travelers safely home. Many are still manned and are extremely quaint and colorful - like little storybook cottages set apart on tiny rock out-croppings - ready to tell their tales of time past. Enormous, old mansions, dating back to the Revolutionary War, which have entertained the presence and conversations of generals and presidents alike sit high atop some of the bluffs along the Hudson. Many of these manicured residences were also built by the influential industrialist who made New York what it is today.

The river was running strong to the south when we woke the next morning so we decided to wait for a couple of hours until the ebb ceased and the flood started. The tide was close to its low and had left an ugly mudflat on the opposite side of our dock but there was plenty of water under our keels so we could exit at will. Large logs floated by and fishermen dotted the little point of Cat's "Kill" or Cat's "Creek", trying their luck for a pan size or larger bass. A deer swam the river in front of us and a sailboat hailed us on the radio hoping that we could create a large enough wake to float them off the sandbar prison that had captured them in a moment of inattentiveness.

Eventually the tide turned and we proceeded out of the creek and onto the river for a third day of travel north. Our wake freed the victim sailboat and we were off to our destination of Waterford, New York. It hosts the beginning of the infamous Erie Canal and the place where one fork of this water road leads you to Canada via Lake Champlain to the east and the other leads to Canada after transiting the Erie and Lake Ontario. We turned to port and after transiting a lock and passing the capital of New York at Albany, leaving all the tidal flow and river currents behind, we pulled into Waterford for an extended stay. We would clean the boats, and position and re-provision ourselves for the 24 locks on the historic Erie and the 8 locks of the Oswego Canal.

Waterford gets the congeniality award of any of the towns where we have had the pleasure to be temporary citizens. Our five day stay would allow us to get to know some of the area and experience the friendliness of its people. To begin with, the town provides free dockage with electricity and water for two nights and after that you can stay as long as you need to for an additional $10.00 a night no matter what size boat you are. There are also restrooms and showers just above the docks and a nice visitor center staffed by volunteers who will help you with any of many requests. The grocery stores there leave some of their carts at the dock so you can use them for doing laundry and hauling groceries back and forth from the local grocery store across the bridge. The townspeople sponsored an historic walk along the Champlain Canal with free tee shirts and a nice hot dog lunch to follow for those who completed the trek.

Our grocery shopping trip found us caught in a rainstorm as we raced across the bridge, like some crazy juggernaut in a soap box derby of grocery carts. Last year, when the Erie Canal flooded and traveling boats were floating over the tops of the lock walls and into the countryside and mariners found themselves swept under bridges and trapped by these steel overpasses, the town of Waterford came to the rescue. By housing people, delivering food and water, and providing transportation and encouragement, they established the "Lock Three Yacht Club" to make the several week ordeal tolerable. Thank goodness the weather this year was not as brutal. Due to the previous year's ordeal and in order to attract boats to the canal, our transit this year would be free.

This little town is the gateway to the Erie and has entertained every size and shape and type of cruising boat and yacht that can whittle its height to 21 feet or less. Sailboats must have their masts stepped by this time at a marina downstream and antennas, radar arches and biminis that are not within the specification must be lowered to clear the bridges and lock structures ahead. The gates to "Lock 1" rise in front of the Waterford docks like the doors that held back King Kong from the city of New York. Most boats are heading west on the Erie, which runs east and west and was built in the very early 1800's. The canal itself runs east and west until you make another decision over 100 miles upstream to continue west on the Erie to Buffalo or take the Oswego Canal 24 miles north to Lake Ontario, which is what we had planned. In the beginning ... the Erie Canal was transited by barges pulled by mules - the paths of which still border the old sections of the canal. The Mohawk River, which makes up part of the route was at one time a Native American water trail used by the 6 nations of the Iroquois. There were many British, French, Indian and American battles fought during and after the revolutionary war, in and around the present location of the canal.

The locks themselves are working antiques with brass polished circuitry and gold and blue painted lock houses inset in park-like settings much like diamonds are set in unique and beautiful jewelry. Leaving Waterford, five locks come in rapid succession to lift boats 169 feet. Each has its own personality to include the lock masters and their unique style of communication and cadence of the water flow. Some locks have ropes and some have cables and some have ropes and cables dangling on their walls with which to lash your boat for the ride up or down each water elevator. Some locks are bigger than others and some are deeper than previous or future locks. Some have rough sides of concrete from ages of use and some have been refurbished with smooth metal or concrete sides.

The Erie Canal takes you through the back country of New York State through industrial towns that have become or are on their way to extinction. It is sad to tie above or below the lock for the evening in a town that once flourished along this important route of commerce, which today is transited mainly by pleasure craft. Names like Mohawk Carpet Mills and Beechnut Foods use to employ generations of Americans in these thriving towns which today have become destitute and desolate - soon to be no more unless their leadership resuscitates life back into them with a new paradigm. Fabulous turn of the 18th and 19th century brick homes line the streets, for sale, cheap. The citizens that remain sit on their porches hoping someone will come forward with a solution or commute to distant places for employment. In the rare instance some towns have built docks that cater to us weary water wayfarers and invite us to stay for free; embracing us in hopes that we will leave a little of our hard earned cash behind in local restaurants and grocery stores. Even the kids have become discouraged and in some cases entertain themselves by scribbling graffiti on the vacant buildings and harassing the boaters as they pass by their shoreline of despair. It is sad to see them close to death. The canal itself is beautiful and a trail for bike riding and walking skirts it banks making it a wonderful spot to stop for the night, along the walls of this museum. Cars cruise by us and gawk as we become their entertainment for the evening.

We traveled through Scotia, Amsterdam, Canajoharie, Herkimer, Rome, and Brewerton and then onto the Oswego Canal and the city also called Oswego. Three locks dropped us down to the level of Lake Ontario.

Canajoharie, which means in Indian, "The pot that never needs to be washed", is one of those little cities trying to come into the 21st century. The name comes from a smoothly hewn rock punch bowl that the river has carved in the sedimentary stone bed as it swirls and spills itself over into a set of cascading waterfalls. On the hot and humid day we traveled through there it felt good to hike the river and enjoy the evergreen forests and wild flowers in the hollow of this ancient valley.

Friends of ours from our church in Vancouver, Washington met up with us for the second time on the journey as they visited their son and daughter-in-law to assist with lambing not far away from there. They spent the night on the boats and then traveled up river to Herkimer with us where a car waited for them. Eric, their son, was good enough to take us on a tour of his sheep farm and show us around the area. He and his wife raise lambs, sell wool and yarn and grow most of their food on the 160 acres 1400 feet above the Mohawk Valley. They started with a few sheep and have grown the flock to over 350 - diversifying into other retail items. Chris and Gail got a chance to be surrogate moms to three lambs who had been orphaned when their mom died after giving birth to them, which is usually the case when triplets are born.

Interestingly enough this area is quickly becoming an area where the Amish are settling. Several families in traditional dress were fishing and having a picnic in the small park in front of the docks. The women were dressed in long skirts and had shawls over their shoulders and bonnets on their heads. The men, with their home made denim clothing, long hair and beards and distinctive brimmed hats, stood around contemplating important matters centered around farming while their buggies stood at rest and the horses grazed, unharnessed on the grass nearby. A couple of the young men came down and talked with us. As night fell the horses were harnessed to the buggies and the Amish families huddled into the crowded motor-less vehicles with red lantern lights glowing. The sound of the horses' hooves clippity-clopped across the bridge above us until only the silence remained and then they were gone.

The next day we traveled up river with John and Ricki to Herkimer. After a great meal together they headed for the farm and we settled in for a projected wind and hail storm that was brewing just a few miles west of us. We storm tied the boats along a free concrete wall and prepared ourselves for the high winds and golf ball size hail that were hitting Utica.

The wind came up stiffly and the rain passed through but the squall was over as soon as it started and we were spared the smashing and damaging effect of the hail.

Oneida Lake is a part of the Erie water path before the little burg of Brewerton. Our weather was excellent and we crossed this twenty mile stretch in glorious sunshine and no wind or fog which are both common on the lake. It was Sunday and smaller pleasure and fishing boats were out in force. Brewerton, like many of the cities along the route, has a free dock so we took advantage of the luxury and had dinner at a local pub at the water's edge nearby. Two musicians lulled us into submission as we sat on our boats after a delightful dinner. Their notes resonated over the water, interrupted only occasionally by the squawking of the many geese and goslings that make this their summer home. We like they have escaped old man winter and enjoyed eternal summer by heading south and then north at just the right times. It is hard to believe that when the snow flies and the thermometer drops well below zero the ice blankets this lake with a shield over six feet thick. Cities of ice fishing houses will pepper the steel hard surface of the lake and canal and snow mobiles will take the place of the bass boats that scurry about during the summer in search of lunker size pike and bass.

Our final stop before crossing into Canada via Lake Ontario is Oswego, New York. The town is the home of coast guard station, Fort Ontario, a maritime museum, a wonderful waterfront walk, great restaurants and the Guinness Book of Records holder for the most bars on one street. They sport a wonderful canal wall near town where the tie up is free and within view of Lake Ontario. This was an optimum location to wait for perfect weather to dance with our first Great Lake. If the timing is wrong and the weather, wind and fog decide to play havoc with tiny boats the trip can be a nightmare. A young college friend of our daughter's from Rochester, who is a signer for deaf and hard of hearing students at the Rochester Institute of Technology, drove down to spend the evening with us. It was a real treat to catch up on her life. With her gas tank filled and a hug to send her on her way we went to bed. We had passed through lock 8 - the last drop to Lake Ontario's level, late in the evening, so we could depart at 5:00 a.m. before the 7:00 a.m. standard daily lock opening time. The brisk evening wind gave way to a glorious crimson sunrise with only a ripple on the water. We peacefully motored passed the last exit light out of the harbor as the sun showed its face over the horizon. Each of us had set our own route and due to our differences in travel speed would rendezvous several hours later on the other side. As our wakes followed us into this next chapter of adventure, lightning and thunder flashed and boomed in our distant pathway miles ahead. This was one of those milestones on the loop we had only dreamt about and now with only a half hour behind us and four and a half hours ahead of us we put our nose to the north and prayed the weather would hold.

We are now several days into Canada. The crossing was the smoothest we have ever experienced in all the years of traveling across large bodies of water. The trip on the Trent-Severn has been a remarkable one. The weather is hot and humid. The bugs are as thick as the plagues of Egypt and the vegetation in the canal is as heavy as the lettuce in a tossed green salad but we are having a great time.

Blessings to all.
We have picked up a free internet connection so I'll send this off.

From Ontario on the Trent!
Fondly,
Chuck and Chris

LOOPET 16

LAKE ONTARIO TO GEORGIAN BAY AND LAKE HURON VIA THE TRENT-SEVERN

DEAR Family and Friends
We rose at 4:30 a.m. to get an early start across Lake Ontario and into Canadian waters. The roaming internet we have been so blessed to have will not work for us up there so we will have to hunt up WIFI stations and get emails out that way instead of easy access on the boat. I will write the journey from New York City through the Erie Canal and across the lake when we get to the other side. If you need to get a hold of us use the cell number. Fifty-five nautical miles across so at nine to ten knots we should be there in five to six hours. SeaSea and JUWIKA will arrive soon thereafter. An early start before the wind comes up is the best thing to do.

Blessings to all,
Love,
Chuck and Chris from Oswego NY

Greetings to our Friends and Family,

If you are wondering why we haven't written or answered emails it's because internet hotspots are few and far between. One would have to wander the small cities in search of unsuspecting systems - looking for some router or link-system that is not secured with a password or spend hours at the library or internet coffee shop/cafe in order to keep up-to-date.

Last time I was able to connect to the net I glanced at the number of emails building up and it was around 100 and then the signal was gone. To use the Verizon system that has worked so well in the states would cost - as the lady helping me said - "You don't want to know." So we will send things off and stay in touch when we can.

Tonight we are anchored in a small bay on Simco Lake just about forty miles from the end of the historic Trent-Severn Waterway. This weekend is the celebration of Canada Day - July 1st - on Sunday and Monday is a holiday making the weekend a long and busy one on the water and elsewhere. Canada Day is like our 4th of July; so we will raise a glass to this great neighbor of ours to the north. It really is amazing that we are on such friendly terms and able to enjoy their country the way they do ours. It is a pity that the Canadians didn't have a small, warm colony to the south, but then perhaps we wouldn't have such a friendly exchange; as they depend on: Florida, Arizona, California and Nevada for their winter escapes as we depend on them for unbelievable summer cruising in British Columbia.

As I wrote last time, we were preparing to cross the first of the Great Lakes and that is where I will begin. The lighthouse at the entrance to Oswego, NY lit the way out the channel onto Lake Ontario at 5:00 a.m. The sun had not yet risen above the eastern horizon. The wind was as calm as a baby's breath. All three boats, with red and green navigational lights glowing, departed in single file silently; so as to not wake the town and disturb those who wouldn't poke their heads from under the sheets for several more hours. The distant shoreline was invisible and a light blanket of fog lay low to the water several miles out. We each decided to plot our own courses and run at our most efficient speeds once we cleared the outer breakwater; to meet up many hours later at our rendezvous check in point in Canada. The trip across was uneventful - which is what we prayed for - yet very beautiful; as the crimson sky greeted us and illuminated the boats like a back stage scrim in a fancy Broadway show. After several hours we spotted land on the other shoreline and rounded some low, tree covered islands which would lead us to our destination. A light shower had christened the boat and the black clouds, which earlier had produced a spectacular, booming display of electricity, gave way to warm and penetrating sunshine. We gave thanks for such a remarkable crossing.

We settled for an out of the way little marina at a place called Waupoose for our check-in point for Canadian Customs. Here we called from a pay phone to a customs agent who asked us the usual questions concerning: alcohol, tobacco and firearms, fruit, vegetables and meats. Bill and Gail and Chris and I have checked in many times through British Columbia so our information is current and on file. The process went without a hitch, with no inspection, as we were welcomed to Canada and all she has to offer.

The exchange rate is close to par so the usual discount would not apply; keeping many Americans home from travels north. A few minutes later Paul and Stacy checked in and an hour later Bill and Gail finished the process.

The marina was remote, and at $1.25 a foot, we decided to cross over to Waupoose Island just a short distance across the bay where we could tie to a government float for free. We were told that the island was private and that a sheep farmer ran a flock of sheep there. Often times he used the little ramp and dock to transport his flock to and from the mainland. The dock hands, a couple of boys from the town, told us that he wouldn't use the dock till morning. So off we went to our own private little fantasy island.

Upon landing we were greeted by a large metal energizer rabbit sculpture and a few sheep were grazing under a tree nearby. There were some houses in the distance and an old truck near the dock. The dock was big enough to land a good sized helicopter on. The sun was out, the sky was clear and the world looked wonderful.

Paul and Stacy unloaded their bikes. Bill and Gail lifted their dinghy onto our private dry dock for some needed repairs. Chris and I took advantage of having some firm ground from which we could wax one side of the boat.

Paul and Stacy returned from their ride with sheep "stuff" caked in their tires and with stories of the little dirt road that circled the island. We were going to get our bikes down but decided that we would clean theirs up after our own exploratory trip around the island. Because our bikes and theirs are fenderless, a narrow racing stripe was displayed between Paul's shoulder blades. We would try and do a better job of dodging the unlimited amount of fertilizer, which covered the two-tired tractor road through the grass at the water's edge.

There was an old English style brick home, reminiscent of the one in the Robert Louis Stevenson novel "Kidnapped" and several cottages with doors and windows wide open and no one in sight. Some looked abandoned and others looked manicured, but there was not a soul to be seen. Sheep were everywhere, including under the pier and post foundations of the homes; which provided shade from what had become a very hot sun. Groves of trees were interspersed around the island, which broke up the meadow landscape that seemed to dominate the interior. Mini flocks of ewes and lambs lay in large groupings under the trees warily eyeing us as we approached. They stampeded away as we passed, with their little black, white and black and white spring-loaded offspring bounding away behind them. There was also an old church and several gates, which had to opened and closed as we worked our way around the perimeter of the island.

Through one gate there was an ancient looking barn, partially dilapidated with an open barn door leading down into a cellar. Inside there were more sheep. The latch on the gate was an old fan belt wound around a series of nails to keep things tight and those sheep in that section. A quaint farm house stood by on a small knoll and a statue of the Virgin Mary looked over the whole tranquil operation. After passing through the gate we were immediately greeted by the "Three Little Pigs"; which took a liking to Chris and her back bike tire and started rubbing themselves briskly against it, almost knocking her over. Stuck by the wool of her chinny- chin-chin in the fence nearby was a ewe protected by her lamb. As I approached in hopes to free her, the lamb rushed at me, bounding high into the air like a grasshopper on a hot paved driveway. It was a real three ring circus. Fortunately through all the excitement the ewe pulled herself loose and raced down the road with her lamb. We jumped on our bikes and the piglets galloped after us hoping to escape the confines of their world through the gate that was the exit back to ours. We returned to the dock with some new smiles on our faces after such an adventure on what appeared to be a deserted island.

That evening before dinner I went for a swim and basked in the sun to the sound of the sheep baaing and the waves lapping against the shoreline. It was a perfect picture of peace and serenity. There was dinner on the dock, a peaceful sunset and a perfect night's sleep; and then there was morning.

Everyone awoke to the warmth and humidity of a near perfect day; thinking that coffee on the bridge and a slow wake up would make the new day an extension of the perfect one the day before. As we lifted the blinds to let in the morning sun we were greeted by what appeared to be a plague of flies, bugs and winged creatures of the insect family. There were literally millions of them on Essi-Anna. JUWIKA and SeaSea were also frosted with the same icing. To open the door meant that a clouded flurry of them would invade the interior to join hundreds that had already found their way through the small cracks and crevices of Essi-Anna and the other boats and were collecting on the inside of the windows. I made a dash outside as hundreds of bugs smashed beneath my feet and hundreds of others fluttering around me like autumn leaves in a wind storm. The boats were crawling with bugs. We were prisoners in our own homes. The girls squirmed as they watched the hoards of insects crawling on the fiberglass - making it alive and black and ugly.

Just as we decided that the only way to exterminate them would be to turn on the wash down pump and hose them off, finishing the job by sucking up the remainder of the soaked swarm with the shop-vac to keep them from plugging up the drains; we looked out and saw the sheep farmer approaching in his small boat – barge in tow, arms waving for us to move immediately. He looked like he meant business and wanted the space where we were tied. Engines were started in an instant and we were gone, bugs and all. They were under foot, on the seats and in, on and around every part of us and the boat. This was the mother of all infestations and our questions as to why we were the only ones on the island were answered.

We rounded the island on our escape route from bug Hell and headed toward Picton, Ontario, which would have to be negotiated through a passage exposed to Lake Ontario. She got in her licks this morning and dished out a little punishment of uncomfortable beam seas for an hour or so before we ducked into protected waters around the point. We rocked and rolled and pitched, with the wind and spray helping us get rid of some of our castaways. But the majority held on tight and followed us to our anchorage outside Picton. After dropping the hook just off the channel leading into Picton and six hours later, after much cleaning, we finally had things back under control. Except for an occasional survivor, life was good again. Thank You, Moses! Let my people go without anymore bugs.

A short dinghy ride and walk to town produced a wonderful almond filled pastry for Chris and one of the finest butter tarts I have ever eaten. To me, mincemeat tarts and butter tarts are two of the great treasures of Canadian cooking. Many more of these delightful sweets would be consumed before crossing back over the border.

The next day we made a gorgeous run from Picton to Trenton, Ontario where we would start the transit of the Trent-Severn Waterway. We had purchased our passes in March and had been reading about this canal system that would eventually release us into Lake Huron, some 240 miles to the northwest. It is a system of 44 locks that was built between 1820 and 1920. When it was finished it was used for protection, commerce and now pleasure. Most of the locks are still hand operated - manually cranked by the lock attendants to open and close the water gates and lock doors. They must be maintained as originally designed and built in order to keep their historic status. Each has a lock house and an adjoining park that is manicured and adorned with Canadian pride. For .85 cents a foot you can tie along the walls leading to and from each lock - no water or electric included - and spend the night or day exploring the little towns that usually are adjacent to these fabulous water elevators. The Trent, as we affectionately call her, is full of life and each little town is alive with activity. Bike paths skirt the canal and make it very easy to explore the countryside. The parks have picnic areas and the entertainment for many of the villagers is to come down to the locks and talk to those making their way up or downstream. The attendants are very helpful and always assist with a little push here, or the handling of a line there, making the experience very enjoyable.

The waterway itself is a potpourri of lakes, man-made canals, marshes and rivers. Many of the canals and lakes are chocked with weeds; requiring us to stop ever so often to reverse our props and quickly spin them forward again to release the salad of grass and vegetation that builds up around the shafts and props. Some of the lakes are huge with moderately deep water, and very rocky, tree-lined coves that remind us of the Northwest. Cedar trees and fir trees cover the small islands and shorelines and the loons echo their haunting calls in the quiet of the evening or morning to remind us that we are so blessed. Turtles, carp, bass, pike, crappie, beaver, muskrat and otters, cranes, gulls and osprey make the waterway their home. Ontario even has a poisonous rattlesnake, which is on its threatened endangered list.

One evening we sat on SeaSea and watched three fishermen fill buckets with crappie. Like poetry in motion they ritualistically hauled in a fish every minute using the same consistent, rhythmic movements.

Some of the canals are cut through sheer rock and are so close to the trees that you can touch them on both sides. The water being a consistent six feet gives us a generous two feet of clearance; if there isn't a log or deadhead lurking below that has been dislodged from the muddy bottom by someone exceeding the six mile an hour speed limit in some of the sections. A few of these narrow canals are only wide enough for one boat to pass. So when entering them from one end or another a security call is made to make sure no one is coming the other way.

The thousands of rocks and tiny islands make navigation challenging but everything is well marked and the awesome beauty of the place is as pleasing as the eye can endure. Wilderness cottages are perched atop gray granite outcroppings and stand alone, taking up in some cases, most of the footprint of the island. They are isolated from the rest of the world except for access by small boats from the mainland. There is no tide so permanent homes and rustic, aged log cabins, cottages and RVs are at the water's edge and at the mercy of the locks and associated dams which control the water level along the canal and in the lakes. There are thousands of them - cottage being only a figure of speech to describe even those palatial estates adorned with variegated "colorful" flower pots, pools and decks. There are always Adirondack chairs, which sit waiting for someone to sit and gaze at the waterway.

Some of the lakes rent house boats; so we share the waterway with these "wall bangers" as they are called. Because the operators are weekend warriors and the house boats themselves, like giant sails in the wind and out of control most of the time; they bang back and forth as they come to dock or enter or exit the many locks. For the most part we haven't seen too many houseboat cowboys but we are always on our guard as one approaches.

Chris and Stacy have skippered our boats through all the locks on the Trent and the Erie; making their total "lockings" some 76 without a single hiccup or mishap. They are praised by the lock masters. I have been told several times, while working the lines in the lock that I have hired a "first rate captain". Chris has done a remarkable job and has stopped taking any advice from me. She has earned that right.

Two of the locks we have transited - one going up 65 feet and one descending 49 feet are called hydraulic lift locks. Instead of the conventional, let the water flow in and out to raise and lower you locks, these unique systems work like two giant cake pans partially filled with water that are lifted or lowered by huge pistons attached to them in the middle. They lower and raise the front and rear hinged side of the pan to allow the boats to enter at the water level you are on. Once the boats are in and tied to the side of the pan the hinged door is closed and the pans go up or down - boats floating inside - much like you would go up or down standing in an elevator. On the trip down you drive into the pan, which is some 50 feet above the level you will drop to below so it appears you are driving off the end of a flat world. On the trip up the same feeling is true, except that at the top of the lift when you look off the back of the boat you are over 60 feet in the air. It is a very different feeling as it appears that your boat has become an airplane.

The villages along the Trent have their act together. They have done what the towns along the Erie need to do. We spent two days in Frankford at a fabulous, free fiddle festival with professional fiddlers, dancers and entertainers arriving on patio boats along the canal from all parts of Canada. Sunday morning the fiddlers played for an ecumenical service under the fiddle tent and there was a pancake breakfast and lots of homemade pie.

The next stop at Campbellford we were treated with a chocolate factory and a cheese factory as well as a scenic bike path that took us across a suspension bridge and gorge under which flowed a raging river.

Peterborough had a little lake in its downtown area where we found anchorage for three days, protected from the wind in view and sound of the rainbow colored fountain just off our stern. Their chamber hosts a festival of lights each weekend during the summer with fireworks and free live music in the park. The park was a hundred yards from where we were anchored and the fireworks went off from a small barge in the middle of the lake we were anchored in. The entertainers for the evening were Herman's Hermits who played until dark when the fireworks lit up the sky above us. They also had a Greek festival the same weekend, an unbelievable Saturday market and the largest museum of canoes in Canada.

The museum displayed canoes of all types and from all regions of Canada; both old and new; from tiny skin Eskimo kayaks to huge cargo canoes that could carry 8000 lbs and were used by Voyagers during the time of the Hudson Bay Company.

A few nights anchored out after leaving Peterborough and we were in Fenelon Falls where Stacy and Paul had arranged for us to tie up at a dock owned by relatives of people they had met earlier on the route in Virginia. Barb and Norm are experienced boaters who own a 42 Hatteras long range cruiser and have done the Great Circle 1 and 3/4 times. They are in the process of converting over to land yachting and had just purchased a beautiful 38 foot motor coach. Ironically they had spent time at the Happy Wanderer with friends, which is where my folks have their winter place.

Their dock is nestled in a cliffed, rocky gorge just west of Sturgeon Lake. It is made of solid concrete with cleats stout enough to allow all three boats to raft together. They had 30 amp shore power for all three boats. The promontories around their place are home to the cliff divers or jumpers or lover's leapers of Fenelon Falls. The weather was hot and humid and the dock and deck and river made it a perfect spot for swimming and staying cool.

The girls each had an air mattress that allowed them to float freely in the current - legs tethered to ropes tied to the dock to keep them from going too far downstream. One afternoon Bill and I towed their little air mattress flotilla upstream toward the falls and let them float leisurely down stream toward the dock. Their laughter could be heard as some of the leapers challenged them to join in the jump. There were no takers.

Each night before bed we would cool ourselves down in the water before retiring for the night; fans blowing overhead and around the bed to keep the hot humid air at bay. I even dove from the top of Bill and Gail's boat to prove that even though I am one year older as of June 15th I am no smarter. I did a pretty good dive, Gail said, and she caught it on film. I also dove under the boats and removed a little grass which the prop spins hadn't touched.

After dinner out with Barb and Norm and a grateful goodbye and offer to reciprocate their hospitality in the Northwest or in Georgia, we passed through the Fenelon Falls lock toward the downhill locks on the last leg of the Trent. Our goal was to clear seven locks and anchor out Thursday night on the other side of Simco Lake and close to Orillia. We would try and get one of the last "buy two nights and get one free night" slips at the Orillia Marina early Friday morning. This is where we would hopefully stay for the long Canada Day weekend - and that is where we are. As I write this I am sitting on our bridge with Essi Anna tied to a twenty-five foot long slip which is all they had left, looking out over the marina quickly filling with party goers from all over Ontario. Boats are coming in like the tide in Nova Scotia and the bagpipers are playing just yards away, accompanying a group of young people dancing the Highland fling. I have eaten one butter tart already and Chris has purchased some éclairs for the evening dessert. An occasional firecracker is heard in the distance as Canadians ramp up for the 1st and this happening weekend. The Canadian flag is flying over the main dock and the local news station has pulled out all the stops with news celebrities and dockside coverage of the event including a giraffe neck, looking camera boom recording the pulse of the docks as each boat sets up their celebration central. The marina will be packed and the festivities in the park at our boat's doorstep are par for the course along the Trent.

Happy 4th to all of you. Happy 1st to us! Our American flag flies proudly beneath our Canadian shade umbrella of red and white maple leaves. May God continue to bless each of you and us as we celebrate our freedoms and remember those who have given so much to ensure them.

God Bless America and God Save the Queen!

From:
"Oh" Can-eh!-da"
Love,
Chuck and Chris

More of the Trent Severn

Greeting to Family and Friends from Killbear Provincial Park, Parry Sound, Ontario.

The wind is howling as we sit at anchor admiring some of the most beautiful sandy beaches on Georgian Bay, Lake Huron. I am preparing to take the girls ashore in the inflatable while the guys sit on the boats and keep anchor watch. Killbear Provincial Park, as it is called, is a huge camping and recreational area for Ontarioites who come here from as far away as Toronto to enjoy the one, two, and three or longer weeks of their summer "holiday". These Canadians are a hearty lot who have a love affair with their lakes, rivers, bays, creeks and forests. They love to fish standing in the water, swim in the balmy 60-70 degree water, drink beer while basking in the water and stroll the shorelines of their fresh water beaches in bikinis and swim trunks; while thunder and lightning crash and flash all around them and rain threatens to negate the promise that God made to Noah. I suppose it is because the winters here freeze everything up solid and they are trapped inside for a goodly part of the year unless they are snow-mobiling polar bears who travel these same waterways on trails made of ice.

For two of the three past nights we have had severe thunder storms and high winds. The anchors have held well and we have fared well; except for being awakened by artillery quality booms in the middle of the night and flashes of blinding lightning that fill the sky in an instance and then leave you groping in the dark. We listen to the weather religiously now that we are on much bigger water and respect the wind. The security of the canal has spoiled us. Today it is whipping up a saucy soup of nine foot waves just miles away outside our relatively protected harbor. Inches of rain gets dumped in a matter of hours and flags on the boats flap like the ears of a wet Labrador shaking itself after a swim.

Laundry day three days ago in Parry Sound was a testament to the nature of the Ontarioites fervor for the outdoors. We were accompanied by a mob of them in the laundromat that was drying mattress pads, clothes, sleeping bags and a sundry of other camp or cottage gear; only to return to their temporary housing for another round of the same the next night. The kids were running around, still in their roasted marshmallow stained PJs, while mom helped dad with the clean-up and discussed mutiny.

More about Parry Sound later but back to where we left off - Canada Day in Orillia! Orillia's celebrity all star is Gordon Lightfoot. For those over 60 and under 45 you may not know who he is, so for homework ask one of us in that age group. The town itself puts on a huge Canada birthday bash and the municipal marina is full of life. The adjoining park is the center of the festivities with a wonderful, old fashioned parade, First Nations craft booths, the usual trailer fast foods, entertainment venues throughout the day and the serving of a gigantic Canadian flag cake made by the local Mariposa Bakery from 30 large size sheet cakes made it a great event. The culminating activity of the day was a sing-a-long which sounded more like the ruckus in a hen house being invaded by a weasel and some spectacular fireworks, which I must say were the best we've seen.

The problem with the whole event is that people drink too much, too fast, too late and that keeps the rest of us up. One evening I had to break up a party at 3:00 a.m. The next night the poor man beside us almost had a heart attack as the two boats next to him cursed and jousted to see who could be the most obnoxious well into the next morning. The police finally arrived and broke things up, evicting the rascals.

Due to the poor quality of our sleeping hours Chris and I complained to the harbor authorities and asked if they could grant us one night free which would allow us to speak kind words of our time in Orillia. In addition we pleaded the same case for our compadres and so we all were given the gift of a gratis night as the docks emptied following what really was a great stay, some scrumptious butter tarts and a challenging botchy ball tournament where the girls beat up on Bill and me!

The next morning was beautiful and sunny. We were on the last leg of the Trent- Severn headed for the final descent to Georgian Bay via a few more locks and the "BIG CHUTE RAILWAY"! This legendary transport system on the way to and from Georgian Bay is an experience of a lifetime and will put a smile on your haircut if you ever get the chance to transit it.

A behemoth yellow iron carriage that resembles a bare bones, altitudinous railway car rides on rails over a granite hill leading from one side of the Severn River to the other. It was built as a temporary boat transport over land instead of a lock and was also built to keep the lamprey eels from migrating into the Great Lakes which a water lock would have allowed. Bill says that he can remember reading about this in his 5th grade reader which tells you how long it has been there. The novelty stuck and a lock was never built so the Big Chute is the only way that boats on the waterway, ranging in size from jet skis to 100 footers can continue their journey to or from Georgian Bay.

We spent the night on the blue line above the Big Chute, which is the name given to the staging place for all locks, hydraulic lifts and the railway on the Trent. This is not to be confused with the adjacent concrete lock walls where you can stay overnight. After the locks close at 7:00 p.m. you can move to the blue line so the lock masters know you are ready for transit. Usually you get on the first load going over the hill in the morning if you have positioned yourself there. We arrived the afternoon before we wanted to be loaded so we could watch the process and become acquainted with the routine. It was fascinating to watch and at the same time there was some apprehension. The tolerance for error is zero - just as it is for doctors delivering babies. Millions of dollars worth of vessels depend on these operators knowing their jobs; and they do.

The process goes like this:

- The giant carriage is pulled up the slope or is gradually lowered down the other side with an elaborate system of pulleys, winches and disc brakes located in a wheel house at the top of the hill.
- The rails go from one side of the mountain to the other and extend into the water to a depth that allows the boats to drive/

float on and off of the slings which support you during the transport.
- The railway operators choose from the boats waiting in order to maximize the load and call you over a PA system.
- When you are called and the carriage is located partially submerged in the water on your entry side you drive the boat into the carriage and the slings are raised just at the right locations under your hull to support your boat during the trip over the hill.
- Your keel sits on the wooden platform, which makes up the floor of the carriage as one leg of the support while the rest of your boat is supported by the slings.
- If your props or shafts extend below your keel they hang your tail end over the back of the carriage as to not damage them. This creates the feeling that you are off balance and that you may slide off the back of the carriage as it rattles up and down and over the mountain.
- The railway wheels run on two sets of tracks which at certain points on the transit take you high into the air over the road and solid pink, gray quartz and granite mountain below you, to the other side.
- The operators are on a little walkway right beside you and you are free to roam around your boat's deck snapping pictures and wringing your hands while at the mercy of these experts.
- On the other side the carriage is partially submerged again and you float off the slings, which are lowered beneath you and away you go – engines restarted and gearboxes engaged.

The whole process takes around 10 minutes excluding loading and you travel some 200 feet in elevation.

Rating this experience is like trying to explain to someone the feeling you had when you first saw Peter Pan fly!

Leaving the Big Chute we wound our way amongst more quaint cottages nestled on rocky outcroppings and precipices; their backyards the evergreen and deciduous forests of pine, cedar and white birch with tons of poison oak and ivy growing like Christmas stockings hung on thousands of mantles; their front yards the narrow waterway that we entered some 240 miles ago; full of water lilies, rushes and wild irises. This journey was supposed to take us two weeks and we have been entertained by, "Her Lady the Trent", for close to a month. We would soon say goodbye to fireflies at night and festivals at every bend - hospitality being the Trent-Severn's middle name.

We refueled at Port Severn before exiting the last lock that dropped us to the level of Georgian Bay which makes up the extreme NE end of Lake Huron. It is an archipelago of 30,000 islands, fishing camps, small towns and remote bays and anchorages. It is a paradise for exploring mixed with challenging navigation and lots of wind and weather. Careful attention to markers and buoys is essential as you wind your way through mine fields of island size boulders lurking just below the surface of the water. Loons make these coves and passage their home and are often seen putting on a display of wing flapping as they appear to be creating some kind of pecking order. Females glide effortlessly across the mirror glass waters with a couple of jet black baby chicks, in tow or riding on their mother's back, as they call to one another in their distinctive voices.

LOOPET 17

GEORGIAN BAY, LAKE HURON TO BYNG INLET ONTARIO

Dear Family and Friends,

Leaving Port Severn, Chris gave a sigh of relief and a smile of satisfaction for navigating the 44 locks without a single mishap or even a close call. She was flawless in her handling of the boat. There was no time for much reflection though as the waterway leading away from the lock and into the bay is strewn with rocks complicated only by narrow passages, hairpin turns and low water - respectfully named "The Potato Patch". In the year 2000 the water level in Georgian Bay was below the level recorded on navigational charts and some of the areas we were passing through, if only one foot shallower, would not be able to be navigated. Fortunately this year water levels are a few inches above chart datum and every inch counts.

Our destination for the first night would be an anchorage on Beausoleil Bay which is a huge island provincial park with many places to drop our anchor, boat camping sites, two youth camps and massive numbers of hiking and biking trails. It is located close to the small resort town of Honey Harbor which can be reached by way of "Little Dog or Big Dog Channels" by dinghy.

Georgian Bay can be traversed by way of a small boat route which winds in and around the 30,000 islands, only poking its channel into the main and exposed body of Lake Huron when rocks and land formations do not allow you to travel inside. There are many narrow inlets that take you back into the interior towns at the heads of these bays. The other route is to run outside the islands as you pick your way back through the rocks at strategic points in order to run up these inlets. There are advantages to both and we have done a hybrid of the two; beauty on the inside and speed on the outside. Of course the wind and waves outside can make for a very sloppy trip if the weather doesn't cooperate.

Many of the pristine beaches and islands are owned by First Nations Tribes and there is a small fee for going ashore and enjoying a walk or sun bath on sandy beaches and in blue waters that remind you of the Caribbean. Beausoliel was not one of those owned by the First Nations peoples so we explored ashore - hiking over the Canadian Shield rock that makes up the area we are traveling through. There is little soil atop this granite surface so the vegetation sinks its roots deep into every crack and crevice it can find and holds on for dear life against the gales that sweep across this landscape in the winter. Winter here is as cold as an empty heart. The trees are distorted and lopsided like ancient travelers, heads lowered and backs bent, from the constant pressure of the storms that buffet the shorelines. These islands are busy places with many vacationers using the rustic facilities, so we went in search of quieter places.

Beckwith Island would be our next stop - owned by First Nations Tribes. We anchored in a small cove on the east side for protection against the west prevailing winds. Even though we were tucked inside, strange roller beam waves rocked us all day and night, making it a very irritating place to stay in spite of its beauty. So when morning broke we decided to head for Frying Pan Island and the famous Pickerel restaurant named, "Henry's," across Georgian Bay and to the north. Beckwith had taken us to the south side so we would have to scoot north with beam seas slapping our port sides for 18 miles, which in boat jargon means, three hours on the back of an angry bucking bull. The wind was supposed to be light but as is the case, you know what the real weather is when you find yourself in it. After leaving the lee of the island and an hour into the trip the seas were building and the boats were pitching like a rocking chair out of control. We decided to change our course and run with the waves on our port rear quarter and head for a small passage called Twelve Mile Inlet at O'Donnell Pass. It is a narrow gauntlet of rocks and ocean spray as the waves crashed over the reefs making the foul ground visible. The night before, I had prepared two routes just in case of a change in the weather; so our entry into O'Donnell was studied and safe. We made our turn between big waves and the ride became much more tolerable. At the light on O'Donnell Point the passage ahead looked like it was a dead-end wall of rocks; but right in front of us were the correct red and green markers which lead us through the blind S turn into tranquil waters. We relayed the route information back to SeaSea and JUWIKA who were behind us, and in another forty minutes everyone was safe and inside.

Marker after marker, narrow passage after narrow passage and island after island; we finally arrived at Frying Pan Bay and set our anchors for the night with plans for dinner ashore at Henry's. They have a dock there but the little bay we were in was within walking distance of the restaurant, so why pay for dock space when that is why you carry an anchor. In a little cove next to us was an old variety/ice-cream/liquor store and gas dock surrounded by a graveyard of broken down vehicles, snow mobiles and outboard motors which had all met their maker on some hidden danger beneath the water, snow or ice; a good reminder to be careful.

Each boat cooks every third day, but when we are in the area of a world famous establishment like Henry's we take advantage of a meal out. People fly in from all over the place on small float planes which arrive like the coming and going of flocks of geese, eager to devour battered or pan fried fillets of pickerel accompanied by coleslaw, beans and fries.

Henry was the founder; who had his fish camp here many years ago and would cook for an occasional passerby who happened upon his remote cabin. Today, it is big business. The fish was well lubricated, the setting and company was excellent and the entire experience was memorable. We even dueled with the owner's daughter over another few pieces of fish and had some good laughs.

A quiet night at anchor, a fun dinner out and off we went toward Parry Sound. We would stop a short way from that destination and anchor for one more night before we would have to re-provision, pump out our holding tanks and spend a night on the docks. That evening we tucked into our own private bay on the lee side of Dunroe Island five miles from Parry Sound and set our anchors in this little nook occupied only by a few cabins, a resident loon family, a beaver mound and now us. The shallow water around the large rock in the middle of the bay had absorbed the warmth of the sun, making it a great place to swim and wade. A loon's nest sprinkled with shell fragments was at the water's edge and fresh water clams dotted the sandy bottom below. Chris, Gail and Stacy got out the air mattresses again while Paul and I built a fire pit for a barbeque we would have later. After the work was done I got out the fins and snorkel gear and dove around the island to check out the life below the surface.

We had a fabulous dinner on the rocks! We each retired to our boats just in time to see massive thunder clouds building in the distance. Before long booms could be heard and as night closed in around us, flashes of lightning kept cadence with the ever increasing explosions. There was no wind and we thought the storm was passing to the north so we went to bed. At midnight we were awakened by what sounded like a freight train roaring through the trees; and the lightning, thunder and rain jumped on us like fleas on a stray dog. The other boats were up too - watching their anchors and keeping tabs on our positions. With radios on 72 we talked with each other for a couple of hours as the boats made circles like competing figure skaters. Around two in the morning the storm turned itself off like a faucet and we retired for the night - the second time. The gentle slapping of the water against the hull, darkness, silence and the call of the loons were all the sleep aids we needed. We knew our anchors were well set and deeply embedded after such a ride. A glance toward the cabins on the distant hillside told us that there was no electricity and off we fell to sleep.

The sun strained its way into a cloudy day as we made our way to Parry Sound. Channel 68 is the standard hailing channel for marinas so I contacted Parry Sound town docks and in we all came. It was so carefree to be tied to the dock after such a tumultuous evening at anchor so we leisurely explored town and had breakfast out. We dumped our accumulated garbage, which is always a byproduct of anchoring out a lot. We prefer a more solitary setting and it is much cheaper too, so whenever we can unload our garbage in a proper fashion we do.

When I started the previous chapter we were in Killbear. Tonight we are two days past there in a little town named Britt, Ontario, several miles up an inlet from Georgian Bay. Most of yesterday and last night was spent with five other Canadian and American boats in the well protected Hopewell Bay.

Bears had been seen there in the morning so we all explored the shoreline in our inflatables looking for the mom and her cubs. Were they gone?

Our journey today was a combination of the inside and outside routes, even though the outside route paralleled and wound us through the granite reefs of the nearby shoreline so closely that you could count the freckles on the rocks. This is a place where no mistakes can be made and where you pray your boats don't have a power failure. The wind from the west blows the water over the rocks below the surface and onto the exposed granite, producing spray and a rough ride in the shallow channel we call "safety". The wind today had whipped up its own version of a spin cycle. We had passed through the narrow S gate at "Hang Dog Pass" where boats over 40 feet are not supposed to go but since we were 39 and SeaSea was 44 and JUWIKA was 32 we averaged the boats' lengths together and figured we could make it. It was much less confining than "Canoe Pass" that we had negotiated the day before and wondered what all the "hoopdeela" was all about.

Rounding the corner and heading along the reefs we counted off the reds and greens; with SeaSea in front using the most updated electronic charts running, which I had purchased in Fort Lauderdale, Florida. JUWIKA took up the rear a couple of miles behind. Bill, Paul and I had met with some Canadian chaps the day before on our boat while the girls were at a floating tea party hosted by Stacy. We were told that the men were not invited to the tea and would have to find another boat to meet on where stories of adventure could be swapped and cigars could be smoked while sipping on a cold beer and sharing information about the leg to be traveled. Ron and Ron, who lived in the area and were traveling together, confirmed that we had the latest paper charts for the next leg; reviewing them with us to pass on local knowledge. They confirmed the electronic version as well, warning us of the mine field of foul ground that lay ahead.

Leaving the two Rons and their wives the following morning, Paul and Stacy, in the lead, picked their way along the route. We confirmed and relayed information back to JUWIKA through the miles of hairpin turns and rocky corridors which made up the channel. Working through the wickets, we arrived at the entrance to Byng Inlet and out of the heavy beam sea slop just as we heard JUWIKA on the radio say that she was at markers "8" and "9" and had just lost her engine. Bill quickly dropped the anchor to keep from drifting onto the rocks and fortunately it bit well. When we heard the call we quickly responded and confirmed that they were indeed dead in the water. We assured them that we were on our way back out as Chris turned the boat amongst the rocks and headed back into the rough water; greens now on the right and reds on the left. Bill and I worked on towing bridles so we would be ready to hook them up and get to safe water as soon as possible while Chris worked her way out the channel. Bill and Gail's boat had turned its nose to the wind and was pounding in the waves but not drifting. Fortunately markers "8" and "9" had adequate maneuvering room around them on one side; the other side strewn with numerous exposed and hidden dangers.

Our plan was to circle JUWIKA, come around her stern and pass by her starboard side without being too close; Bill would throw me a line and I would have to connect JUWIKA to Essi-Anna quickly before the line became strained and the rope was jerked from my hands. Bill, waiting for us and wanting to salvage his anchor, tried to work his way forward, hand over hand on the anchor rope but to no avail. The wind was blowing too strong and the anchor was set deep into the lake's bottom so we would have to try and pull the anchor loose with our boat and then have Bill retrieve it hand over hand while they were being pulled forward. As we put pressure on the bridles JUWIKA's anchor rode became tight but the anchor would not pop loose. The bow pulpit on JUWIKA became strained and began to break. We needed to get underway before floundering in the waves and perhaps getting the lines tangled in our props, which would mean disaster. I yelled to Bill to cut the anchor loose. Quickly Gail produced a big, sharp fillet knife, the rope was severed and JUWIKA's anchor went to Davey Jone's Locker. In spite of the harrowing experience, I couldn't help but think that this would provide Chris and me a great opportunity to sell one of our two extra anchors we had bought as a result of our St. Augustine sailboat fiasco.

SeaSea had followed us out at a safe distance and was giving Chris information on the radio and helping her navigate safely back through the wickets while I worked lines on the swim platform and Bill steered the same path in our wake. The boats pitched and tossed as we turned our beams into the oncoming seas and began the tow at three and a half knots. JUWIKA was 50 feet behind us on the heavy wash cycle. Essi-Anna kept time on the spin cycle as water washed over the swim platform and over my feet. Chris concentrated on staying in the channel. Stacy and Paul led the way as Bill and Gail steered JUWIKA behind us trying to follow in our track. Two hours later, after a lot of teamwork, prayer and divine intervention, our prayers were answered and we were inside safe water and heading for SeaSea who had found an anchorage and was waiting for us to drop JUWIKA off on her side. We would have to glide her next to SeaSea and then release her as Bill and Gail threw lines to Paul and Stacy, bringing her to a halt alongside. Other than the wind blowing hard as JUWIKA landed and SeaSea's bow pulpit coming within inches of Gail's head and their galley window; thanks to Paul's speedy footwork to fend off, she landed safely and that part of the ordeal was over!

The problem was a clogged fuel filter from all the rocking and rolling, even though Bill had changed it three weeks earlier. Paul, Bill and I put together another anchor setup with parts from a small marina nearby and our 33lb. Claw, which duplicated the one that sits on the bottom at the markers on this journey that everyone will remember in their minds for a lifetime. Paul is a mechanical genius and this is only one of many times he worked his magic to get someone back up and running.

That evening we all went out to dinner at the Little Britt Inn and celebrated safety; giving God thanks for safe passage and a quiet and peaceful anchorage away from the outside rocks and reefs.

Today is rainy, windy and cold. We just filled with fuel at $1.12 a litre and rather than going back out on anchor we decided to stay the night on the dock at St. Amant's Marina. This is a rare occurrence. JUWIKA and SeaSea are at anchor a short distance away. Bill and Gail just dinghied in to use the WIFI we got with our night's dockage so we are sitting here with the heater going, drying out clothes and reflecting on how thankful we are for the safety we were afforded. Hopefully tomorrow will be a sunnier day!

From Byng Inlet, Ontario with much love and gratitude,
Let us know how you are doing!
Blessings,
Chuck and Chris

Dear Family, Friends and awesome cruising partners still on the loop,

Chris and I left the boat in Little Current, Ontario until next summer and took a cab a couple hours north; flying out of Sudbury, Ontario to Palm Springs last Saturday a.m. to be with my mom and dad.

My Mom had brain surgery and is recovering in a skilled nursing center. It was imperative that dad had support and with the rest of the family dealing with important, personal issues (having worked through the pre-operation illness and process with them), it was our turn to stay the course.

We will return home to Washington when Mom and Dad are ready to return home to their place in Vancouver. Good Lord willing that will be in a month or so.

More information later.

Pray for speedy and complete recovery as well as peace and joy during the process.

Blessings,
Chuck and Chris

Loopet 18

Byng Inlet on Georgian Bay to Little Current, Ontario

GREETINGS Family and Friends,

It is now the 3rd of October and the last leg of our trip before "Life threw us for the Loop" has not been written. Sorry for the delay but literally, "More water can go under the bridge when you are on land than when you are cruising." Land life is complicated with too many chairs to sit in and too many clothes hanging in the closet and too many trinkets on shelves that are there only for the show and have no practical purpose except to look pretty.

It was July 18th at Killarney, Ontario when I finally got a chance to talk with my Dad.

We had been at anchor for close to a week and were at the doorstep of the North Channel as my Mom got ready to go into surgery for Hydrocephalus – liquid on the brain – which from all indications and previous diagnosis was causing much of her weakness, confusion and the discomfort she had endured for too many years. A temporary lumbar puncture had produced miraculous, "awakening" results so this more invasive "Ventricular puncture" was supposed to produce permanent equivalent lasting results – not without risk – for an 82 year old. All our hopes were high – wanting only the best for a wonderful woman who had suffered too much, yet continued to thrive when all odds were against her. She feared nothing – especially death – yet her hopes were to stay with her family and lead a productive life as long as God's clock on her body continued to tick.

The surgery was July 16th and in the early hours of Tuesday morning Mom experienced three unexpected seizures. She was in ICU when I called Dad on Wednesday, July 18th. His voice was clear that things had not turned out as expected. I told him I would call him again Thursday morning and see if things had improved.

Frustration, pain and concern for Mom's well being were evident as I asked him if we should end the trip and come to Palm Desert, California, to be with them in their winter home, far from their summer home and family in the Northwest. Their time down south had been extended in order to complete the procedures and recovery for Mom before heading north. Time slipped by and delays due to health issues extended the time scheduled for the surgery. Now the hopes of a new and better life were being dashed against the rocks, much like the waters of Georgian Bay pummel and erode the hardened granite as the winds blow across wide, deep expanses, creating a foamy confusion in navigating already disturbed waters in fragile fiberglass boats.

Dad's answer was different than usual – the chosen route, foggy and shrouded with uncertainty, but his words rang out like a red navigational gong leading us from treacherous water into a safe harbor, "I think that would be a good idea, son.", was all that needed to be said. The decision was made before the words left his lips. We would be packed and ready to leave our journey and friends behind before the sun rose the next day for something much more precious and important – my Mom and Dad.

The Loop journey continues! We had no idea that our lives and our adventure would take such a dramatic turn.

We left St. Amant's in Byng Inlet under beautiful, sunny, powder blue skies, headed for Beaverstone Bay some 40 miles away. The rain had subsided the night before and the weather forecast was for light winds as we exited the same narrow entrance we had pulled JUWIKA through to safety two days before. We would have to duck in and out of treacherous, narrow boulder strewn channels; navigating the last 15 miles by way of a newly charted route of open water and a keyhole entry channel leading into protected waters. We had reviewed these with local yachtsmen while the girls whiled away the afternoon over tea on SeaSea some days gone by. The trip was uneventful with several options for anchorage planned should the weather deteriorate before reaching our destination.

The scenery in this area of Georgian Bay is different than the previous leg in that the Canadian Shield rises higher above the water and the granite takes on a soft pinkish hue. A closer inspection of the surrounding cliffs revealed ribbons of quartz laced throughout. A variety of trees stand in forests much like those of the Pacific Northwest and copious gardens of wild blueberries take their foothold higher above the water's edge; wherever an indentation in the plated rock allows decaying matter, moss and windblown debris to collect, creating a natural vessel filled with the richest of potting soils. Small streams and lakes dot the landscape – water lilies and bulrushes abound.

The blueberries that abound here are different from the dark blue/black huckleberries Chris and I grew up eating as kids. They grow low to the ground and have a milder flavor yet they are very delicious and plentiful as long as you haven't been the second one to visit the fields, shared by: bears, chipmunks and other critters of the forest. We took the opportunity to enhance our diet with fresh berries on our breakfast cereals, blueberry scones and desserts for many days while we traversed this beautiful area.

Just a short 20 miles from Killarney we dropped anchor in the lee of a series of small islands. It is one of the most scenic areas we have been in and one that made our hearts reflect on home and the cruising we do in Washington, Alaska and British Columbia. All the water is fresh and the environment seems much more sterile than the saltwater coastlines of the Pacific Northwest. There were no bears roaming the beaches in search of a mussel and crab dinner beneath the boulders that lace the shoreline. There were only a few deer, no seals or whales, no otters and fewer birds than we encountered on the Mississippi and other legs of the journey; with the exception of the ever present gulls which seem to follow us wherever we go.

A trip to shore and a closer inspection of one of the many remote and private cabins which dot the shoreline revealed numerous rakings of claw marks across the rustic log siding – evidence that black bear are present though never seen by us. Mice are prolific; their little telltale licorice colored droppings were everywhere. We were visited by a mischievous weasel family as they checked us out on their way to their favorite rocky playground.

The sun baked down on huge boulders, arranged in circles in the shallow water creating bathwater warm tubs which served as gigantic therapy pools. I took advantage of the opportunity to get into the water; followed by dragging myself up onto a smooth, barren, granite hot plate sculptured perfectly for my shape; for a penetrating radiation of heat which cooked any kinks and tension from my very soul. Chris and I felt like turtles basking on a log as we closed our eyes and let the warmth soak in and through us.

Dinghy forays ashore for hikes and berries, visits with other boaters at anchor close by and brief talks with some locals who were burning garbage in a burn barrel at their cabin made two days go by like water under our keels and then it was time to move on.

This area is also an area where many people charter boats for a week or so. Before long our little anchorage behind the islands and out of the prevailing winds became a bit more congested as four other boats pulled in, two of which were charters and two local cruisers.

We had heard chattering on the radio and saw at a distance other boats pass close to our little paradise, continuing on into Collin's Inlet and beyond. Many we knew as acquaintances from previous anchorages and docks. They were moving on to Killarney and then the famed North Channel – pushed by their own timetables and migratory instincts. That evening we had snacks aboard SeaSea as Stacy worked her hospitality magic and invited our temporary neighbors in our little bay for a social hour on their aft deck.

Earlier in the day we had taken our dinghies on an exploration around and through the narrow boulder strewn passages and came upon a group of guys sending up smoke signals at the trash barrel; where they rid themselves of paper and other burnables which they didn't want to boat out. One of them owned a remote fishing cabin on the lake from which he and his family and friends had fished and vacationed for years. He shared stories of the lake's water level dropping drastically and pointed out evidence of the old waterlines and the receding depths which now make this area much more hazardous to navigate. He also shared tales of the cruelly cold winters in this remote area, accessible only by boat in the summer and snow mobile in the winter; where generators, candles, lanterns and wood stoves are the only forms of light and heat for the cabins. Cabins is a relative term as many of these winter homes are quite exquisite even though they lack all the on grid conveniences of the homes of us city mice. Apparently, one of the owners of a nearby cabin was a wealthy neighbor, who was associated with the Seagram's trademark; often times came up before the winter hoards arrived and cut, split and stacked wood for his friends, so they would be cozy and warm upon their arrival. This was a friendly gesture for one so well to do.

The next day it was time for us to move on. We were heading for another anchorage a short hop away which would offer us more protection from the wind which was supposed to shift and rise on us over night. The morning was warm and sunny without a cloud in the sky and without a whisper of breeze. It was a perfect morning to slide through the narrow passages and shallow water which ran between the rocky bluffs leading to Collin's Inlet and another archipelago of islands and boulders. The water is sky blue in this area and the shallows are choked with weeds. The cautiously navigated, short jaunt brought us to our next stop in no time. We slipped down a long finger of water on a dead end bay only to find a very small sailboat tucked in behind the point of one of the islands. It was one of the boats we had met at our last stop; the owners of which had cruised this area for many years and had fallen in love with the place. They had actually purchased land on the American side of the North Channel where Lake Huron and Lake Michigan meet. There they built a pole barn to store their 24 foot sailboat, which by the way was in pristine condition. Each summer they spend time gunk-holing the North Channel and Georgian Bay. Their names were Ralph and Pixie and they delighted us with their tales of adventure both here and on the second of their floating loves; a splendid canal boat on the romantic Canal du Midi, in southern France. They both were accomplished yachtsmen (she was a captain) and authors (he was the author); as well as being professionals in other fields. Over a glass of wine they shared tidbits of their journeys with us. They had published a couple of guides, one of which we instantly fell in love with, on cruising the ancient Canal du Midi, which dates back to the 1600's. Here we come, France!

Upon our arrival, Chris and I decided to duck a little deeper into the finger between a bluff and an island. With Chris as a bow lookout and me watching the depth sounder we could see that the bottom was coming up and the water was infested with the dreaded weeds we had encountered on the Trent-Severn. Just as we were coming to a halt and started backing up into the 15 foot water mark, Ralph came on the radio and said they had actually almost gotten stuck the previous year in the octopus-tentacled grasses and weeds just ahead of us. He agreed that the spot we were now hovering in was a better choice to drop the hook. SeaSea and JUWIKA followed suit and dropped their ground tackle, one – two, behind us, and we all settled into this perfect little cove before it was time to make lunch. I wriggled into the wet suit and went for a long swim to the other boats; and then climbed some cliffs to pick blueberries for tomorrow morning's hotcakes. Meanwhile Chris lounged in her air mattress armchair I had bought her; tethered to the swim platform and swinging in rhythm with Essi-Anna, reading another book in the warm midday sun. We know this doesn't hold a candle to what Heaven will be like, but it sure was a good appetizer.

Later in the day we skimmed across the weed beds in the inflatable and poled our way into shallow leads a quarter of a mile from our little anchorage. We picked and ate berries. Then we spied on a mink family whose home we discovered under a huge flat rock at the water's edge. We sat there in silence as these inquisitive, sleek little masters of stealth popped in and out of sight amongst the rocks, wondering who these strange intruders to their peace, serenity and security were. That night we revisited their home and watched them by flashlight while, what sounded like a wolf, howled its eerie melody in a far off hollow. The wind had not yet materialized and a million stars lit the sky like brilliant white sparklers on the Fourth of July. Sleep, as usual, was sweet; as the slowing cadence of the boat swinging on anchor closed our eyes. They were not to open again until the sun would keep its promise of a warm awakening once more.

We were only a stone's throw from Killarney now but our religious, a.m. visit to the radio and our conference with Bill and Paul made it clear we were in for a blow associated with lots of rain and heavy lightning and thunder. Our passage was a protected one except for about four miles of open water just before Killarney. Killarney is situated on a narrow channel with virtually little or no room for anchoring. We had heard that one of the major transient marinas had closed down and that the other one was booked solid. So we took into account the forecasted winds and decided to tuck into another little bay behind Keyhole Island just before the open water of Lake Huron leading to Killarney. After dropping the anchor we called the marina and they actually had space for us the following day. One more night on the hook and we would end the week with a day at the dock where we could water up and fully charge the batteries again. During the entire journey of some 6,000 miles we had saved thousands of dollars in dock fees by anchoring out. It is something we much prefer and with the new claw anchor back on the bow pulpit of Essi-Anna we had the confidence to sleep soundly in almost any kind of weather and under most conditions. It was another, amazing day of exploring and berry picking; to include a delicate patch of wild raspberries; poling our way around beaver dams and through beds of blossoming water lilies in the inflatable. We had dinner together and saw a movie before bed as another beautiful day ended.

As we went to bed the wind came up a bit and an occasional rumble of distant thunder told us the forecasted storm was brewing. We all let out a bit more anchor rode and pulled the covers over our heads in a good night gesture. Morning broke with a dark and foreboding sky. The black clouds billowed over the distant mountains from the north and the penetrating winds found their way into our peaceful little sanctuary. A few raindrops began to fall and then claps of thunder could be heard moving in our direction like the roaring of heavy, steel military tanks as they make their way into battle. Streaks of lightning flashed around us and in a matter of minutes the boats were slammed with gale force winds. Our positions on our anchors swung 180 degrees in an instant. The sheer, 300 foot granite wall that had been a magnificent backdrop and view from our bow was now at our stern and even though a fair distance away was now what we would slam our stern into in very short order should our anchor give way. The powerful wind came in gusts and at times punched us, retreated and then punched again making the boats shudder under the immense strain of our life line to the bottom. The rain started to pour out of the sky as though a heavenly ocean had lost its bottom and the boat windows began to fog up so that JUWIKA and SeaSea were blurred in the deluge.

I called to the other boats and told them I was going to start my engines so I would be ready should our anchor start to drag. I knew that if for some reason the shackle broke or the anchor popped loose I would have no time to start the engines and respond before being driven into the wall behind us. Should need be, we would battle the wind with the power of the boat to assist the anchor. We all chatted back and forth on the radio as the boats tugged and tossed in the wind waves created by this threatening but brief squall. The anchors held. The winds and clouds passed within a half an hour. The waves melted back into the depths of the lake and the sun poked it friendly face back into our lives as we headed into the baby-blue eyed, open waters of Georgian Bay on our way to Killarney five miles away. We had made another safe and adventurous passage.

Killarney is a quaint little town on a channel leading to more beautiful scenery and anchorages. It is reminiscent of what La Conner, Washington, one of our favorite stops in the Northwest, may have been like before too many people arrived. For the first time in a week we saw cars again and roads here actually led someplace. The waterway is a major thoroughfare traveled by most boaters who are heading to and from the North Channel which starts just west of Little Current, Ontario about 20 miles toward the setting of the sun. The water is crystal clear and unbelievably pristine. The buildings which line this narrow waterway town give the flavor of a village on the coast of Nova Scotia with their net shed looking roofs and ancient looking docks jutting out into the channel, beckoning travelers to stop and spend some time and money. It is far from touristy but laid back and relaxed; with fresh white fish served from a red school bus restaurant; eaten off of paper plate boats, on outside picnic tables with buttery scoops of Farquar ice cream, served for dessert or an appetizer from stilted lopsided building at the water's edge. These treats were the delight of our palates, after having been at the mercy of our own cooking for the last week.

The weather had turned for the better and the wind was on a retreat. Paul and I sat in the lounge overlooking the channel and caught up on emails as we discussed the trip and where to go from here. Bill and Gail would pick up Bill's brother and a friend and proceed through the North

Channel at a different pace than our two boats would travel. JUWIKA had to be in Petoskey, Michigan, on Lake Michigan and back in the U.S., where Bill and Gail would leave her for ten days to do a road trip to a family reunion in Wisconsin. Whereas; we on SeaSea and Essi-Anna would leisurely meander through the North Channel and rendezvous with JUWIKA: after visiting Mackinaw Island; clearing customs at Drummond Island; making a long run down Lake Michigan to Chicago, where we would continue on together to our final haul out location at Springbrook Marina 50 or so miles down the Illinois River.

The phone call to my Dad Thursday changed all that in a few words. "I think that it would be a good idea if you came home son." he said.

It was late in the afternoon and we had to act quickly to put all the new plans in motion. This is an area that gets extremely cold in the winter – the water freezes over and boats are stored on dry land. So we would have to find a place to haul Essi-Anna out. Another alternative would be to make a very fast run to Lake Michigan and have Kenny, (our boat hauler), meet us there with his semi and carry us home. This would mean we would return Essi-Anna to Poulsbo from a location at the north end of Lake Michigan. This option would be very costly and this option would delay our response to my Dad and Mom's needs to get there as soon as possible. It would take at best, and if the weather cooperated, about six long days to get to Lake Michigan.

Several other phone calls requesting winter storage in the area all directed us to a place called Boyles Marina and Storage. Pat and his family came highly recommended and have winterized boats and stored them for a couple generations. My call to them assured me they knew what they were doing. When I asked Pat if he had room for one more for the winter in his indoor storage building, he said, "Bring it on". I explained that we would leave Killarney early in the morning and make the 25 mile run to Little Current where we would have Essi-Anna ready for them to winterize and store. We also inquired of them if they knew where we could get on a plane to make the trip to California and if there was any place to rent a car or if there was a shuttle to that airport.

Pat said the closest small airport was at Sudbury, Ontario, two hours to the north and the only way to get there was by taxi. He gave us the numbers and within a matter of half an hour we had made arrangements to fly from Sudbury to Toronto to Las Vegas to Palm Springs. We would arrive at 2:30 a.m. Saturday morning where we would then take a taxi to the care center where Dad had said they were transferring Mom.

Sudbury was a familiar name to Chris and me, since we had passed through there in 1997 on our camper trip to Prince Edward Island and Nova Scotia. The landscape is one of stunted trees and barren landscape that looks like the moon. At one time this region was actually used for moon walk training due to its similarities.

All the arrangements were made to get there. Now the work of packing only necessary things we would need at home for the next year and giving away or getting rid of all perishables, food and anything else that would freeze and break was the next task at hand. It was six o'clock in the evening by now and time was precious. It felt like our little island of peace and serenity had hit an iceberg and everything we had planned just hours before came to a screeching halt as water rushed into our eyes – realizing the pain Mom and Dad were going through and the abrupt ending to what had been a storybook fairytale of adventure.

Ship's stores to include: all canned, refrigerated, bottled, dried and frozen goods were divided up between our friends, with the left over bags of things they could not store went to the young guys working on the docks. Electronics had to be disconnected and everything on deck stowed below decks. All cleaning supplies that would freeze and break had to be discarded and the water tanks had to be drained. An oil change on the generator had to be done. Fortunately, I had just done the engines so fresh oil would sit in them for the long cold winter. The boat had to be cleaned and readied for storage. There was a lot to do and little time as the clock ticked down the hours and minutes until our lonely, solo, early morning race to Boyles.

In addition, we had to pick and choose what we would pack. The boat had been loaded in Olympia close to a year earlier with all the necessary possessions to make this passage. They had been carried across country on the back of a semi trailer and now we had to pare down our return to four check-on suitcases and two carry-ons. The rest would have to stay with Essi-Anna until the summer of 2008 when we would return to make our run back to the U.S. and truck her home from the Illinois River.

Late that Thursday evening, with most everything done, we laid our exhausted heads down for our last sleep aboard and let the soft lapping of the water and gentle rocking of the waves put our minds and bodies to rest.

Stacy and Gail had planned an early breakfast for us and after having devotion with them and crying some pent up tears and exchanging hugs with our boating family, we cast off lines and pulled away from the dock on a silent, tearful and reflective dash to Little Current. The wind was blowing gently, the sky was blue and we were silent; knowing the decision we had made was the only one to make, and the right one, in spite of the emotions of being jerked back to reality by the storms of life's loop on land that now flooded our souls.

The last year and close to 6000 miles of living from day to day without a calendar or the worries of all life's other trappings puts you into a rhythm that is hard to explain. Where to anchor and what to eat, reading, games, living in and with history and geography, new friendships, meditating, different scenery and battling the elements during a year of shorts and tee shirts and endless summer is a luxury that is far from reality on land; even though a watery reality is waiting to strike her blow around every bend in the river or behind each difficult open water crossing. No one got hurt, no one got sick; not even as much as a cold. The boats ran almost flawlessly and our friendships grew with every passing mile; realizing that we needed and wanted to spend time together. Memories were made that can only be surpassed by the emotions, love and support that continue through the close relationships we have as family and friends.

LOOPET 19

MY MOM AND LIFE WITHOUT HER OR THE LOOP

W E arrived in Palm Springs at 2:30 a.m. on Saturday morning of August 20, 2007. It was over 100 degrees as we made our way across the tarmac to the terminal. Our luggage had been lost so it did not meet us. This was just another one of those things that happens with land transportation. We caught the last taxi to Manor Care Rehab in Palm Desert where we had a joyous reunion with my Dad and Esther; our daughter who had flown down to give Dad support until we got there.

Mom was sleeping peacefully. But the all night stories of her ordeal and uphill battle made it clear that the journey for her and Dad, as her faithful care giver for the last year, had been one strewn with sleepless nights, difficult days and hard choices. Esther left after the weekend was over, returning to her own brood of swashbuckling little men. Chris stayed on a week with Dad and me to spend time with Mom as we all worked to nurse her back to health so they could make the journey home to Vancouver. She was unable to sit or eat without help and unable to walk at all. Her conversation was very weak with only the blinking of her eyes at times; to signal a yes or a no. But our hope for another miracle was strong and she seemed to be willing to make the effort.

Dad and I continued to spend long days and evenings caring for Mom; often times saying goodnight long after she had fallen asleep and the lights were out in the other rooms. For a month we battled infections and medication changes and six more days in the hospital, therapy sessions and visits to the doctor. Daily massages, stretching of her legs and tendons, polishing her nails and creamy foot and hand rubs, lavender on her pillow, devotions and reading to her and dueling with the insurance company for even the smallest of things became part of our daily routine.

Little pleasures like a "Frosty" from Wendy's made Mom's day. As time went on, Dad and I, acting as her full time nurses except for a few hours of sleep at the Happy Wanderer, were able to get her strong enough to make the journey home on a nonstop flight out of Ontario, California.

My brother and sister and their spouses, Matt and Marsha and Kori and Steve would meet Dad and Mom at PDX and take them home; where Matt and Marsha and Chris had modified their home to assist in her continued recovery. Our oldest daughter, Anna, and her husband flew to Ontario and met them and Jeff travelled on the same plane to Portland with Dad and Mom. Meanwhile Anna and I drove their loaded, north bound car back to Vancouver. Greg and Linda would be down the next day to help with Mom's care.

The reunions with her family: kids, grandkids, brothers and sister and friends were full of love and memories and talk of the future. But the strain of infections on her body over the last year and the complications associated with brain surgery at 82 were more than she could endure.

Mom knew where she was going and knew where she had been. The circle of her life would soon make a complete loop while those of us left on our loops continued our journeys with gaping holes in our hulls and only her memories to patch the pain.

A boat in Ontario, Mom's journey uncertain and ours still to complete both on land and on the loop hammered home the reality of our own mortality. The charts that guided our lives seemed to be the wrong revision, with the new ones not yet installed. We were searching new and comfortable passages as we struggled with the lessons life and the loop were teaching us.

Anna and I returned from California, with the car two days later. Three days after that Chris and I were returning home from a board of directors meeting of the Lutheran Church Northwest District which had been held in Southern Oregon. I had just talked with Matt and Dad and they said Mom was getting ready for bed. All was well, she was peaceful, and there was no need to come and see her tonight.

We said we would be there when she woke in the morning. Ten minutes later Matt called and said Mom was not doing well and we should come as quickly as we could. Another unexpected storm had reared its ugly head over the mountains and attacked her life, like the spontaneous storms we had experienced on the loop. The I-5 Bridge was congested and what should have been only a few minutes turned into thirty. Time goes so slowly for some and so quickly for others. The cell phone rang again and there was no need to rush anymore. Time had become eternity for her and the clock had stopped for us – even if for only that moment.

On Sunday, August 26th, after a previous night of constant prayer, as her roommate at the care center told us later, Matt and Dad held Mom's hand and prayed and talked to her long after her eyes had closed. Moments earlier she had looked into their faces and said she needed to go; thinking she meant she had to use the bathroom they called for help from the care center staff. In reality, as they soon understood, she was saying her goodbyes in the way that Mom always did things – with grace and calm and a peaceful spirit.

Time had not been gracious enough to me to allow one last kiss and one last smile from her strong and angelic face. I had been fortunate enough to spend a month with her, telling her I loved her and lifting her and feeding her and forcing her bitter tasting medication down her and laying down next to her and reading to her and joking with her and just watching her as she silently slept. She had called me to her bedside several times and told me she knew what I was trying to do for them.

When Dad and I asked her what she wanted she had told us that she, "Just wanted to spend time with us." She was not afraid and she knew that her loop was closing. The same rainbow which God gave Noah as a sign of hope and promise to all of us – an incomplete loop of awesome color which we had seen after the storms on our Great Circle journey - could only become a complete and beautiful circle for her if she let go of her body and our hands and looked for one final time to the cross. She had set us free to live another day and she had taken the hand of Christ.

I'm sitting at my office desk in one of the 37 chairs that are in our home – six weeks after my mom crossed into eternity and reflecting on everything she meant to me. Logan and Sawyer – two of our three grandsons are coming over for us to watch while their brother Noah goes to get his teeth checked. When he was a little guy he fell and some of his teeth were knocked out. The new ones are having a hard time coming in. That's one of the dangers of living on "hard land".

I think Sawyer has a cold – I saw his nose running the other day - so I will probably get one from him since he is always poking his fingers in my mouth when I hold him close and tell him I love him.

Logan will tell me, in his broken English, common for one so hard of hearing; about his birthday which is coming up the 26th of October and then he'll get excited as he tells me in his own deaf language about the squirrels in the park he feeds just before going into his speech classes and he'll want me to take him to gymnastics on Friday to see him – as he says – "jumping".

We still don't have a permanent pastor at our church – it has been over a year since Bill and Gail left St. John.

Winter Hospitality Outreach starts soon and we will spend sleepless nights awake, while the homeless men in Vancouver who sleep at a local church rest peacefully out of the cold.

The grass needs mowing but the lawn mower won't start – I guess I'll have to buy a new one. The old Snapper is 25 years old. Maybe it will stop raining long enough to get it done.

Relatives are sick and being prayed for. Death has visited our family and life continues to go on for those who miss those who have gone on before us.

We are traveling to Bend with some good church friends this weekend. In a few weeks Matt and Marsha and Chris and I will drive a car south along the narrow, but scenic road down the Baja to Cabo San Lucas.

Anna and Jeff have finished the gorgeous remodel of their vintage home in Portland. People will stream through this weekend; gleaning ideas for their own projects.

Christmas will be here soon and Chris will be into her grandma babysitting mode. I will package and lift colorful, joyfully wrapped presents, which will travel with love to all parts of the world as I become the Christmas elf, working alongside Esther and Steve at their UPS stores.

Life is so good but so different; more expensive and more complicated on land than aboard Essi-Anna. We can see why some of the long-haired, carefree on the surface, laidback loopers we met along the way just keep on making the circle. Maybe they continue to travel the loop because they have no one waiting for them on land or maybe because they are still looking for a different meaning in life or maybe because they really do have it all together. Perhaps they have learned to trade the unimportant trappings of life on land for the simplicity and adventure of life on the water; which many find too spartan, too irresponsible and too remote to make a diet of it for a lifetime.

Whatever the reason, we had heard our names called to live the life of good pirates for a year. It was so full of every good thing that we are eternally grateful for the journey.

I sat in the hall of the rehabilitation center that night – what a difference a thirty minute delay on the freeway can make - with different tears than I now have in my eyes as I write this un-ended chapter of life and the loop. Family passes in and out of the silent, dimly lit hallway door to say their last goodbyes; even though their words are no longer audible in Mom's world. Even so they must be said.

I didn't go in to see the place where she had been. She wasn't there. My memories of her would be those she so gracefully brought into my life and the vision of her shining face – full of health and life and peace that she now has in the presence of our Lord. I had said my words when she could hear them; while I could see their impact upon her face.

Just beyond our tears, the grand and glorious sun on the water was brilliantly shining for Mom. The loop she now traveled had no starting or ending point; far exceeding the one Chris and I had so appreciatively traveled aboard Essi-Anna.

LOOPET 20

Closing the Loop – The Final Chapter

LITTLE Current to Blaine, Washington and Home Waters
It is now March of 2008. The weather is starting to improve and thoughts of closing the loop and returning Essi-Anna to home waters is heavy on our minds.

Mom has been gone for some seven months. Chris's mom joined her a month ago after a long and exhausting battle with kidney and heart failure. To lose two moms in less than a year is a heavy burden. What a reunion for them.

Essi-Anna sits in sub zero weather in her strange and dry winter storage home in Little Current awaiting our decisions. Our legs have become more stable on land and duty and devotion to our life on land has infiltrated our hearts and minds and erased some of the desire to pull roots again, travel across country and resume the journey on the loop.

Bill and Gail completed the journey as we had planned – pulling JUWIKA out of the water on the Illinois and trucking her home with Ken who had delivered Essi-Anna to Davenport. Paul and Stacy had said their goodbyes to them at Peoria, Illinois and journeyed further south to the Mississippi and then the Tennessee where they parked SeaSea near Chattanooga for the winter, returning home to Athens, Georgia.

The trip for them since leaving each other in Killarney had been one of beautiful but busy anchorages in the North Channel: a historic stop at the Grand Hotel on Mackinaw Island; an uneventful reentry into the U.S. at Drummond Island; and long days battling heavy weather as they traversed huge and treacherous Lake Michigan before rendezvousing in Chicago.

When we asked them for their appraisal of their last leg of the loop they were pleased they had done it but reiterated that it was far from the best part of the trip.

Chris and I had pondered over many options as Essi-Anna still sat silently in Little Current awaiting our decisions.

1. We could make the return flight to Little Current in June and continue the trip to the Illinois River where we would pull Essi-Anna out of the water and truck her home. This would get us and the boat back in the fall of 2008.
2. We could make the return trip to Little Current; refit Essi-Anna, head east retracing some of our trip and pick up the Rideau Canal which would take us through Ottawa, Ontario and eventually to the St. Lawrence. From there we would explore eastern Canada as far as Prince Edward Island on the Atlantic and then sell the boat out east. This would mean a couple more summers away from home and family and couple more winters for Essi-Anna in cold storage.
3. We could sell the boat in Little Current and buy a small boat on the Columbia River, ending our cruising life for the time being. This would still require us to make a trip out there to pack up a truckload of personal effects that would not be part of the sale.
4. Lastly we could make arrangements to ship Essi-Anna directly from Little Current, having Pat and his organization at Boyle's Marine disassemble her, pack her up, load her and ship her across Canada to Blaine, Washington. This would get her home in June of 2008, ready for the summer cruising season in the Northwest.

We finally settled on the later. We were far from ending our cruising life. To so abruptly end the life of adventure on the water, which flows through our veins like invigorating blood would be like succumbing to some degenerating disease.

A call to Pat to share our thoughts confirmed that this could be a real possibility. He had worked with a very reputable trucker who shipped big boats across Canada. Pat would contact him and get the details on how this would work.

Little Current is on Manatoulin Island, the largest island in North America surrounded by fresh water. The only way off of it is by ferry or a small bridge to the mainland to the north. The ferry was out of the question and the width of the bridge was questionable as to its ability to accommodate Essi-Anna.

The back country roads in this area eventually connect with larger arterials which would take our girl across Canada and back home. Pat would also drive to the bridge and measure it to make sure the boat could pass though it without any problem before starting the disassembly process. Should it be too narrow our only other option was for us to run the boat to another location at the north end of Michigan and have Kenny pick us up there.

Fuel prices had spiked heavily so we knew the bid to transport Essi-Anna would be a costly one. The trip to Davenport had come in at around $12,000.00. The trip home, excluding Pat's work would, ring in at a little under $19,000.00. Our initial cost analysis of buy versus ship before beginning the trip had gone out the window. Our pocket book was thrown for a loop as well but to leave her out there was not an option. To purchase another boat of her character and condition would cost us more than we wanted to spend.

We made up our minds that our lives on the water would continue with her and that she would grow old with us in the Northwest. She had supported us flawlessly throughout the loop and for the last 11 years as we traveled as far north as Petersburg, Alaska and many forays to Northern British Columbia so to abandon her was out of the question.

All specifications confirmed and the transport scheduled we awaited the departure date from Little Current. It would take some four to five days before we would meet Essi-Anna on the Canadian side of the border just north of Blaine. She would roll across the wilderness, prairies and Rocky Mountains on her way back home.

We sat at the commercial border crossing on Tuesday morning, June 24, 2008 and watched down the truck clogged highway for any sign of the boat. Chris's Dad, Lee, was with us. Having lost Betty a few months prior, he was excited to spend time where his mind could take in the beauty of the islands and all they have to offer. He and Mom Miller had spent several summers cruising with us so he understood that with the pleasure of cruising comes the work of preparation.

At the age of 87 he was part of the recommissioning crew in Blaine. We had made arrangements with a marina to sling us into the water where we would put the wheel back on, fire up the engines and motor a short distance to the Blaine Marina; where we would take the next week cleaning her up and getting her ready to head south to the San Juans, Gulf Islands and Victoria, B. C. for the annual "Splash" weekend. The Victoria Splash is a magical event the first weekend every August where people from all over Canada and the U.S. gather to experience a premier performance of the Victoria Symphony on Sunday evening. A huge barge is moved into the inner harbor. Boats and shoreline hordes descend upon the city in anticipation of an extravagant weekend of music, food and fireworks in the shadow of the towering elegance of the old Canadian Pacific Railway Hotel – The Empress. Double-decker buses and the pomp and pride of the divinely lit Parliament Building add to the backdrop of this very British city.

Ten o'clock was the scheduled time for meeting the boat. As though on cue, we saw Essi-Anna rolling slowly towards us, stern first, aft of a large diesel tractor.

I had called customs the day before and told them of our situation and asked them to advise me on the protocol to be used for re-entry. They said to get in front of the boat, talk to the customs agent at the commercial gate and clear Essi-Anna for the trucker who would follow us through the gate to the U.S. side. I had all my documentation and Pat had filed all necessary paperwork for her to stay in Canada over the winter so everything was in order.

After a quick call to the trucker on the phone, we pulled in front of him to wait our turn in line. The single file opened up into four lines and check in slots which were restricted by heavy metal height and width stanchions.

As we approached the customs booth my eyes fell upon the immoveable width restrictions in all lanes. Three of the lanes read 14'6" – an impossibility for Essi-Anna to pass through as that is her beam. My heart sank. As the truck in front of us moved forward to talk to the customs agent I could read our width restriction sign. Divine intervention had given us a final blessing on the trip. It was the only gate that read 15'. To turn around would have been impossible and to back out of this tangle of commercial traffic would have taken hours and hours to accomplish.

We slid through the gauntlet with thanks and a prayer with three inches to spare on each side. The customs agent asked us a few questions and after scanning his computer screen and with a smile flagged both of us through without a hitch.

We stopped in a lot on the U.S. side of the border and shook hands with the trucker. Essi-Anna was filthy and covered with a fair number of species of insects found in Canada but there she was; not a scratch, not a ding, not a dent.

He told us that his pilot cars were unable to cross the border and that basically he would make the illegal dash for the marina some three miles away with us in the lead. He had reviewed the route and knew there would be no problem with clearances. He also told us that if the state patrol stopped us he would be heavily fined and the boat would be held up until we could arrange for pilot cars to take us the next mile or so to the water.

As had been the blessings afforded us on the loop, we were not stopped. We arrived at the marina and were slung immediately into the water. With a handshake and a check for $19,000.00, Essi-Anna was back in home waters. Essi-Anna's road trip had closed her final chapter on the loop.

The tides of emotion rushed through our minds and bodies like the tide floods and ebbs through a narrow channel, foaming and bucking and swirling into whirlpools large enough to swallow you in one bite. There is danger in those tidal changes, before and after the slack water makes way for safe passage. Places like: Deception Pass and Dent Narrows, Hole in the Wall, Green Rapids and Dodd Narrows can be made when the water is calm for a few minutes; before the fury of the current turns them into an out of control carnival ride that can dash your life upon the rocks or roll you over and suck you down, never to see the light of day again.

There Essi-Anna sat tied to the working dock just port of where she had been slung into the water. Her usually shiny hull was covered with road grime, and grease and splattered with bugs.

She was disassembled and hardly looked like herself; needing much attention and care before she would be ready to motor south. Her insides were stuffed with all the trappings of a year spent on the loop: bikes, the motor and inflatable, boxed up charts and books, electronics and all that was necessary to make a journey we had left almost a year ago.

Our lives had crashed into life's rocks several times since we left her in Little Current. We suffered the loss of both our Moms and the funerals that followed, trying to resurrect joy in the lives of our Dads after their first mates had gone overboard after sixty plus years of navigating life as a team.

Chris and I had both had a hard time adjusting to life back on land. Responsibility at every bend in this new river meant making decisions more complex than battling the unpredictable and exciting each and every day on the loop.

To wake up each morning with your sole purpose of surviving until the next day and making decisions as to where the anchor would drop and how the weather would impact our safety and what was for dinner, had now been traded for a life of responsibility to and for others. We were no longer seafaring mariners making our way through life with only an occasional glimpse of the lives we had left in Washington State while on the loop.

We had talked heavily of selling it all and leading the lives of buccaneers aboard a larger boat, which would take us to other parts of the world. We had actually ventured to Seattle and Bellingham to look at a Nordhavn and a Fleming but in-spite of all our dreaming, the answer seemed to always come back – no!

Family ties run strong and to selfishly check out of the lives of our Dads, our kids and our grandkids to pursue more fantasy just wasn't reality for us. We had been afforded the opportunity to live the life of pirates for a year. We wanted to pass on the love for such adventure to the next generation and in order to do that we would have to invest time in their lives. We would return to being summer scallywags, enjoying the world we had left, "Before Being Thrown for the Loop".

Life on America's Great Circle Loop was over and a new chapter of our lives would begin with the cleaning and reassembly of Essi-Anna.

The wheel installed on the bridge, after much sorting to find it in the cabin below, a turn of the key to move and get underway to the marina; we came up short. The batteries were dead. We had to make more decisions. With tears in our eyes, yet smiles on our faces, we sat silently on the deck and let the screeching of the seagulls and the gurgling of the rising tide capture our spirits once again, with the realization of how fortunate we really had been and are. We had experienced a loop in life that is only possible for a handful of people. We had ridden the waves of fear and joy and pain and bliss. From the time we had dipped our keel in the Mississippi till now we had lost much but gained even more. Our lives had been changed forever.

We looked at each other with awe, contentment and peace; grateful for the past and excited about what the future held. The memories of the loop refreshed as our minds revisited the journey that had now come to a close. The faces of our moms and the journeys they had completed in the last year were still clear in our hearts and would never fade like the dull shine on Essi-Anna's hull that now reflected the aging faces of those who had come to meet her in this place. We had been, "Thrown for the Loop". The sun was shining brightly and the warm breeze seemed to whisper a calm message of renewal. We let the moment be what it was, old friends who had been reunited to put our lives back together and continue the loop we call life.

The Journey at a Glance

- Left home August 28, 2006 and returned to California July 20, 2007
- Essi-Anna made it home June 24, 2008
- Anchored 70% of the time
- Held up by weather – 6 days
- Came home twice for Chuck and three times for Chris
- Left the boat in Madeira Beach, Florida for Christmas and Norfolk, Virginia for quick trip to our home in Cabo San Lucas, Mexico
- Ran in fog – 2 days
- Ran in rough seas and skinny water lots
- Ran aground once in sand but got off on our own (no damage)
- Shallowest water for the longest time entering Cedar Key on the Gulf – 5'
- Changed oil – 4 times at anchor
- Journey length approximately six thousand miles
- Wore long pants – 8 days
- Most awesome moment – Entering New York Harbor after a beautiful run on the Atlantic Ocean and seeing the Statue of Liberty

Budget at a Glance

JUWIKA's costs were substantially less due to completing the journey on the Illinois River and not having to make an emergency trip home and storing the boat in Canada. In addition she is a single screw diesel boat.

Insurance and Transport	$32,000.00
Fuel	$18,000.00
Maintenance and Repair (spun shaft)	$5,000.00
Lodging and Dock fees	$10,000.00
Food and Restaurants	$8,000.00
Air and Car	$7,000.00
Additional Insurance	$3,000.00
Charts and Software	$1,200.00
Total:	$84,200.00
Experience	Priceless!

Day snorkeling on the Florida Keys

Dismal Swamp on the way to Norfolk, Virginia

Georgian Bay shortcut. Tight squeeze

It doesn't get any better than this!

Just feet from our baptism in the Mississippi

JUWIKA on the marine rail

Lighthouse on the Hudson River

Loading Essi-Anna in Olympia, WA

Lots of rocks in Georgian Bay

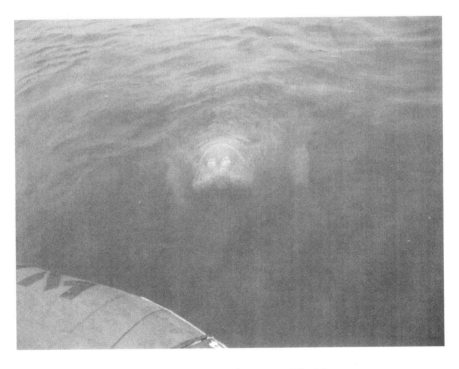

Manatees at Crystal Springs, Florida

JUWIKA entering Peterborough lift lock

Navy ships everywhere!

Rescue on Georgian Bay

Mississippi Queen

Wow! New York City - Us in Time Square

300 blocks of shaved ice to make a bobsled run in Dunedin, Florida

Alligators everywhere!

Anchored in Little Diversion Canal on the Mississippi

Annapolis graduation

Bare bones "Looper"

Kentucky Lake Lock

Curing Tobacco in Kentucky

Mile high apple pie at Kaskaskia Lock on the Mississippi

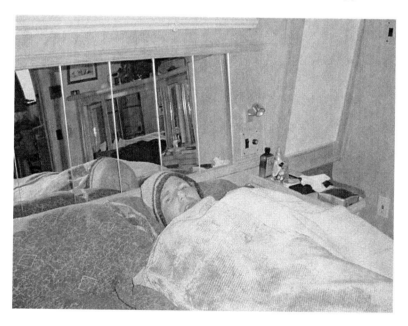

Keep moving south - winter is coming! No heat at anchor!

Trapped in our anchorage by a tug tied to a tree on the Tenn-Tom

Calm after the storm on the Gulf of Mexico

Going ashore on the Florida Pan Handle

Hurricane Alley Florida

Shells along the Florida coast

Relaxing before our big day on the Gulf of Mexico

Waterford, New York - Entrance to the Erie Canal

Grocery shopping was always a trek.

Lots of Insects

Chris on Waupoos Island, Ontario

SeaSea, Essi-Anna and JUWIKA on the Trent

About the Author

Captain Chuck Hewitson and his wife Chris keep their boat at the Poulsbo Yacht Club on the Puget Sound in Washington State. They are experienced mariners who retired from careers in teaching and a successful, private electronics company with Chuck's brothers. For the last thirty years they have traversed the waterways from Olympia to Alaska, spending summers somewhere along the Pacific Northwest's scenic and wild Inside Passage.

They are active in charity work, having served on various boards, both private and public. When they are not cruising they spend time in Vancouver, Washington and at their home in Cabo San Lucas, Mexico doing volunteer mission work.

Chuck holds a 100 ton inland waters and an OUPV near coastal captain's license. They also run a private charter business in the Pacific Northwest.

They have been blessed with two married daughters and four grandsons who have also gained a respect and love for the cruising lifestyle.

CPSIA information can be obtained at www.ICGtesting.com
Printed in the USA
BVOW050034111011

273272BV00004B/8/P